*The Future of the*
*International*
*Strategic*
*System*

Chandler Publications in
Political Science

Victor Jones, *Editor*

# The Future of the International Strategic System

EDITED BY

## Richard Rosecrance

*Cornell University*

Published under the auspices of the Institute of
International Studies, University of California, Berkeley

**CHANDLER PUBLISHING COMPANY**
An Intext Publisher
SAN FRANCISCO • SCRANTON • LONDON • TORONTO

Library of Congress Cataloging in Publication Data

Rosecrance, Richard N.
    The future of the international strategic system.

    (Chandler publications in political science)
    "Published under the auspices of the Institute
of International Studies, University of California,
Berkeley."
    Bibliography:
    1.  Strategy.      2.   Atomic weapons.      I.   Title.
U163.R67              355.02'17              72-161297
ISBN    0-8102-0437-1

Copyright © 1972 by Chandler Publishing Company

All rights reserved

International Standard Book Number 0-8102-0437-1

Library of Congress Catalog Card Number 72-161297

Printed in the United States of America

*Book designed by R. Keith Richardson*

# Contents

## Preface

The study that follows began as a project of the International Security Program of the University of California, Berkeley, and is being continued as a central focus of the Peace Studies Program at Cornell University. Essentially, the collaborators were convinced that too little attention was being given to problems of what may well be in the future a multipolar strategic world. The United States and the Soviet Union have tended to view international stability as fundamentally a bipolar problem, a problem, to be sure, which might be complicated by the actions of fledgling nuclear states. The spread of nuclear weapons has been considered dangerous, however, not because it threatens to change the nature of the game of international politics, but because it threatens bipolar stability. On the whole, the perspective of the essays which follow is different: the world is seen either as multipolar or as a strategic environment in which multipolarity could easily develop unless resolute actions are taken by the two major nuclear states. The present concerns are twofold: (1) What would such a multipolar strategic world be like? (2) What, if anything, can be done to make it more stable?

The editor is indebted, not only to his colleagues, but also to those who offered advice and criticism and provided research support. At Berkeley, Professor Ernst Haas made our joint inquiry a project of the Institute of International Studies and gave valuable assistance at every point. Mrs. Cleo Stoker and Mrs. Sheila Moses offered greatly needed administrative and editorial aid. Jeffrey Hart and Richard Witherspoon contributed research assistance. At Cornell, Professors Milton Esman and Franklin Long, along with Professor George Quester, have made it possible for the Peace Studies Program to continue and to deepen the research and hopefully fruitful speculation which is represented here.

It is fitting that we dedicate this volume to our children, for they will bear the brunt of trying to understand and cope with the coming multipolar world.

Richard Rosecrance

*Ithaca, New York*
*February, 1971*

## Notes on the Contributors

*Kenneth E. Boulding* is Professor of Economics at the University of Colorado and author of *The Meaning of the Twentieth Century* and *Conflict and Defense*. He has spent his career in searching for methods of peaceful resolution of conflict at both the national and international levels.

*Donald G. Brennan* is the editor of *Disarmament, Arms Control and National Security* and a research associate of the Hudson Institute. He has written widely on strategic topics.

*Richard N. Gardner* is Henry L. Moses Professor of Law and International Organization at the School of Law, Columbia University. He is a former Deputy Assistant Secretary of State for International Organizational Affairs, and has authored *Sterling-Dollar Diplomacy* and *In Pursuit of World Order: U. S. Foreign Policy and International Organizations.*

*Ernst B. Haas* is Director of the Institute of International Studies, University of California, Berkeley. A student of integration theory, he has written *Tangle of Hopes: American Commitments and World Order, Collective Security and the Future International System*, and *Beyond the Nation-State.*

*John C. Harsanyi* is Professor of Economics and Business Administration at the University of California, Berkeley. He has written widely in the field of game theory and the application of game-theoretic models to social problems.

*Malcolm W. Hoag* is a Senior Staff Member of the Economics Department of the RAND Corporation. A specialist on strategic matters in Europe and the Far East, he has written many articles on the strategic balance and the nuclear spread.

*Morton A. Kaplan* is Professor of Political Science at the University of Chicago. His seminal work, *System and Process in International Politics*, dealt with the problems of a world in which nuclear capabilities were possessed by each member of the system. He reconsiders these problems in his essay for this volume.

*George H. Quester* is Associate Professor of Government and Research Fellow of the Center for International Studies, Cornell University. He is a specialist on deterrent processes and on the spread of nuclear weapons. He has written *Deterrence before Hiroshima* and *Nuclear Diplomacy: The First Twenty-Five Years.*

*Richard Rosecrance* is Walter S. Carpenter Jr. Professor of International and Comparative Politics at Cornell University. He has written on international theoretical matters and edited the volume *The Dispersion of Nuclear Weapons: Strategy and Politics.*

*Reinhard Selten* is Professor of Economics at the Free University of Berlin and is a well-known game theorist. He has written *Contributions to Experimental Economics* and *Price Policy of Multiproduct Production in Statistical Theory.*

*Reinhard Tietz*, of the University of Frankfurt/Main, is a staff member of the German Research Society.

*The Future of the*
*International*
*Strategic*
*System*

Richard Rosecrance

# *Introduction*

Many studies have been written on the spread of nuclear weapons.[1] On the whole, these focus upon the impact of nuclear dispersion on the probability of central nuclear war between the United States and the Soviet Union. If there is a link between local nuclear war and central nuclear war, then any greater probability of the former increases the chances of the latter. Traditionally the argument is offered that the spread of nuclear weapons will raise the statistical probability that some nuclear weapon will go off somewhere on the globe. If one weapon goes off, then the nuclear inhibition is broken, and it is much more likely that other nuclear weapons will be used. A process of vertical and horizontal escalation is then posited in which the United States and the Soviet Union eventually become embroiled in strategic conflict.

These arguments are worth attending to and repeating if only because the world is now presented with the spectre of nuclear spread far more pervasive than that which it has witnessed previously. Today there are only five nuclear-weapon powers: the United States, the Soviet Union, Britain, France, and China. The last country joined the nuclear club in 1964. This list represents an over-all rate of no more than one acquisition every five years since 1945. Since 1952, on the other hand, the rate has been much slower, more on the order of one new member every nine years. Present portents, however, suggest that the future rate will be much higher. Israel is certainly on the threshold of a bomb capability. India can produce a bomb within a year should it choose to violate international obligations,

[1]See, for example, L. Beaton and J. Maddox, *The Spread of Nuclear Weapons* (London: Chatto and Windus, 1962); R. Rosecrance (ed.), *The Dispersion of Nuclear Weapons* (New York: Columbia University Press, 1964); L. Beaton, *Must the Bomb Spread?* (Harmondsworth, Eng.: Penguin Books, 1966); W. Bader, *The United States and the Spread of Nuclear Weapons* (New York: Pegasus, 1968); A. Buchan (ed.), *A World of Nuclear Powers?* (Englewood Cliffs, N.J.: Prentice-Hall, 1966); G. Quester, "The Nuclear Non-Proliferation Treaty and International Atomic Energy Agency," *International Organization* (Spring 1970).

1

and within three to five years if it honors its existing reactor commitments. Japan and West Germany have the reactor capacity for peaceful purposes, which if turned to military production would enable them to become major nuclear powers within a decade. Brazil has claimed that it must use nuclear explosions for peaceful economic purposes and has refused to sign the Nuclear Non-Proliferation Treaty. Pakistan and the United Arab Republic have not signed because of the abstention of India and Israel. As the spread of power reactors proceeds, other states will be placed on the threshold of nuclear-weapons production. Other European countries, South Africa, and Australia will eventually acquire options on the bomb. As the world moves into the generation of breeder reactors in the nineteen-eighties and -nineties, plutonium may even become plentiful; this development would reduce power costs, but would also put nuclear weapons within the grasp of twenty or more states. Giant desalinization reactors, producing and consuming enormous quantities of electricity, will also produce large amounts of plutonium, and thus contribute to this process.

## ADVANTAGES OF NUCLEAR STATUS

It would be premature and even erroneous to claim that the short-range impact of such changes will be to upgrade the status of minor powers to greater equality with the two nuclear superstates. At the same time, nuclear weapons do change the status of their possessors. No nuclear state's homeland has ever been attacked, though the forces of nuclear states have been involved in limited combat in other areas of the world. It is difficult to imagine a limited war being fought over the inert body of a state whose nuclear weapons might be used to prevent or terminate that war. The spread of nuclear weapons, therefore, probably reduces the number of areas of the world in which conventional wars might occur. From the perspective of an individual state contemplating acquisition of such weapons, moreover, it is possible to see reasons for going nuclear. The international status attributed to a nation tends to go up as it gains nuclear capability. A nuclear state is likely to see itself as freer from alliance ties and alignment bonds; therefore, its political latitude is likely to increase. Further, whatever doubts a fledgling nuclear state may have about its own capability, it is likely to find major nations taking its capabilities seriously. One has only to recall the shift in estimates of Chinese power and potential that occurred with its nuclear detonation. When the United States unveiled its first-generation ABM plans, it was apparent that the system was designed to cope with a missile attack from China. Implicit in the argument for a China-oriented ABM was the notion that, if it did not have such a system, the United States might not be able to dissuade its South and Southeast Asian friends from yielding to Chinese pressures southward. United States policy makers apparently believed they had to employ new systems and concepts to deter the world's fifth nuclear power.

The advantages accruing to a new nuclear state can be seen from another point of view. It might theoretically be argued that a state which acquires nuclear weapons will actually suffer a net loss in national position: it may lose the benefits of protection by major nuclear states, while gaining only that protection that comes from its rudimentary capability. There are two rejoinders to this contention, however. The first is that states which have acquired nuclear weapons have not, by that reason, lost the favor or protection of their major power guarantors. Neither France nor Britain was denied nuclear guarantees from the United States when they acquired separate atomic capabilities. Under General de Gaulle, France appeared to rest content that the United States, in its own interest, would always support France in a major conventional or nuclear crisis. If the argument were true, there would be no need for Paris to tailor its policies to strict NATO patterns. Since 1969, moreover, France's greater "integration" with NATO has certainly not been prevented by her developing nuclear capability. In the British case alliance solidarity is even more marked. Britain cooperated more fully with the United States in military and strategic terms after the development of her "independent deterrent" than she did before.

The Chinese instance might seem to be contrary to these precedents, but in fact it is not. Russian disagreements with China did not center around the Chinese desire to acquire nuclear weapons, but related rather to the Chinese worldview and approach to foreign relations.[2] Chinese antagonism toward the Russians stemmed in part from Russia's unwillingness to embark upon a more ambitious policy of challenge to the capitalist Western world and her willingness to accept "peaceful coexistence."[3] This is not to say that the Russians were happy with Peking's nuclear program or that they would not like to limit China's nuclear progress today. But nuclear weapons were not the source of the Sino-Soviet dispute; they were merely a reflection of it. If there had been no other grounds for rupture, it is unlikely that nuclear weapons themselves would have produced an attenuation of alliance bonds.

Even India would not be likely to find her relationship to the Soviet Union and the United States grievously affected by a bomb decision. It is unlikely that either great power, fearing to lose leverage in Delhi, would cut off aid as a result of such a step. The Indians, mindful of the Soviet and

[2]See Donald Zagoria, *The Sino-Soviet Conflict: 1956–1961* (Princeton, N.J.: Princeton University Press, 1962), Chapter 5.
[3]Zagoria, pp. 165–169.

U.S. response to the Indo-Pakistani War of 1965, are not apt to be swayed
from a nuclear course by the concern to maintain support from Moscow and
Washington. Rather, they would question how much that support would be
worth. Perhaps paradoxically, neither the United States nor the Soviet
Union would be likely to follow their policies of 1965, terminating arms aid
and deliveries. Further, the Indian bomb decision will obviously be presented in a Sino-Indian context in which it will be seen as an equalizer of
China's nuclear advantage. If neither the United States nor Russia is willing to give an iron-clad nuclear guarantee to Delhi, both countries are in a
difficult position to object to India's efforts to make up the deficiency in
power against China. As far as Pakistan is concerned, Delhi will argue that
India is the *status quo* power, and thus that India's capability against
Rawalpindi would be detrimental only if Pakistan were bent on changing
the *status quo* by force. While an Indian bomb will certainly bring Pakistan
and China closer together, it is unlikely to lead either the United States or
the Soviet Union to clasp Pakistan to its bosom. It seems probable, therefore, that a nuclear India would lose few of its remaining links with the two
major nuclear powers.

   The second factor mitigating the disadvantages that nuclear status might
involve is the secular decline in alliance credibility. Even if it were true that
states which gained nuclear weapons would have to give up major power
guarantees, the result would be the loss of a distinctly depreciating asset.
Since the United States and the Soviet Union have both attained major
retaliatory capabilities, it has become clear that neither would be able to
make hard-and-fast commitments about nuclear support for allies under all
circumstances of enemy attack. For a major power like the United States
or the Soviet Union to resort to nuclear weapons in response to a serious,
but still nonnuclear, threat to its allies would be to risk mutual suicide.
Until nuclear weapons were used by the alliance guarantor, there would be
no direct threat to the homeland of either major power. The use of such
weapons, however, would raise the threat of escalation, both in terms of
destructiveness and geographic scope. Nuclear guarantees in an age of
"mutual deterrence" look increasingly less credible. Interpreted symmetri-
cally, this condition probably means that the Soviets have more latitude in
the use of pressure against the Western alliance than they have realized; it
also means that the United States has more scope in capitalizing upon dis-
content and revolutionary ferment in Eastern Europe than it has sought to
use. If nuclear alliances manifest declining credibility, even if nuclear status
injures relations with a major guarantor, the loss cannot be great. Guarantor stock is going down, fledgling nuclear stock up on the international
power exchange.

## PROLIFERATION AND STABILITY

It is therefore likely that we shall see many more nuclear decisions in the years ahead. The final impact of those decisions, however, is not easy to estimate. If the ultimate horror is a nuclear war between the United States and the Soviet Union, and if, as many people assume, nuclear weapons are more likely to be used among ingenue powers than by established members of the nuclear club, then the impact upon central stability will be determined by the relations between old and new members. If there are firm alliance or alignment ties, then any conflict of the newer members embroils the older ones, perhaps on opposite sides. If alliance relationships are declining or nonexistent, the possibility of local nuclear attack may not present a greater threat of all-out nuclear war among major powers. This suggestion in turn raises the question of respective rates: the rate and direction of nuclear proliferation on the one hand, and the rate and direction of alliance dissociation or discohesion on the other. Up to 1971, it appeared that the decline in the force of alliance ties might be proceeding more rapidly than the spread of weapons. If the prospects of a much more rapid spread are correct, however, and if the spread does not lead to any marked attenuation of alliance relationships, at least in the short run, it seems likely that the problem of the dispersion of nuclear weapons will be more serious in the future than it has been in the past.

One of the justifications for this book, moreover, is that up to now the magnitude of our concentration on nuclear proliferation has been nearly inverse to the magnitude of the problem. From 1958 to 1960 there was a great deal of discussion about a very rapid spread of bombs, a spread which some claimed would lead to use of the bombs in war no later than the mid-sixties. Radical therapy was suggested to halt proliferation. American defense planners strove either to dissuade European countries from acquiring bombs or to pool the bombs in what was then called the Multilateral Nuclear Force. By the end of 1964, however, the fever had abated. No longer was there a great urgency to prevent the spread among allies, or to constitutionalize it in multilateral groupings. With the signing of the Nuclear Non-Proliferation Treaty in 1968, the world was even more content: Now countries would join in a general pledge against acquiring weapons. Since states would be hesitant to break a solemn treaty, for many the NPT seemed to be the solution to the danger of nuclear dispersion. In 1971, however, it appears that many states may move to *de facto* if not *de jure* capabilities: They can acquire the materials and the detonation mechanisms for fabricating a bomb within days or weeks of making a decision to do so. The spread is taking place ineluctably under the guise of adherence to the treaty. Perhaps paradoxically, when the world most attended to the portents of spread (in 1958–1960), bombs were not spreading rapidly. Now that the world has been lulled into a false sense of security about the likelihood of spread, the bombs are beginning to proliferate underneath the table. Today it is worth devoting more attention to the problem that they will present.

## PROLIFERATION AND MULTIPOLARITY

Past accounts have usually concentrated on the impact of nuclear proliferation upon central nuclear stability. How would the acquisition of bombs by additional states affect the probability of war between the United States and the Soviet Union? This is not a negligible question, and it is one that several of the ensuing papers address. There has been considerable speculation about such questions in the past. In addition, however, this volume raises the question of another effect of proliferation: Is it possible that eventually the game of international politics will be transformed from a two-party or bipolar contest into a quintipolar, septipolar, or even multipolar competition? Is it possible that there will be a spread of major-weapons capabilities to other states so great that China, Japan, Germany-Western Europe, perhaps eventually India and even other states, will become so militarily and technologically developed that they can take their place beside the two greatest powers, the United States and the Soviet Union? If such a transformation of the international system takes place, the rules and guidelines for international strategy that have been offered since 1945 will become quite obsolete.

It is easy to see why this is so. The model of deterrent stability that has been employed since World War II is bilateral. One power threatens; another power deters the threat. The two communicate their strategic intentions to one another. The arms of one are intended for possible use against those of the other. The two can measure themselves against each other and reach some understanding of the force and doctrine which they need to ensure stability. Indeed, the development of strategic doctrine since 1945 has been concentrated almost entirely in the field of bilateral relations among superpowers. The doctrine of limited war also grew out of the two-party confrontation: If the choice was solely between inaction and Armageddon, there had to be another alternative. Oddly enough, moreover, despite the appearance of China, France, and Britain on the nuclear stage, the arms race continues to be studied in its bilateral aspect. The Strategic Arms Limitation Talks have sought to arrange arms equilibrium between the United States and the Soviet Union, with little attention to the burgeoning problem of China. Yet, if the two powers do not take China into account, equilibrium will be difficult to achieve. Further, the presence of a third major nuclear power complicates relations with the Big Two. How will one of the two giants know whether increases in the strategic force of the other are intended for possible use against China or against itself? Rearmament to ensure a deterrent against China under all circumstances may be seen as directed against the superpower opposite number. In theoretical terms, of course, the deterrent threshold must rise with the acquisition of new nuclear states, for each power must be capable of retaliating against an attack launched by all other members of the system. In short, we may already be moving into a system of presumptive tripolarity while our calculations are still founded on a bipolar basis.

The consequences of such a system could be malign or beneficent, depending upon the nature of alliance ties. If tripolarity means essentially two powers ganging up against one, arms race and political tensions can be expected to rise. At some point if the two allies become extremely strong, the third may have to resort to desperate measures to break up their combination. This could engender even greater political and military instability. On the other hand, if there are no alliance relationships in a tripolar system, the result could be even greater stability than under conditions of bipolarity. Since each power would only worry about an attack by one other power, he would not have to accelerate his deterrent preparations. Moreover, if that one other power attacked, the aggressor could not rely on the peaceful inclinations of the third state. The third power, staying out of the fray, might threaten or attack the weakened victor at the moment of his triumph. Tripolarity, under these circumstances, poses the intractable dilemma of the victor's inheritance, and may restrain bilateral conflict.

As the number of major players increases, however, system impacts change. Two different alliances of two powers each could help stabilize a quadripolar system, while tripolarity would be unsettled by the alliance of two powers against one. Offensive alliances would be destabilizing, while defensive or collective-security alliances would be stabilizing. Alliances among the stronger states are destabilizing, while alliances among the weaker states are likely to be stabilizing. In any event, as new powers are added to the strategic game, bipolar outcomes no longer apply.

Burgeoning multipolarity may differ from bipolarity in other respects. Bilateral deterrence theory has contended that one state could be "deterred" from aggressive action by the threat of nuclear retaliation on the part of its superpower opponent. The nuclear aggressor could be clearly identified; his rival would be the only possible responder. In a quintipolar or septipolar nuclear context, however, it is possible that one would not know the source of attack. If so, the threat of certain and immediate retaliation would not carry the kind of credence it would possess in a bipolar context. It is possible that desperate aggressors might attempt to make gains when a confrontation was in process between two other states, hoping to attribute the aggressive attack to one of the protagonists. A possible failure to reliably identify an attacker within a short period of time is just one of the many quandaries of the potential nuclear multipolar world that lies ahead.

Another uncertainty has to do with differences between the major and minor power games in international politics. In some measure it is true today that there are at least two games of international relations: There is the nonnuclear game, where conventional opponents in non-European areas of the globe jockey for position and sometimes make war. And there is the nuclear game, where deterrence is king and where thus far there has been no war. But there have been world crises, and there have been periods of instability and uncertainty. In the minor-power subgame, as we have seen, a nation can argue that the acquisition of nuclear weapons will strengthen its position against possible nonnuclear opponents. Once a nation goes nuclear, however, for good or ill it becomes also a member of the supergame, the nuclear game. While it may have improved its position in the subgame, it may be in a very unfavorable position in the supergame.[4] It may therefore be true that while its impact upon the subgame is not destabilizing, the spread of nuclear weapons may erode stability in the supergame.[5] Further, since the spread of weapons has basically the impact of extending the supergame, it may extend that game more rapidly than doctrine and posture can accommodate. As far as the supergame is concerned, relationships are no longer bilateral. We move from a two-party to an $n$-party game. Deterrence theory, fundamentally dyadic in character, does not tell us proper strategies for an $n$-party game. It may be, therefore, that entirely new strategies will have to be found for a multipolar world. While it would be premature at this point to speculate on the nature of those strategies, it is just possible that a multipolar world will have to rely as much on reward and reinforcement strategies as on punishment strategies.

The work that follows is divided into three parts. The first section, on military analysis, considers the impact of strategic factors in a world in which major nuclear capacities are more widely diffused than they are at present. It poses the question as to whether such a world will be more or less

[4]If its major opponent is a nuclear power, it is possible that the acquisition of nuclear weapons could also improve a state's position in the supergame. This is *not* the same thing, however, as saying that the supergame will now be more stable.

[5]Stability would be increased in that conventional wars that might have taken place would now not take place. It is difficult to imagine a conventional Egypt invading a nuclear Israel and *vice versa*. Once bilateral nuclear capacities have been developed, however, their technical vulnerabilities may lead to pressures for preemptive attack; the incentives to use such weapons may increase. It is surprising, but most nuclear countries today do not even conceive of using nuclear weapons against a nonnuclear country. When their opponent develops weapons, however, they must conceive of use of unlimited weapons against him.

stable, strategically, than the present system. In some cases where new instabilities are foreseen, recommendations are offered that would help to mitigate the impact of nuclear spread.

The second part considers multipolarity from a game-theory or location-theory perspective. If wars are partly caused by inequities in power, and the spread of weapons makes for a greater equality, will the future world be more stable than the one we presently know? For the purposes of answering such a question, the world is conceived first as an over-all game, and then as a supergame. From an analytic point of view, the spread of weapons may offer certain stabilizing effects to the over-all game, but it is likely to introduce uncertainty and instability into the supergame. One theorist concludes that the spread of weapons will undercut the viability even of superpowers, rendering all states only conditionally viable.

The third section deals with the problem of deterrence and reward. Do the difficulties of bilateral deterrence theory apply in a multipolar world? If strictly military variables are inadequate in stabilizing such a world, what are the prospects of nonmilitary techniques? Finally, the concluding chapter is designed to draw together the diverse strands of analysis, to state in what respects a future multipolar order may be more unstable than the bipolarity we have known to the present, and to speculate about ways in which it might be made more stable.[6]

[6]The Appendix provides the mathematical apparatus on which the Selten-Tietz game-theoretic conclusions of Part II are based.

# PART I

# Military Analysis

CHAPTER 1

Donald G. Brennan

# Some Remarks on
# Multipolar Nuclear Strategy

The purpose of this essay is to discuss a number of issues that arise in nuclear strategy when several countries (rather than two) are the principal actors. Although we have had more than two nuclear countries for quite some time, most of the strategic writing in the West has, for good and obvious reasons, concentrated on the case of two nuclear opponents. I shall discuss here some aspects of the case of several nuclear powers.

It is not possible to give an exhaustive treatment of the range of possible multipolar strategic nuclear situations. The range of individual strategies that might operate within a given country is at least as great as the range that might be considered within one of the present superpowers, and individual secondary states would be at least as subject to unpredictable trends and fashions as are the superpowers. There is of course no necessity for any two states to operate on the basis of the same strategies and strategic views; thus, a comprehensive description of even the relatively plausible combinations of circumstances involving only, say, six countries, could easily exceed the scope of a fat volume, to say nothing of a brief essay. However, I believe it may be useful to discuss the key technical and perceptual issues, and to illustrate some of the more interesting possible cases of the interactions and uses of strategic forces.

I shall assume a reader with some familiarity with basic bipolar strategic nuclear considerations. So far as specific time frames and assumed "nuclearization" of the world are relevant, I shall consider primarily the later 1970s and beyond, and a world of six or eight nuclear powers. However, many of the considerations we shall discuss could be perfectly relevant to the present five nuclear powers, particularly in cases involving confrontations of other than the two superpowers themselves.

The author of this paper is a staff member of the Hudson Institute. This paper represents the views of its author. There has been only limited circulation of the paper to the Hudson Institute staff and no formal review procedure. No opinions, statements of fact, or conclusions contained in this document can properly be attributed to the Institute, its staff, its members, or its contracting agencies.

## SOME TECHNICAL ISSUES

The kinds of uses and implications that several national nuclear forces can have are importantly influenced, and in some cases even dominated, by the technical characteristics of the forces. For example, one of the important characteristics that will influence the significance and the possible interactions of such forces is their degree of protection against attack from other nuclear forces. Each of the two present superpowers has devoted major resources to developing strategic forces that cannot be easily eliminated, even in an all-out surprise nuclear attack by the opposing superpower. Secondary nuclear states may develop strategic nuclear forces that are equally well protected, and the implications of the forces involved will depend considerably on the specific characteristics of the force.

Many different degrees of protection are possible. At one end of the scale, it is possible that a number of countries in Western Europe, including specifically the United Kingdom and France, might combine to constitute a European nuclear force that would, in effect, be a new superpower, having resources and characteristics analogous to the Soviet and American strategic forces, and in particular having a comparable degree of protection. However, the present West European forces are not especially well protected, and some of the countries in our hypothetical future environment might well have forces similar to, for example, the current French force, which could probably be completely destroyed by a relatively small number of weapons (say, ten) delivered by either of the present superpowers. (The advent of French missile-launching submarines may well change this situation.)

The kinds of techniques that might be used by future nuclear powers to protect their forces will not necessarily be the same as those used by the present superpowers. Submarines of suitable design are likely to remain attractive as a relatively invulnerable mode of basing strategic forces, but they are also likely to remain relatively expensive, and may not be as extensively used by secondary nuclear states as they are by the United States and the Soviet Union. Within the next several years, it is possible that some countries might find it attractive to emplace missiles in hardened silos similar to those used for the U.S. Minuteman forces, but potential developments in missile accuracy (miss distances of a few hundred feet or less may be achieved by 1980) will ultimately make this technique of limited attractiveness. At least some nuclear states might be attracted to the use of land-mobile missiles as a way of providing concealment, an option that would be more attractive for larger, less populated countries. (It is difficult to make mobile missiles highly resistant to blast overpressure, and thus a small country deploying such weapons might be vulnerable to area attacks with pattern bombing.)

A scheme that is intermediate in quality between submarine systems and fixed, undefended land-based systems, but which may be no more expensive than some forms of land basing, is the placement of missiles on surface ships. This possibility is often rejected in casual discussions as being excessively vulnerable. In fact, however, a suitably operated surface-ship system could be of considerable effectiveness. The Multilateral Nuclear Force (the MLF), widely discussed as a proposed United States-European venture in the early and middle 1960s, was, at least in the later years of discussion, intended to be a system based on surface ships. The sheer number of surface ships operating on the world's oceans (there are several hundred thousand) would make it difficult for a prospective enemy to locate such a ship. It would also be possible to construct the ship in such a way that identifying its real purpose from external observations, would be difficult.

Another basing scheme that might possibly appeal to some secondary states would be to use bombs stored in orbit. This system would of course contravene the Outer Space Treaty, but this fact might not be decisive. In the past, the present nuclear powers have not found orbital basing attractive on purely technical grounds, and it is unlikely that an orbital system will seem highly attractive to the superpowers on technical, economic, or political grounds in the near future. However, the same considerations may be equally strong for secondary nuclear powers in the future, when it is to be expected that the cost of placing payload in orbit will be greatly reduced. Thus, this possibility cannot be wholly excluded.

Active defense is one of the ways widely favored by analysts for protecting some components of the U.S. strategic forces. "Active defense" usually means ballistic-missile defense (or "ABM"), but defense against bomber attacks still has some relevance in this connection. Advanced forms of active defense (the term "active" is used in contrast to "passive" defense, as in the use of concrete shelters or dispersal of population) depend on technology that is available at present only to the two current superpowers. I do not expect this situation to change in the near future, but it is possible that useful forms of active defense may become accessible to secondary nuclear states by the 1980s, even without aid from a superpower. If so, active defense may be one of the means available for protecting strategic forces in secondary powers as well.

It should also be noted that active defenses can be used by the present superpowers to limit damage to some degree from attacks on cities, although their use for this purpose is somewhat more controversial.[1] As I shall later indicate, such defenses can importantly influence the possible uses and significance of opposing nuclear forces. The achievement of such

[1]See, for instance, Johan J. Holst and William Schneider, Jr. (eds.), *Why ABM? Policy Issues in the Missile Defense Controversy* (Elmsford, N. Y.: Pergamon, 1969). Chapter 5, by this writer, discusses the issues in the city-defense controversy.

defenses by secondary nuclear states at useful levels of effectiveness is not impossible, but perhaps less likely than the achievement of defenses purely for the protection of nuclear forces.

It is worth noting explicitly at this point that one of the important technical characteristics of potential future nuclear forces is the sheer size, or fire capacity, of the force. It is unfashionable to use the term "ammunition supply" in relation to such forces, but it will be useful for the purposes of this paper to discuss ammunition supplies in relation to the possible objectives of these forces, possible defenses of opponents, and the roles and significance of alliance arrangements.

## PERCEPTUAL AND DOCTRINAL FASHIONS

Technical considerations alone will not suffice to explain the roles and significance of nuclear forces. Some interesting examples of the limited applicability of technical criteria can be found in the history of the French nuclear force and in discussions and debates related to this force. Some strategists have emphasized the vulnerability of the French force, at least as it has existed up to the present, to a first strike, especially one at the level that might be launched by a superpower. (It is true that the Soviets, for instance, could probably eliminate the French strategic force by a suitable attack.) These strategists have therefore tended to argue that the French nuclear force is of no significance, a "zero" on the international scene. This is quite far from being the case, in several ways.

The most immediate effect of the French force was probably purely internal: it stiffened the backbone of the French bureaucracy. Many senior officials of the French government apparently believed that the French nuclear force increased their government's freedom of action, and it gave (or should have given) France something of a preferred position in the world, especially in Europe. Such beliefs, collectively held throughout a bureaucracy, can become something of a self-fulfilling prophecy, and indeed did so in the French case. De Gaulle's withdrawal from the NATO integrated commands, for example, while rooted in some genuine sources of complaint, would likely have been much more difficult if it had not been for the French strategic force, and the belief in at least some quarters of the Foreign Ministry that it increased their freedom of action. The French force was also an important factor in the ability of the Gaullist government to persuade itself that it was entitled to a primary role in the affairs of continental Europe. While such attitudes were not universal outside France, to put it mildly, in France their presence almost certainly contributed substantially to the success (from de Gaulle's point of view) of his foreign policy.

Thus, one must judge that the French nuclear force would have been important to de Gaulle's purposes even if it had been nothing but a sheer façade, the "fakeness" of which was visible to the entire world.

However, the French force was not only a façade vis-à-vis the outside world. As with other national nuclear forces that may possibly emerge, it was partly—and perhaps largely—designed for French needs regarding powers other than the superpowers, given the possibility of relatively local conflicts. In particular, the French force was undoubtedly established with an eye on Germany. For the purpose of protection from a neighbor that can be expected to be without nuclear weapons of its own for a very long period of time, questions of vulnerability to attacks by the superpowers are of little interest. Even if such a neighbor had some nuclear armament, it might not be of a scale or quality to make plausible a successful attack on a force that might well be highly vulnerable to a major attack.

Another interesting example of the relevance of perceptual fashions can be found in relation to the French force. Since the debate about ballistic-missile defenses became an important part of the international political scene, it has become commonplace to hear it said that a major Soviet ballistic-missile defense system would "nullify" the value of the French strategic force. This is not quite true, even in the framework envisaged in such remarks, because the Soviets could not be completely confident of intercepting every weapon the French might fire at them, and this fact alone might well influence the course of a crisis involving France and the Soviet Union. However, the interesting aspect of the remark is that it has become fashionable only with the advent of ballistic-missile defenses and the impending advent of a French missile force. It is interesting that such an observation was almost never heard during the buildup of the French strategic-bomber force, although it is true, and fairly widely recognized, that the Soviets have a *massive* air-defense system—much more dense in relation to the planned future French missile force. Why is it that the political-strategic community is now willing to downgrade the threat of French missiles against a Soviet Union equipped with missile defense, when the French bomber force was not similarly disparaged in relation to a much heavier Soviet air defense? I believe it is fair to answer that this is nothing more than a change in perceptual fashions.

The relevance of such fashions to the subject of multipolar strategy is that the fashions can and do influence the fundamental interactions of such forces and the strategies that will be considered for their use. At the most basic level, such factors as the number of countries possessing nuclear weapons and the circumstances under which nuclear weapons might be used relate to prevailing perceptions about the admissibility of using such weapons. If they are regarded generally as objects of opprobrium, having no significant political use and good only for deterring the use of such weapons by others, and if no particular prestige is attached to national ownership of such weapons, then not many additional countries would be motivated to acquire an independent nuclear-weapon capability. It would, in that case, be relatively unlikely that the weapons would actually be brought into play in a conflict. But if nuclear weapons come to be regarded as "just another weapon," readily useable both for political purposes and for deterring nonnuclear attacks—and if in addition they are widely regarded as "quality" weapons symbolizing an advanced state of technology —then many additional countries would acquire their own national nuclear weapons, and the likelihood that they would be used in some conflict would be much higher. Obviously, an intermediate degree is possible, and the present world situation lies somewhere between these extremes.

The prevailing perceptions themselves may, of course, be influenced by specific nonnuclear defense problems. To illustrate, consider the situation prevailing in the late 1960s, when the United States was very heavily involved in Vietnam. If the North Koreans had chosen that period to reopen the Korean conflict, I am confident that there would have been much serious discussion in the American government about the use of nuclear weapons against North Korea to compensate for the fact that we were already extended in Vietnam and it would have been exceedingly difficult politically to conduct two such nonnuclear campaigns simultaneously in two different theaters. In other words, U.S. willingness to use nuclear weapons in North Korea might, among a number of other factors, have been influenced by the nonnuclear conflict in Vietnam. I do not know how the resulting U.S. debate would have come out, but it is certainly clear that—in that hypothetical context—nuclear weapons would have seemed more "useable" in Korea than they would have if the Vietnamese conflict had not existed. It is easy to find other examples in which the admissibility of nuclear use could become linked to secondary nonnuclear issues.

One of the most important doctrinal fashions that will impinge on the interactions of multiple nuclear forces is the extent to which deterrence is emphasized in relation to defense. The relative importance attached to deterrence on the one hand, and to defense on the other, will in the first instance depend upon prevailing states of technology. If strategic nuclear offensive forces are very efficient in relation to achievable active defenses (mainly air and missile defense), as was the case in the 1950s and early 1960s, then deterrence will dominate most strategic considerations and active defense will play a relatively small role. If, on the other hand, active defense were very effective in relation to prevailing offensive-force technology, then considerable additional emphasis would be given to defense as a component of over-all strategic forces. If offensive and defensive technology are of roughly comparable effectiveness, as has been the case (at least for the superpowers) in the middle and late 1960s, then the relative emphasis to be given deterrence or defense will depend very much on the prevailing fashions.[2] And it may well happen that doctrinal fashions concerning this point will differ substantially from one country to another. Indeed, through the 1960s attitudes in the United States concerning this point differed sharply from the corresponding views in the Soviet Union. I shall return to the significance of defense in a multipolar context later in this discussion.

## SOME FORCE INTERACTIONS AND USES

In this section I shall take up some of the kinds of nuclear confrontations that could take place in a multipolar nuclear world. For the most part, I shall consider a world of two superpowers and a number of secondary nuclear powers. It will be useful to consider three major categories of interactions or confrontations: (a) cases involving the two superpowers alone; (b) cases involving one superpower and one or more secondary powers; and (c) cases involving two or more secondary powers only. In order to keep the discussion within reasonable bounds, it is necessary to consider simplified and idealized cases, but the nature of the elaborations that would be required for more complicated circumstances will, I hope, mainly be clear.

### Two-Superpower Cases

Whether the secondary nuclear powers in our hypothetical multipolar world would be important in confrontations primarily involving the two superpowers would depend very much on the details of the forces deployed. Consider, for example, a world in which each superpower had 2,000 well-protected missiles, and suppose there were six secondary powers, each equipped with 100 missiles. Let us assume further that virtually no active defenses were deployed in any of the nuclear states. It is then clear that in confrontations which in the first instance involve only the two superpowers, the presence of a number of secondary nuclear states would not be likely to exert significant influence on the confrontation. (I shall discuss the case of the disguised attack by a secondary power on a superpower in the next category.) The superpowers would probably act in their crisis very much as though the secondary nuclear powers did not exist.

However, this result is sensitive to the ammunition supply and the presence or absence of defenses. If the two superpowers had 1,000 missiles

---

[2]For a fuller discussion of this point, see my chapter in the Holst and Schneider volume.

each, and there were six secondary states with 200 missiles each, and three
or four of the secondary states were hostile to one of the superpowers—and
if that superpower did not have substantial missile defenses—then that
superpower would probably be sensitive to the fact that even a "modest"
war with its adversary might leave it in a weak position relative to a group
of the secondary states. In other words, the presence of the secondary
powers would strengthen the deterrence between the superpowers, at least
in one direction (and quite possibly both). If, however, the superpowers
had deployed substantial missile defenses, they might again be relatively
insensitive to the presence of the secondary nuclear forces.

### Primary-Secondary Cases

Some of the most interesting potential cases are those involving confrontations between one superpower and one or more secondary powers. If
the superpower involved had active defenses that would substantially pre-
clude damage from "small" attacks, the situation would be very different
from the one that would prevail if the superpower had no defenses. In
either case, deterrence would be something of a two-way street, because
even a substantial defense might let one or a few weapons "leak" through.
But deterrence of the superpower by the secondary power would surely be
far more persuasive if the superpower had no substantial defenses.

Some effect of this kind (relating to defenses) would be associated with
the extent to which the forces of the secondary power were protected
against attack. If the forces of the secondary power could be substantially
eliminated by an attack from the superpower, it should make the secondary
state nervous about any confrontation with the superpower, although the
superpower could not have confidence that it could wholly eliminate the
secondary force, or that some of the weapons of the secondary force would
not be fired before being attacked.

Something of an intermediate case would result if the forces of the secondary power were adequately protected from attacks by other secondary
powers, even though they might be vulnerable to a really large-scale attack
by a superpower. If the superpower were thus obliged to expend much of
its ammunition to even have a hope of eliminating the forces of the secondary power, the secondary power would derive a good deal of deterrence
from this situation. It should be clear that the extent and effectiveness of
defenses in the superpower would potentially interact with the degree of
vulnerability of the forces in the secondary state.

One of the traditional "scenarios" involving the interaction of primary
and secondary nuclear states is that of the disguised, or "catalytic," attack. The idea behind such attacks is that a secondary state might strike
one superpower (or, perhaps, both superpowers) in such a way as to make

each superpower attacked believe that the attack had been launched by the other, thus presumably inducing a large-scale but completely mistaken war between the two superpowers.

This concept has sometimes been discussed as if a catalytic attack "out of the blue" could provoke a major nuclear war between the superpowers. In actuality, this seems rather unlikely. Both superpowers are well aware that other nuclear states exist, and if a "small" nuclear attack were to occur "out of the blue," the first reaction in either nuclear power would probably be an investigation of the possible source of the attack, together with prompt communication seeking information from the other superpower. Therefore, a disguised attack is unlikely to be effective in triggering a war if it were to occur in a relaxed period.

However, a disguised attack might have very different consequences in a period of extreme crisis, one in which the decision makers in the superpowers were figuratively "poised over the buttons" in the expectation that war was about to begin at any moment. The kind of circumstances that might arise were nicely illustrated in the Cuban missile crisis. In President Kennedy's first public statement about the crisis, he said that any missile launched from Cuba at any point in the Western Hemisphere would be treated as an attack by the Soviet Union calling for a full retaliatory response on the Soviet Union. It is interesting to speculate whether, before making that statement, President Kennedy considered the possibility— which then was certainly remote—that a Chinese missile-launching submarine might then have been in Caribbean waters and could have simulated a missile attack from Cuba, New York, Washington, and perhaps a few other cities. Given the tension that prevailed at the time, and the nature of Kennedy's statement, I believe that not many such weapons would have been required to have triggered a massive American attack on the Soviet Union. Further, it is interesting to speculate whether, if the Chinese had had suitable capabilities at that time, they would have been tempted to try to exploit President Kennedy's statement. Perhaps not, but then perhaps so.

This example should make it quite clear that the possibility of a disguised attack in an intense crisis is a serious one. Again, however, the presence of substantial defenses could make a major difference in the feasibility or likely success of such an attack. Even moderate defenses would probably mean that a few weapons would create no damage whatever; and if a small attack were effectively blunted by defenses, it would not lead to the same pressures for a response that the loss of even a few major cities would induce. Of course, a sufficiently large attack could begin to penetrate even a substantial defense, but the difficulty of disguising the source of an attack would increase sharply with the size of the attack.

Disguised attacks, intended to produce a catalytic war, have been known throughout history, and thus do not constitute a fundamentally new strategic problem, although of course the possible scale of effects is new. The case of anonymous attacks, however—that is, attacks not made to appear launched by someone else but in which the identity of the attacker is concealed—appears to be a fundamentally new strategic problem resulting from nuclear multipolarity. The reason that this is a new thing in the world has to do with the fact that, before nuclear weapons, an attack that could reliably be anonymous was also reliably small in its effects. With nuclear weapons, however, a single weapon, emplaced in advance by clandestine means, could easily destroy a major city. Just a single such weapon might therefore have highly significant political effects, and a few could have major consequences.

For example, suppose that one superpower is engaged in a highly unpopular war with a small, not necessarily nuclear power, and suppose that there are six or eight nuclear states in the world known to be very hostile to the continuation of that war. If the superpower involved were to receive an anonymous message stating that one of its cities per month would be destroyed until it discontinued the war, and thereafter one of its major cities *was* destroyed, continued prosecution of that war would be made politically very difficult for the superpower. Continuation of the war after the loss of two or three cities in this way would require political determination so extreme that it would seem to be national fanaticism.

On the other hand, it should be noted that for a secondary nuclear power to engage in such a tactic would involve a major risk of detection. It is not to be expected that this tactic will become common in the nuclear age. However, the possibility of this tactic represents, in a very real sense, something new under the sun. I believe that it has not been widely enough recognized and discussed in the strategic literature.

I have discussed this possible problem as one involving a superpower and an unknown secondary nuclear power, but of course there is nothing inherent in the situation that relates in an important way to the size of the countries concerned; the roles of the two countries could be reversed, or anonymous attacks be conducted by one secondary power on another.

Whatever the size of the countries, the attacked power does not have any easy choices about responding if it is genuinely unable to penetrate the anonymity of the attacker. In most cases, the only response that would be likely to be politically feasible would be a surrender to the demands of the anonymous blackmailer. The only alternative would appear to be attacks of some kind, nuclear or otherwise, on one or more states that may not have had anything to do with the anonymous attack. For instance, the victim of the attack might destroy one city in each of the two or three or four countries it judged most likely to have been responsible, and announce that a repetition of the anonymous attack would bring on such retaliation again, directed at the same or possibly other states. Let us call this the "blunderbuss response." It is very clear that a state engaging in a blunderbuss response to an anonymous attack is unlikely to lead an international popularity poll, and this response would be likely to stiffen what might otherwise be a flabby alliance among the opposition. However, there are, as I mentioned, few alternatives. It is possible that in particular situations a better one might be found.

## SECONDARY-SECONDARY INTERACTIONS

We have seen that, in interactions involving a superpower with one or more secondary nuclear powers, questions of technical characteristics of the forces, such as the ammunition supply and the nature and degree of protection, could have some influence on nuclear confrontations. On the whole, however, one would expect that "most" such confrontations—in some suitable sense of "most"—would not depend very strongly on the technical characteristics of the forces involved, since one of them would be so much greater than the other. In relationships among the secondary nuclear states alone, since the size of the various forces involved would be at least relatively closer to each other, there would be more plausible situations in which the technical characteristics of the forces involved (including ammunition supply) could influence the nature of the interaction. Apart from this observation, the kinds of confrontations that might be encountered among the secondary states would not differ from those already considered for nuclear relationships among the superpowers alone or between a superpower and one or more secondary powers.

The observation, however, constitutes an important qualification. Consider, for example, two potential secondary nuclear forces, one owned by Israel and the other by a consortium of Arab states. The exact degree to which either or both of these forces would be vulnerable to attacks by a superpower, or susceptible of being intercepted by the defenses of a superpower, would generally be of little consequence for the kinds of interactions that would be most likely to be of importance. (There could be exceptions to this principle.) However, the exact degree to which these hypothetical forces would be vulnerable to each other, or the exact extent to which the forces of one might be intercepted by the defenses of the other, might well heavily influence, or even dominate, the nuclear relationships of the states concerned.

For example, if both of these hypothetical forces had the property that half of either force (if fired first) could reliably eliminate all of the other (a situation that would be technically possible), one could virtually guarantee that these forces would not remain unused through the first intense crisis that occurred after their deployment. In such a crisis each side would become highly aware, not to say preoccupied, with the fact that to wait for its opponent to strike first would guarantee losing to the opponent and the opponent would escape unscathed. The opponent involved, of course, being aware of this nervousness on the part of its adversary, and understanding clearly that the other state could equally win decisively at negligible cost if it undertook the first strike, would also be getting very nervous, and considering initiating the first strike itself. This kind of interactive mechanism, called by T. C. Schelling "the reciprocal fear of surprise attack," is an example of what is often called a "preemptive instability," that is, an instability due to the technical characteristics of the forces confronting each other that leads to pressures for preemption in a crisis.

Preemptive instabilities are very unlikely to figure importantly in the interaction of a superpower with a secondary state, and I should judge that, if the superpowers retain some competence in such matters, preemptive instabilities are even unlikely to be important for the superpowers confronting each other. However, they may well be of considerable importance between secondary nuclear powers.

In many cases, preemptive instabilities might not loom as an important factor for secondary forces. Such would be the case if, for example, the forces involved were virtually invulnerable to attack, and if the decision processes and command and control systems governing the systems were equally invulnerable—a combination of circumstances that can by no means always be expected of secondary forces. Of course, if some secondary nuclear force had been acquired chiefly for political and prestige reasons, and the force had never loomed as an important actual threat to some other force, questions of preemptive instabilities would also be substantially irrelevant. However, the hypothetical Arab-Israeli case sketched above should suffice to indicate that the problem could be a real one.

It is interesting to note that preemptive instabilities, if they occur, result mainly or wholly from technical characteristics. Such cases would therefore constitute instances in which purely technical factors could increase, perhaps markedly, the likelihood of war. For some reason, the idea that purely technical effects of this kind can themselves become an important factor leading to a war seems unreal to many traditional political analysts of international relations. The effects involved, however, could be very real indeed.

The context of several secondary nuclear powers is a good one in which to illustrate one of the important differences that can arise according to whether strategic nuclear philosophy prevailing in the several states involved is primarily offensive, or defensive. (I assume here that there is some ultimate feasibility of defenses of substantial effectiveness for these states.) If the prevailing fashion is one of primary reliance on deterrence by offensive forces, and if each of several states does not wish to be in an inferior position to any possible combination of its potential opponents, then the situation is certain to produce unlimited arms races in offensive forces if more than two states are involved. This situation would result, of course, because, for at least some purposes and under some circumstances, the nuclear offensive forces of several potential enemies can be added together to constitute a single and much larger nuclear force.

However, if the prevailing fashion is one of defense, then the defenses of several different countries would not in general add together to constitute a single and more powerful defense. Thus a situation involving several secondary states could be stable against arms races in an environment emphasizing defensive forces, even if each of the states were determined not to be in an inferior position to any potential combination of adversaries. (This effect was pointed out to me some time ago by Alvin Weinberg.)

### Miscellaneous Interaction Effects

The question sometimes comes up as to whether traditional "balance-of-power" calculations will be made as *nuclear* balance-of-power calculations in a multipolar world. It is my belief that this is not likely to happen often, if at all, but the possibility cannot be excluded.

Again, the question is very much bound up with the technical characteristics of the forces and postures involved. Some examples may help make the considerations involved clearer. Suppose there are six secondary nuclear states, each rather small in area and having only ten major metropolitan areas, so that each country can be substantially destroyed by ten well-placed weapons of high yield. Let us assume that each of these nuclear powers has 100 missiles, each of which is absolutely impervious to attack. Finally, let us assume that there are no active defenses in any of these states. Then it is quite clear that nuclear balance-of-power calculations would play no role in that situation. Each of the secondary powers has an overkill capability against all five other secondary states taken together—in fact, twice over. There is no strategic point to be served in considering groupings of these nuclear forces. If there is also a superpower on the scene that some of these secondary states would like to "balance," and if that superpower has, say, 2,000 missiles and has a defense that could intercept at least 1,000 missiles fired at it, then the superpower is not going to be in the least "balanced" by any feasible grouping among the six secondary states. If the superpower does not have the defenses, then its sensitivity to coalitions among the secondary states would depend chiefly on the extent to which it is sensitive to the difference between being targeted with 100 missiles or 600 missiles. It is not difficult to believe that the United States, at least, would not be sharply sensitive to that difference, at least in a wide range of circumstances.

To return to the collection of secondary states alone, let us now consider a situation in which each of the countries has 100 missiles as before, but in which each country has a defense that could intercept, say, 150 missiles. In that situation, one would expect a good deal of diplomatic activity designed to produce favorable alliances and coalitions and inhibit the establishment of coalitions pointed the wrong way. In such a case, nuclear balance-of-power calculations could easily have some significance.

But it seems to me that on the nuclear level the circumstances in which such calculations will be significant are likely to be rare, at least in comparison to the frequency with which traditional balance-of-power calculations will be significant.

Another miscellaneous effect I wish to mention here is that there can be important serial effects involving several nuclear states, if an actual nuclear war takes place. For example, if there are, say, eight nuclear states, then the relationships among all eight can easily be modified as a result of a nuclear war involving only two of the states. As an easy example, suppose the two superpowers were the states having the initial war and were largely destroyed, and suppose that some of the secondary states had been client states of the superpowers. It is clear that a quite different set of relationships would exist after the war. Serial effects could easily be influenced by technical factors, such as ammunition supply and the vulnerability of the forces concerned.

## STYLES OF WAR-FIGHTING

It is probably appropriate to point out here that the ways are quite varied in which strategic nuclear forces might actually be used in a war involving two or more nuclear states, and that these ways can interact with the political uses and significance of the forces, although it is perhaps not too likely that they will interact very much in this manner.

A fairly common image of strategic nuclear war between two nuclear states is that one country will fire most or all of its missiles at the other country, perhaps mainly at military forces, and that the country attacked will then retaliate, using most or all of its surviving forces, perhaps firing mainly or wholly at cities. It is conceivable that a war might actually go this way, but it is also conceivable that it may not.

The kinds of confrontations which would most likely immediately become all-out strategic nuclear wars are those involving some vulnerability of the forces. For example, if state A is contemplating an attack on state B, and the nuclear forces of state B are significantly vulnerable to attack (that is, if they can be appreciably reduced, or perhaps even wholly eliminated, by an attack from state A), then the argument in state A will go as follows: "If we attack the forces in state B as heavily as we are able, we shall insure that the damage they can do to us in retaliation is at least limited to the capability of their surviving forces. If, however, we begin with a very limited attack, perhaps just a missile or two to demonstrate to them that we are very serious and want them to back down, we may signal to them that we shall eventually attack them in a large-scale way. Then, if we convince them of this possibility by that limited attack, they would attack us in turn—with a nearly or wholly undamaged force, so that we should be much worse off than if we had struck their forces all-out first." This line of thought will argue for an all-out attack if any attack at all is to be undertaken.

I believe that such arguments are very unlikely to be persuasive in cases where a maximum attack on the enemy's strategic forces would leave those forces substantially intact. However, it is possible to argue that even if the enemy forces could be very much damaged, but if your own forces were vulnerable to some attrition, then it would still be desirable to initiate an all-out attack promptly, if any attack at all is to be undertaken. But in this case one would target the cities and population of the opponent so as to ensure that the opponent would be in a relatively weakened position in the postwar world. I believe that this line of thought is not likely to be important in any nuclear state in the near future, but one cannot exclude the future possibility of such reasoning—and of actions based on such reasoning.

If a strategic nuclear attack is not all-out, then it will be limited in some degree. The range of possibilities is from one single weapon upwards, and the targets attacked may be military, nonmilitary, or mixed. A limited strategic war would be mainly a competition in resolve and determination. Presumably, if such a war were to take place, it would be about some essentially political issue, and the nuclear attacks would be used in an attempt to coerce a resolution of the war on terms that would presumably have some relationship to the issues that started the war. If strategic nuclear war ever comes about deliberately as "the continuation of politics by other means," as opposed to arising through inadvertent escalation from some crisis or from some essentially technical accident, it will have this kind of relationship to the issues that led to the war. However, it is quite possible that such a situation may never come to pass.

## CONCLUSIONS

There are very few over-all conclusions that I can draw from a study of nuclear strategy in a multipolar context. Relative to purely nonnuclear conflicts, the maximum possible damage of a nuclear war is of course enormous. However, it does not seem possible to me to conclude that wars would be more or less likely to be limited, more or less likely to happen, or more or less destructive. In common with many other students of these matters, I believe that the world will become more dangerous if more countries come to own nuclear weapons; but this is not a new perception and it does not arise specifically from a detailed examination of strategies.

But this examination of multipolar strategic problems does reinforce my belief that active defense—missile and air defense—is important for the United States. The greater the number of nuclear countries that could potentially attack the United States in a crisis, the more it seems to me we should have defenses capable of making a genuine difference. We can have them if we choose to have them, and I believe we should.[3]

[3]See Holst and Schneider.

CHAPTER 2

Malcolm W. Hoag

# *Superpower Strategic Postures for a Multipolar World*

## PROLIFERATION AND INTERDEPENDENCE

Predicting the extent and character of long-run nuclear proliferation, and prescribing policy measures that are designed to affect proliferation and resultant multipolar power relationships, are precarious activities. For each country concerned, there are many important variables the future character and magnitude of which are highly uncertain. Forecasters have to put their predictions in probabilistic terms, and deal with subjective rather than objective probabilities at that, which compounds their problem. In all the relevant nations, the issues will turn upon the subjective assessments of decision makers in an environment of complex bureaucratic interactions. Predictions about the results will, in consequence, be prone to error.[1] Furthermore, the subjective probabilities are highly interdependent. What one powerful nation does can powerfully influence other nations in their decisions about military nuclear programs.

Because this interdependence is so central it probably yields the most fruitful approach toward policy prescription and cautious prediction. Such an approach will necessarily focus, especially at this time, upon key policy variables that can be altered in the short run. To do so may appear to be to evade long-term policy problems because prediction is so difficult. Such is not the case. No useful forecast for the 1990–2000 decade, for example, could avoid specifying the crucial determinants during 1970–1990 that shaped conditions in 1990. Given the need to specify the interim

[1]Thus, in "1970 Without Arms Control" (Washington: The National Planning Association, 1958), the authors suggested (p. 41) that the world might have had as many as eight to ten nuclear powers by 1970.

The author is a senior staff member of The RAND Corporation. Any views expressed in this paper are those of the author. They should not be interpreted as reflecting the views of The RAND Corporation or the official opinion or policy of any of its governmental or private research sponsors. Papers are reproduced by The RAND Corporation as a courtesy to members of its staff.

determinants, but an inability to predict with confidence any single "scenario" for 1970–1990, a responsible forecaster for 1990–2000 will present multiple forecasts linked to alternative scenarios. In confronting the distant future, his problem is comparable to that of the military planner. Such a planner must prepare alternative contingency plans, knowing that no single plan will be appropriate over the entire range of equally probable conflict situations that he can envisage.

To focus on the transitional period immediately ahead is especially apt at this time. The early 1970s will call for national nuclear decisions of far-reaching significance. The Nuclear Non-Proliferation Treaty (NPT) has gone into effect, but would-be nuclear powers have not signed and ratified it. Its importance is manifest. More importantly, the decisions to be made on strategic postures by the two superpowers, decisions emerging either from the U.S.-U.S.S.R. Strategic-Arms-Limitation Talks (SALT), or from national planning, will have a vital impact upon the type and pace of nuclear proliferation.

New technological alternatives for strategic-force deployment—or for nondeployment by mutual abstention—account for the sweeping import of superpower choices. MIRV (Multiple Independently Targetable Re-entry Vehicles from a single missile launcher) and ABM (Anti-Ballistic Missile defense) systems are especially important. Such technological developments (including an ABM that could be "thin" in antimissile depth and yet provide some area coverage for an entire continent) are almost as revolutionary in their impact as the earlier marriage of the ICBM and the thermonuclear warhead. The debate about strategic-force postures and plans, in consequence, has once again become lively, as it was during the late 1950s and early 1960s.

The strategic-posture decisions of the superpowers will influence the character of nuclear proliferation as well as its pace. In the context of arguments about the NPT, in particular, pace has been emphasized almost to the exclusion of character. The nonnuclear powers, who are being asked to renounce a nuclear option and thus to limit "horizontal proliferation," as measured simply by the number of nuclear powers, have asked in return that the existing nuclear powers limit "vertical proliferation" by reducing some of their nuclear options.[2]

No request could be more natural; all proud nations resist formal discrimination against themselves. And the request for evidence of reciprocal restraint is in keeping with sincere desires to achieve global arms control. At the same time, some meaningful limits upon vertical proliferation by the superpowers (for example, zero ABM) could spur rather than deter

[2]See Elizabeth Young, "The Control of Proliferation: The 1968 Treaty in Hindsight and Forecast," *Adelphi Paper 56* (London: The Institute for Strategic Studies, April 1969).

some vertical proliferation on the part of the horizontal proliferators. The relationships between limits on superpower vertical proliferation and horizontal proliferation are complicated, with some influences working in opposite directions.

Limits upon superpower vertical proliferation might help check proliferation among nations whose potential nuclear ambitions are centered on achieving retaliatory capabilities against nonsuperpower neighbors. The next nuclear powers are likely to come in opposed pairs—Israel versus the United Arab Republic; India versus mainland China, but then Pakistan versus India; Australia versus mainland China; and so on—with resultant strategic programs that are oriented almost exclusively to immediate regional fears. As long as such programs remain so centered, the only possible adverse effect of setting limits to superpower vertical proliferation would be the undermining of the credibility of superpower nuclear guarantees to allies and nonnuclear neutrals. Otherwise, the "demonstration effect" of superpower willingness to limit their nuclear options would be helpful in inducing other nations to limit their options.

But what if the retaliatory ambitions of new nuclear powers expand to include retaliatory second-strike capabilities against one or both of the superpowers? After all, each of the current nuclear powers falls in this class. Mainland China supplies the clearest case of a nuclear power that must strive for an "all-azimuths" retaliatory capability. Its government must worry at least as much about the possible threat posed by the Soviet Union as that posed by the United States. The French case is now ambiguous. Having proclaimed an enlarged objective for an all-azimuths retaliatory capability,[3] its government, even before the departure of President de Gaulle, appeared to be modifying this objective on grounds of both cost and a less unfavorable attitude toward the competing doctrine of "flexible response."[4] Among the current nuclear nonsuperpowers, only Great Britain has its retaliatory objective clearly oriented toward but one of the superpowers.

About the aspirations of new nuclear powers, the only easy speculation is that most of them will begin with retaliatory objectives limited to one or more of their nonsuperpower neighbors. A few, if they begin at all, will of necessity aim higher. Sweden supplies the obvious example. In the debate within Sweden, both proponents and opponents of a nuclear option have taken it for granted that the possible threat comes from the Soviet

[3]Chief of Staff General Ailleret, " 'Directed' Defense or 'Defense in All Directions,' " *The Review of National Defense* (December 1967); subsequently confirmed by President de Gaulle, *The New York Times,* January 30, 1968.

[4]General M. Fourquet, "The Use of the Different Force Systems in the Framework of Deterrent Strategy," *The Review of National Defense* (May 1969). Presumably this article had been reviewed within the French government months before its publication.

Union. The debate about the character of a possible Swedish nuclear program has turned upon the type of weaponry, strategic or tactical, rather than upon the foe it would be designed to counter. Another example is a possible United Western European Force, where the weight of conjecture falls not upon the nature of the threat but upon the feasibility of a truly United Western Europe as a sovereign power able to command such a force. The prospect of a Western European Force appears nebulous and distant, rather than specific and near.[5] Nonetheless, it certainly belongs on the list of possible forces whose retaliatory objectives, by geographic definition and inheritance, would clearly be ambitious.

Rather than speculate further about nuclear ambitions, it is more rewarding to consider the controllable policy variables that can influence their extent. Some of these variables do not deal directly with strategic postures. Thus efforts to secure a NPT and get it ratified have gone hand in hand with other, unilateral efforts to keep the costs of nuclear acquisition high. Information about improved technology for producing nuclear materials and weapons has been safeguarded within tight security limits, and various trade controls have been employed to hinder the export of items that would assist military nuclear programs abroad. In themselves, trade controls have sometimes irritated foreign powers so much—witness the ban on export to France of large-capacity computers for advanced scientific usage—that they may have reinforced rather than weakened national incentives for nuclear programs. More generally, such nationalistic measures have made other nations less willing to accept so sweeping a renunciation of future options as the NPT implies.

However unfortunate their impacts upon foreign pride, the controls remain highly desirable. The main criticism against them is that they were not uniformly or completely applied. Some nations were discriminated against; and some critical items were provided (for example, KC-135 tankers for the French strategic-bomber force), while other, less critical items were denied to the same recipient. These controls were nonetheless justified, despite the foreign resentments that they aroused, one of them being a heightened resistance to the NPT. So be it. Foreign policy is not so simple that whatever maximizes the prospects for securing adherents to the NPT can, by that one criterion alone, be said to maximize meaningful arms control.

[5] About this possibility, one notes that its supporters start by assuming a marriage between the strategic forces of France and Great Britain. These are precisely the nations, among the current members of the Common Market and the candidates for membership, who have been the least enthusiastic about converting the European Economic Community from a customs union to a sovereign power. And can anything else than one unquestionably sovereign center of authority (a President) be consistent with the life-and-death decision power over a nuclear force?

Just as national trade controls can sometimes conflict with gaining adherents to the NPT, so, more powerfully, can desirable adjustments in strategic postures. Some limits on superpower vertical proliferation are feasible and desirable (1) in their own right, and (2) in making it easier, by demonstration, for other nations to adhere to NPT or other arms-control limitations. The latter demonstration effect is important, but not all-important.

The NPT is no mere piece of paper, despite its escape clause in Article X ("Each Party shall in exercising its national sovereignty have the right to withdraw from the Treaty if it decides that extraordinary events ... have jeopardized the supreme interests of its country"), and despite valid skepticism about the effectiveness of international inspection of nuclear facilities for peaceful purposes. If it were only that, Japanese and West German opposition would not have been so intense. These governments have been deeply concerned about possible long-run adverse implications of ratifying the NPT, and not merely because they fear commercial discrimination in peaceful applications of nuclear energy. Given the great emotional resistance to Japanese and West German nuclear armament, both within their own electorates and abroad, leaders of these nations realize that any subsequent attempt to evade the Treaty or invoke the escape clause would result in extraordinary political difficulties. Other nations would face similar, if not such extreme, difficulties. Hence the political implications of commitment to the NPT are important for all nations, if more for some than for others. Securing adherents to the NPT should therefore be regarded as an important, but not all-important, objective for United States foreign policy. How heavily should this objective be weighted in determining United States arms-control and force-structure policy?

## LIMITING "VERTICAL PROLIFERATION"

Answers to this question will become clearer as the strategic-arms-limitation talks proceed. These positions will establish vital precedents. An especially convenient focus for discussion is the position most favored by articulate U.S. public opinion, because it would maximize limits upon superpower vertical proliferation.

There are numerous variants of this popular position.[6] Yet some themes are so central and common that, with slight risk of caricature, they can be conveniently summarized. It is assumed that the bipolar strategic balance

[6]For one important example, see Carl Kaysen, "Military Strategy, Military Forces, and Arms Control," in Kermit Gordon (ed.), *Agenda for the Nation* (Washington: The Brookings Institution, 1968).

between the superpowers is now stable. Usually this assumption is not spelled out rigorously, but seems to mean that neither superpower, by striking first under any circumstances, could (1) eliminate the capability of the other for "Assured Destruction" of most of the urban centers of the attacking power, or even (2) mount any counterforce attacks that would destroy more retaliatory capability than the attacker used up in his first strike.[7] The dominating fear, of course, is that the new technology (above all, MIRVs for the offense, and ABMs for the defense) may destroy this stability, and will certainly lead to an expensive and mutually threatening new round in a strategic-arms race the end of which is difficult to foresee.

Given so prevalent a fear, it is not surprising that those who share it typically do not merely favor a mutual ban upon MIRVs and ABMs, but are willing to risk a ban that incorporates no provision for inspection. They deem unilateral observation capabilities, without any ground inspection, adequate. As recently as 1967, when President Johnson proposed SALT, an official spokesman for the U.S. Department of Defense remarked, "We hope to avoid bogging down in the perennially difficult issue of international inspection." This remark bothers even so militant a supporter of limits upon vertical proliferation as Mrs. Young: "It was perhaps rash of the United States to agree to a [NPT] Treaty which permitted the Soviet Union to avoid all forms of international control, including those to which others were to be submitted. This could be the thin end of a wedge of noncontrol, and to the extent that security depends upon knowledge, it was a bad precedent."[8]

The central arms-control issue could not be better put: "security depends upon knowledge." The deterrent whose existence remains unknown to the enemy, as in the famed "Dr. Strangelove" illustration, does not deter. Similarly, a mutual ban upon weapon systems whose observance is not verified cannot be trusted. The inspection problem is central. Why, then, was a United States spokesman in 1967 willing to consider an outcome from SALT that would impose mutual limits without provisions for inspection on Soviet territory?[9] Probably the date 1967 supplies the best

[7]For one illustration of underlying models of unstable and stable strategic equilibrium, see M. W. Hoag, "On Stability in Deterrent Races," *World Politics* (July 1961), especially pp. 513–515. To convert this old numerical example of movement from unstable to stable missile postures back to feared instability, one need merely assume ten re-entry vehicles per MIRVed missile while leaving the other parameters unchanged. Such a specter, which is useful to illustrate a concept, but is singularly unrealistic in not changing the other parameters, seems to be exactly the oversimplification about total strategic postures that is prevalent. Hence its current relevance.

[8]Young, p. 17. The quoted U.S. official was Paul C. Warnke, then Assistant Secretary of Defense for International Security Affairs.

[9]Thus the Soviets during the 1961 negotiations rejected the U.S. proposed clause: "Such verification should ensure that not only agreed limitations or reductions take place but also that retained armed forces and armaments do not exceed agreed levels at any stage." The Soviet

answer. An official United States position then no doubt reflected an interagency compromise over alternative positions that had been drafted, and fought over, for many months. The strategic and technological perspective of the mid-sixties made a no-inspection provision much less questionable than it is today, for several reasons.

First, of course, a freeze in the number of strategic missiles on both sides would have been markedly more advantageous to the United States at the end of 1967 than at any subsequent time. The United States had already attained its programmed goals for numbers of ICBM launchers (1,054) and Fleet Ballistic Missiles (656); while the respective Soviet numbers (520 and 130) were only transient points on a steep up-curve for programmed Soviet strategic strength.[10] Officials, even if they then underestimated its future magnitude, were aware of the looming Soviet build-up. To avert it was worth paying a heavy price in terms of foregoing otherwise desirable United States goals in the negotiations.

Second, the character of the deployed land-based missiles on both sides—one silo = one missile launcher = one re-entry vehicle—was unambiguously clear, both then and for a few years afterward, so that unilateral inspection by satellite or other means was demonstrably feasible. Unilateral inspection of defensive installations by similar means yielded no such clear-cut results, but was less critical. Thus, yesterday's hot debate about whether the Soviet "Tallinn Line" system was designed for air or for missile defense has tended toward the opinion that it had no significant ABM capability. But only some on-site inspection could have removed yesterday's crucial uncertainty about the "Tallinn Line" capability, just as only it could resolve today's debate about whether Tallinn's original design permitted subsequent up-grading to a significant ABM capability, without appreciable change in its outward appearance. Finally, the most critical test for unilateral inspection—whether it could detect with high confidence any evasion of a MIRV ban, including evasion of a ban upon MIRV testing—was less dubious in 1967 than it is today.

For these and other reasons, the mid-sixties interagency debate within the United States bureaucracy resulted in a 1967 position that relied upon unilateral inspection. Because any arms-limitation agreement with the Soviets would have to pass its supreme political test within the United States before a sceptical United States Senate, verification of limits by

rejection was complete: "However, such control, which in fact means control over armaments, would turn into an international system of legalized espionage, which would naturally be unacceptable to any State concerned for its security and the interests of preserving peace throughout the world." Arms Control and Disarmament Agency, *U.S. Documents on Disarmament, 1961* (Washington, D. C.: U.S. Government Printing Office, 1961), pp. 442–43.

[10]The Institute for Strategic Studies, *The Military-Balance, 1967–1968* (London: ISS, 1968), p. 45.

means of unilateral inspection alone would not have been approved without searching scrutiny within the Executive Branch. This scrutiny, compared with popular discussion, could draw upon better intelligence and techno-logical information. Consequently just as the official 1967 position re-flected a compromise among perspectives taken in the mid-sixties by dif-ferent agencies within the government, the popular public position in 1970 probably reflects, with a communications lag, the official 1967 position. Can it pass scrutiny for 1972?

Public debate, given the legislative timing that happened to bring the Safeguard deployment before Congress in 1969, has concentrated too much upon ABM. The desirability and feasibility of a MIRV ban supplies a better focal point for the debate about strategic stability. It does so be-cause the presumed existence or nonexistence of particular *kinds* of MIRV capability by one superpower will make particular *kinds* of ABM capa-bility on the part of the other superpower desirable or undesirable, since such an ABM capability will be assessed as an efficient (cost-effective) or inefficient use of total strategic expenditure. If one wants to police agreed limits upon ABM deployments, especially without on-site inspection to dis-tinguish clearly between air-defense and missile-defense capabilities, the most powerful reassurance may be provided by offensive deployments that make ABM deployments in violation of the agreed limits inefficient.

A weakness in the popular public position that seeks a total ban on MIRV and ABM capabilities is a failure to distinguish among different kinds of such capabilities, a consequent lumping together of future pro-grammed U.S. and Soviet capabilities as if they were similar, and a tendency to assume that any MIRV or ABM deployment by the one superpower creates an incentive rather than disincentive for countering ABM or MIRV deployment by the other superpower. Such a failure to distinguish among sharply different kinds of MIRV capa-bilities, with very different implications for the strategic balance, is no longer excusable. The public record is clear:

. . . the United States' decision to deploy this [MIRV] technology was based primarily upon our requirement to penetrate Soviet defenses, not upon its multiple target capability . . . . The explosive yields in our MIRVs are small . . . . [They] will not add significantly to the American ability to destroy hardened Soviet weapons even if all of the MIRVed warheads carried by one booster are fired at the same Soviet missile site. . . . Therefore, I believe that the United States' MIRV must be considered as a stabilizing influence since it preserves our deterrent while not threatening theirs.[11]

[11]Statement of Dr. John S. Foster, Jr., Director of Research and Engineering, Depart-ment of Defense, before the Subcommittee on National Security Policy and Scientific Development of the House Committee on Foreign Affairs, United States Congress, August 5, 1969, pp. 4–5, 7.

With respect to possible Soviet ABM deployments, the programmed U.S. MIRV deployments, now being carried out, will (1) make a "thick" ABM defense of Soviet cities distinctly less effective, and therefore less likely to be deployed, while (2) a specialized ABM defense of their missile silos will not be needed for their hardened missile silos, and therefore will be, roughly, neither more nor less likely. The Soviets need to fear an American first strike no more than before, while they become distinctly less confident about their capability to blunt an American second, retaliatory strike. Because Soviet awareness that their population and industry remain hostage to American retaliatory capabilities is central to perceived stability, one further technological distinction needs mention. Proponents of a MIRV ban sometimes claim that previous multiple-warhead capabilities (MRV) should suffice to deter Soviet ABM defense of their cities, so that MIRV capabilities add little or nothing to this purpose. Such is not the case: " . . . both the Polaris multiples and our other early penetration aids were deployed in a way which placed them relatively close to one another when they arrived near the target. . . . We need, essentially, to be able to spread them [warheads and deception devices] out in space so that one Soviet defensive nuclear burst cannot destroy several American warheads or a whole cloud of decoys."[12] A MIRV capability meets this need.

In marked contrast, "When the Soviets split the SS-9 payload into three warheads, each one of these warheads would be well into the megaton range and would still have adequate capability against a single Minuteman silo. In this regard—warhead size and capability for first strike—our MIRV and the likely Soviet MIRV are not symmetrical."[13] A Soviet MIRV program would (1) make a U.S. "thick" ABM defense of its cities appear less effective to the United States, and therefore less likely to be deployed, and in this respect would be symmetrical with the impact of the U.S. MIRV program on Soviet ABM prospects. However, the likely Soviet MIRV program (2) makes an ABM defense of U.S. hardened missile silos distinctly more likely (witness Safeguard), so in this respect the impact is asymmetrical.

Given the very different character of probable U.S. and Soviet MIRV deployments in the absence of an effective and now unlikely, MIRV ban, only one unambiguous conclusion about the desirability of such a ban, as it affects the bipolar strategic balance, emerges: the deterrent to "thick" ABM defenses of cities would be weakened. An effective MIRV ban would make such defenses much more effective,

[12]Foster, p. 3.
[13]Foster, p. 7.

especially because "testing MRVs would also have to be banned since their purpose can so easily be confused. Also, tests of re-entry decoys, which of course are supposed to look like re-entry vehicles, would also probably be unacceptable."[14] Proponents of ABM already claim that, even when the offense is free to use high-confidence decoys and other penetration aids, "it is about as expensive to nullify a good defense as to build it."[15] If the offense is denied the testing of MIRVs, MRVs, and decoys, stronger claims will be made for defenses. An agreed concomitant ban upon ABM deployments would then be more tempting to evade, and its verification correspondingly more difficult. Such verification, as noted earlier, virtually requires some on-site inspection. Clearly a MIRV ban, an ABM ban, and reliance upon unilateral national inspection do not complement each other nearly so completely as is commonly assumed.

But is a MIRV ban feasible? If it is not, the partly competitive, partly complementary relationships between a MIRV ban and an ABM ban need not be explicated, with all their complications. The standard test for any arms-control limit must be applied: Would a clever enemy have a strong incentive to evade the limit, and, if so, how would he go about it? As to incentives, because their probable MIRV capabilities strengthen both their first- and second-strike capabilities markedly, the Soviets would be tempted to evade a MIRV ban. Their incentive would be reinforced, given their suspicious view of the United States, by their own doubts about the feasibility of a ban.

As to methods of evasion, one can only speculate about which combination among many possibilities the Soviets might be tempted to try. Any attempt would probably first involve a covert phase to establish technological reliability and precision, which in itself would not satisfy military commanders intent on full testing of operational military systems. But, as with Soviet preparations to resume atmospheric tests of nuclear weapons during the lull of the early moratorium, Soviet commanders could be appeased by thorough measures to open a subsequent overt phase with a burst of operational tests. In the covert phase, the Soviets would have to establish the technological reliability of only one additional critical mechanism: a device for imparting a specific differential velocity to a re-entry vehicle already in a ballistic trajectory in space.

The simplest way is (1) to test the ejector mechanism for this purpose with but one ejection per launch: "Tests of such a single re-entry

---

[14]Foster, p. 9.
[15]D. G. Brennan, "The Case For Missile Defense," *Foreign Affairs* (April 1969), p. 435.

vehicle could then give high confidence of a MIRV capability."[16] Suppose that by unilateral observation we detected one launch and the re-entry of one object. Would our observation be so acute that, with high confidence, the imparted slight differential velocity would be observed and correctly interpreted? Or (an idea that might appeal more to military commanders) the Soviets might elect (2) to constrict the differential velocities imparted to a few re-entry vehicles so that they fell in a tight cluster. External observers might then mistakenly interpret the test as being that of a MRV rather than a MIRV. Soviet military observers might be propitiated by reasonable conformity of the impact points within a predicted pattern. Or, within normal "peace-time" space activities, the Soviets might choose (3) to put many vehicles into different orbits by one booster, as is customarily done when different scientific phenomena are to be observed. The precision with which the different orbits were established would be a measure of the capability to establish desired differential velocities in space, and thus of MIRV accuracy. The possibilities are manifold.

In any event, the Soviets may have tested operational MIRV systems already:

We do know that the guidance and control system employed in the SS-9 tests has capabilities much greater than that required to implement a simple MRV. The things we do know about this mechanization are completely compatible with MIRV even though they do not prove MIRV capability. My own judgment in this matter is that the Soviet triplet probably is a MIRV . . . .[17]

Naturally, a spokesman for the U.S. Arms Control and Disarmament Agency expresses a more cautious judgment, but certainly one less favorable to the feasibility of a MIRV ban than his ACDA predecessors in 1967:

There is a difficult and serious problem which we still have under study as to whether—if testing of MIRVs were to be banned at the stage reached now or in the near future—deployment would be possible for one side or the other for its strategic purposes, on the basis of experience already gained. . . . But we are not yet clear whether, under conditions of a moratorium or ban and in event of a deliberate effort to evade, we could detect some testing aimed at further MIRV-MRV development particularly by national means alone."[18]

The feasibility of a MIRV ban is not a settled issue. To this author, however, infeasibility has already been sufficiently established, chiefly because the MIRV concept has been known so long, while its test-

---

[16]Foster, p. 9.
[17]Foster, p. 6.
[18]ACDA Deputy Director Philip J. Farley, as quoted in *The New York Times*, July 25, 1969, p. 13.

ing is a matter of space physics that can be accomplished in diverse ways. For arms control, rather than bemoan a missed 1967 opportunity, it seems far better to capitalize upon expected MIRV capabilities in several ways, including two in particular: (1) limits upon the number of launchers, since fewer are needed; and (2) limits upon the number of ABM interceptor missiles that restrict their coverage to "thin" rather than "thick" dimensions, because mutual MIRV capabilities will help deter heavy ABM defenses of cities in any event. But why any ABM defenses at all? The tiresomely familiar arguments are valid—it is probably futile to expect the Soviets to move from some ABM deployment to zero; while hardness alone, without "hard-point" ABM defenses, will no longer suffice to protect American missile silos. One less familiar argument needs to be added.

U.S. strategic retaliatory forces, in addition to deterring Soviet strategic forces from a massive attack, must still provide backing for U.S. theater (or General Purpose) forces abroad. Ideally, the conventional capabilities of U.S. and allied theater forces would suffice to implement a "no-first-use" doctrine for nuclear weapons, which would minimize their needs for residual dependence upon strategic forces. Practically, our theater capabilities fall considerably short of this standard.[19] If theater forces were threatened or engaged in combat, nuclear weapons might have to be used. Then the least bad among undesirable options might be a controlled nuclear strike ("demonstration") that fell observably far short of general war. Would the Soviets then counterdemonstrate or worse? Nobody knows. But just as even thin Soviet ABM defenses make a nuclear demonstration against their territory a distinctly more difficult operational problem than one directed elsewhere, as well as politically more risky, so should any Soviet demonstration against the territory of the United States. The first area function of a thin U.S. ABM defense is to force the Soviets to consider so high a level of nuclear counterdemonstration against U.S. territory, using high-confidence penetration aids in a heavy attack, that they will be deterred from such attacks even if there are theater nuclear exchanges abroad.[20]

This arms-control position, which accepts MIRVs and thin ABMs, necessarily implies other vulnerability-reducing changes in the U.S. strategic posture beyond Safeguard.[21] Less obviously, it implies changes in U.S. strategic planning, and in capabilities for replanning rapidly,

---

[19]For an analysis and partial prescription, see M. W. Hoag, "What New Look in Defense?" *World Politics* (October 1969), Sections IV, V, and VII.

[20]For elaboration, see Hoag, Section VI.

[21]*Ibid.*

for any given set of strategic forces.[22] If these forces are to back inadequate theater forces with appropriately tailored nuclear-strike plans, many adaptable options for such strikes must be available. Each would be significantly different in some respect, but each would stress preserving rather than destroying enemy hostage populations, with most strategic power withheld for continuing deterrence. The 1961 policy theme of "controlled nuclear response" would be implemented more fully by such options for less-than-general-war strikes.

By the nature of contingency planning, no such set of plans could hope to be complete since one or more of the preplanned options could be depended upon to fit a future crisis. A further ability to replan rapidly to meet the conditions of a particular emergency is desirable. Yet even to choose one option well from a preplanned set of them puts exacting demands upon pre-crisis and in-crisis information-gathering systems (Intelligence) and upon near-instantaneous interaction between the scene of actual emergency and top-level decision-makers (Command, Control, and Communications Systems). For present purposes, we need only note that these requirements arise from regrettable theater-force deficiencies, and tend to be global in nature, given the political commitments and the military dispositions (for example, for missile-carrying submarines) of the two superpowers.

No specter of a never-ending quantitative arms race between the superpowers is implied. On the contrary, assuming that both sides will prudently reduce the vulnerability of their retaliatory forces, the bipolar strategic balance will probably never become dangerously destabilized by impending qualitative changes. These changes call for more complex capabilities, which need not imply increased numbers of delivery vehicles, at a new plateau for bipolar equilibrium. What needs emphasis here is that the probable qualitative changes induced by new technology and bipolar superpower relationships alone, prior to any additional changes made with other powers in mind, will have far-reaching multipolar implications. The by-products of the new bipolar balance, and of the transition to it, will be significant.

## IMPLICATIONS FOR "HORIZONTAL PROLIFERATION"

This position, as sketched above, on feasible and desirable limits upon superpower "vertical proliferation" would clearly not maximize the demonstration effect against "horizontal proliferation."

[22]*Ibid.*

On the contrary, others would claim that the superpowers are setting an example of an arms race rather than of arms-control restraint. To them this position would supply a prominent rationale for not signing the NPT. The nations most eager to cite it, to be sure, might be those who do not propose to sign, or who would sign tongue-in-cheek, whatever the limits upon vertical proliferation. Nonetheless, this demonstration effect must be viewed as a serious, if virtually inevitable, defect of this position.

The link between more nonsigners of the NPT and the actual rate of increase in the number of nuclear powers, however, may be tenuous. One consequence of the vertical proliferation discussed above might or might not be an increase in horizontal proliferation, as more nations acquired neighbor-against-neighbor nuclear capabilities. But a clearer consequence will be a marked increase in the cost of acquiring retaliatory nuclear capabilities against one or both of the superpowers. Even if the number of nuclear powers increases, the scope of nonsuperpower retaliatory ambitions may be reduced for old, as well as for new, nuclear powers.

The prominent example is Communist China. To achieve a secure "all-azimuths" capability, their strategic-system designers will be unable to provide inexpensive means, and may be driven towards prohibitively expensive ones. Their political leadership may then prefer an insecure capability, the possible form and consequences of which we will consider later. First, the expensiveness of a secure capability needs to be illustrated.

Missile survivability provides the most vivid example. Neither of the standard solutions—hard silos or mobility—is technologically easy or inexpensive, especially as higher degrees of hardness or conceal-ment/mobility are sought. Early American missiles were soft and vulnerable, and subsequent design goals for hardness were difficult to attain. The Soviet example is more to the point, because Chinese designs may be derived from early Soviet designs; and the Soviets "bought their equivalent [hardness] to our MINUTEMAN force 5 to 7 years after we did; and with substantial time lag, they have bought and are buying their equivalent to our POLARIS force."[23] In particular, early Chinese missiles may be liquid-fueled, as was more common for the Soviets than for the Americans. Because this type of missile poses such formidable logistic difficulties for protection via mobility, this

[23]Then Assistant Secretary of Defense Alain C. Enthoven, in *Status of U.S. Strategic Power, Part I.,* "Hearings Before the Preparedness Investigating Subcommittee of the Committee on Armed Services, U.S. Senate" (90th Congress, 2nd Session), April 1968, p. 138.

solution to the vulnerability problem may be infeasible for the Chinese for years to come.

One might speculate that the Chinese will follow the Soviet route, with early missile systems whose logistic complexities drive their designers first to deploy them in fixed soft positions, with gradual hardening of missile sites over a period of several years. Yet this prospect should not satisfy Chinese planners. For, considering the qualitatively different character of Soviet and American missile programs, such a fixed-site deployment program would probably at no time offer adequate protection against both superpowers, or at most times against either. In the early (long-lasting?) deployment phase, soft missile sites would obviously be vulnerable to small-yield detonations, which the U.S. MIRV program stresses, provided that they were accurately delivered. The same U.S. program that poses no increased threat to hard Soviet sites[24] offers, against soft targets, markedly decreased costs per target covered. The contrasting Soviet MIRV program, as already noted, stresses large-yield weapons with sufficient accuracy to overcome Minuteman-degree silo hardness. Consequently, a Chinese strategic planner might find even this degree of missile-silo hardness unattractive. At best it might protect his force against one superpower's missiles, but not the other's while such hardness would take much time and effort to achieve.

Superpower technology will thus make "nth-power" survivability problems much harder, at little extra cost to the superpowers beyond the costs of adjusting to the qualitatively new bipolar balance. It may also make nth power penetration capabilities against superpower defenses much harder to achieve, but whether at small marginal costs to the superpowers is more open to question. If, primarily in order to deter limited demonstration strikes by the other superpower and to reinforce the protection of their retaliatory forces, both superpowers move toward thin aerospace (air and ABM) area defenses, the incidental protection gained against nth power strikes could be viewed as a bonus. But if the rationale for thin aerospace defense puts primary emphasis upon protection against nth powers, as was the official case for the Sentinel ABM system whose presentation preceded that for Safeguard, then most of the ABM costs would be chargeable against this purpose. Or if ABM defenses are restricted mostly to the defense of missile silos, with appreciable populated areas left undefended (for example, if later deployment phases of Safeguard are never implemented), neither the costs nor the benefits would be chargeable to defense against nth powers. This last outcome is possible but unlikely, leaving the prospect that superpower aerospace de-

[24]Foster, p. 5.

fenses will have at least a thin area-wide coverage. The attribution of costs for the defenses among multiple purposes will be difficult but mainly of academic interest, so long as annual costs are relatively low for defenses that remain thin.

If the superpowers develop such mutual thin aerospace defenses, modifications may be added because supplemental strengthening against nth power threats can be gained at but small marginal costs. The significance of such modified defenses for the Chinese strategic planner, again, would be appreciably increased by technological differences between Soviet and American defenses. The measures open to the Chinese planner for countering either set of defenses with high confidence (for example, MIRV against ABM) tend to be complex and expensive. The measures that are relatively simple and cheap (for instance, chaff against radars) do not yield high confidence in penetrating defenses, especially against more than one particular set of defenses (for example, more than one band of radar frequencies). To design penetration aids that would be effective against both Soviet and American defenses would be complicated and difficult. High-confidence penetration aids may be priced beyond Chinese means, as certainly the highest-confidence tactic—overwhelming defenses by sheer numbers of penetrating warheads—would be.

The other qualitative systems discussed above—for Planning, Intelligence, and Command, Control, and Communications—have similar implications for nth powers. If there is a need in bipolar terms for limited nuclear-strike options, this need is surely reinforced in a world of more nuclear powers with substantial capabilities. In this more complex world, one superpower imperative must be never to engage in a nuclear exchange that exhausts one's capabilities and leaves one at the mercy of more than one remaining nuclear power. The already strong case for controlled nuclear-strike options, each of which would withhold most retaliatory power, is further strengthened as multipolarity increases. Similarly, the case for detailed operational information at all times, but especially in times of crisis, is strengthened. Knowing not only where and how hard you have been hit, but also, if possible, by whom, becomes more important than ever.

Again, because bipolar commitments and deployments will have generated near-global systems, incremental capabilities against nth powers can be added at small marginal costs. The apparent example is reconnaissance by satellite, which yields global area coverage. The product is an ever-changing inventory of physical objects on the earth's surface, with particular military interest, of course, in changing threat capabilities (for example, number of missile silos). The same information source can supplement other means (say, commercial news) to enable a globe-wide inventory of surface shipping. At the same time, track can be kept from the surface of objects in space orbit. As ABM radar/computer capabilities are added to early warning facilities (BMEWS), launch as well as impact points for objects in ballistic trajectories can be quickly calculated.

But can sufficient track be maintained of objects beneath the surface of the oceans? Four of the five existing nuclear powers seek missile mobility/concealment in nuclear propelled submarines. Such submarines have even greater appeal, in principle, for an $n$th power, because they might conceal the identity of the missile-launcher as well as reduce vulnerability. In practice, this capability must be measured against the antisubmarine warfare (ASW) capability of the United States. Our ASW capability against a future "quiet" and large Soviet threat is uncertain. As technology advances both ASW and anti-ASW potentials, the United States may be moved to invest more or less in ASW capabilities. But, unless the United States finds itself "priced out" of the ASW mission as a whole—as distinct from abandoning the less cost-effective components for performing this mission—it will retain a sizable by-product capability against anyone's "noisy" submarines. Any of the few existing Chinese diesel-electric submarines, if converted to missile carriers, should be easily trackable.

If, recognizing this tracking capability, the Chinese were to seek to maintain one or more missile-carrying submarines constantly on-station off the American coast in order to be ready for quick retaliation, they face formidable expense. Then many submarines would have to be procured for each single on-station submarine, because so much time off-station would be consumed by two-way transits of the Pacific Ocean. If they were to elect the much less expensive option of submarines on-station near their own coast, their on-station force would be days away from firing positions. A crisis momentous enough for them to send a submarine with firing orders would, almost by definition, be a crisis during which opposing ASW forces would be authorized to destroy any Chinese submarines that were moving toward firing positions. The less expensive on-station option is far less reliable.

The Chinese example in general indicates that a secure all-azimuths retaliatory capability against the superpowers would be very, perhaps prohibitively, expensive. The missile-carrying submarine that is not maintained constantly on-station, but rather is sent for an anonymous strike at a predetermined time, supplies a vivid example of an insecure capability attempting to instigate "catalytic war" between the superpowers. How real is this specter? The physical potential, one way or

another, must be granted. The political response of the attacked superpower, however, cannot be taken for granted. Even if the threat remains
anonymous, the least sensible response would be to retaliate against the
other superpower. When in doubt about the source of an attack, the simple
rule of retaliatory prudence would appear to be retaliate against the suspect power with the least counterretaliatory power. If this rule were publicized, should the physical potential for catalytic war be much feared?

An insecure retaliatory capability that does not seek anonymity,
however, is a different possibility and one to be taken more seriously.
One property of a "secure" capability is positive political control at all
times, so that firing decisions can be made or revoked only at the
highest political levels, without jeopardizing the physical survivability of one's capability. Such positive control is sought, among
many other ways, by keeping retaliatory capabilities within one's
territory or on the high seas, or, at most (for instance, for the United
States), within one's own custodial control in the territory of reliable
allies. But an $n$th power that finds a secure retaliatory capability
beyond its means may sacrifice positive control. It may use clandestine
delivery means, whose merit is cheapness, to put nuclear weapons in
peacetime where they are most dangerous—namely, within preselected enemy target areas (cities).

Two questions immediately arise: Why do such a dangerous thing?
How could it be done? The purpose would be to evade superpower
countermilitary offenses and defenses so that physically credible retaliatory threats against a superpower could be made by an $n$th power in a
time of crisis. Thus, suppose Communist China, fearing employment of
American nuclear weapons against her forces in Asia, should announce
that at least ten nuclear devices had already been covertly delivered,
were stored within at least ten large American cities, and would be
detonated if American nuclear weapons were employed against
Chinese forces. Further, suppose that scepticism about a bluff were
countered by an offer to surrender one of the emplaced weapons in
advance. So dangerous but cheap an insecure alternative may appeal
to an $n$th power that finds a secure retaliatory threat beyond her means.

A real physical capability to back such a threat could be created
in many ways, given nuclear weapons. Delivery in peacetime could be
made by any of several smuggling routes: a mislabeled commercial
shipment, a covert landing from an offshore ship or submarine, a
low-altitude flight by light aircraft, or other means. The openness of
United States borders in peacetime is well-known, and, against such
tactics of predelivery, a drastic tightening of border and other controls
in a crisis would be too late. Technically, such predelivery would

appear to be feasible and inexpensive. Politically, it would obviously be dangerous. What sovereign power wants to put its nuclear weapons in the trust of an agent network, one of whose members may defect; to risk border or subsequent detection and seizure, even when the probabilities are assessed to be low; and to be unsure that its decision to detonate or not to detonate will be obeyed? The probable answer is no sovereign power. Nonetheless, given the expensiveness of normal military alternatives, the clandestine delivery of nuclear weapons by an *n*th power cannot be dismissed as incredible. Against this threat, a considerable rather than merely marginal tightening of border and associated controls in peacetime may become desirable.

Fundamentally, protection against this threat, or more generally against insecure retaliatory capabilities, must be provided by compelling counterthreat capabilities. Just as no border can be completely protected against smuggling in peacetime, no defenses can assure protection against missiles that enemy commanders fire upon their earliest receipt of tactical warning (by radar or other signals) before any actual nuclear detonations have occurred upon their territory. The likeliest form that an insecure retaliatory capability will take is one that, in *n*th power declaratory policy, claims to rest upon such risky firing doctrine. To implement it, authority to fire must be predelegated and targets must be preselected. For *n*th countries against superpowers, cities would be the targets by default. If the firing doctrine is implemented, rather than merely used as a bluff in declaratory policy, the worst of catastrophes could result from missile firings based upon false warning.

The superpowers can never be sure that such retaliatory threats are bluffs. Consequently, it would be prudent for them to conduct any countermilitary operations against an *n*th power, if necessary, in a way that minimizes or perhaps eliminates tactical warning (for example, by using ballistic missiles rather than aircraft). More importantly, particularly when discussing the nature and credibility of their nuclear guarantees with allies, superpowers can elaborate the wide ranges of countermilitary options against *n*th powers that lie open to them, short of initiating countercity exchanges. The general nature of these options can be publicized for all to see. An *n*th country's leaders can then appreciate that the onus of initiating city-destruction rests with them if, going beyond bluff, they implement policies for retaliation based upon earliest receipt of tactical warning. The credibility of their declaratory policy will certainly be brought into question, and their tendency to confine such risky doctrine to declaratory rather than action policy should be increased.

For different reasons, the credibility of superpower nuclear guarantees to allies, and still more to neutrals who sign the NPT, will obviously be brought into question. Against $n$th power nuclear threats to neighbors, inaction is one superpower option that is always open. That it will be open is apparent to all. Moreover, if anything, the probability that this option will be chosen tends to be exaggerated in public discussion, which typically lumps all possible nuclear exchanges together under one holocaust heading. Consequently, the United States has nothing further to lose in candid and detailed discussions with its allies about nuclear matters, and much to gain in a deeper mutual understanding and in satisfying legitimate requests for consultation. The detailed discussions that have become routine in NATO within the Nuclear Planning Group supply prototypes that, in appropriately tailored ways, can be profitably emulated in bilateral or multilateral form with other allies. From such classified discussions, allies will at least gain a better understanding of possible American nuclear options, and can better appreciate the applicability and credibility of American nuclear guarantees. Also, they will incidentally gain a more vivid appreciation of the comparative utility and costs of the independent nuclear deterrent that may be open to them.

This perspective will be especially pertinent for allies who might, as a function of American policy, have to consider a nuclear force of their own as an alternative, rather than as a supplement, to the American guarantee. The treaty with the United States that has no terminal date, or no date after which withdrawal notice can be served, is the exception rather than the rule. Where withdrawal from alliance is possible, use of the most powerful American leverage against nuclear proliferation is feasible. Then an ally who chooses to go nuclear could, at our discretion, lose its alliance with and nuclear guarantee from the United States. And so it should. With this powerful leverage added to trade and aid controls, the NPT, and other measures, the extent of actual nuclear proliferation may be less than is commonly forecast. Qualitative vertical proliferation by the superpowers, plus the power of such diplomacy practiced by one or both of them, would probably generate fewer signatories for the NPT, and might or might not lead to an actual increase in horizontal proliferation, measured in numbers of nuclear powers; but it should certainly limit the extent of nonsuperpower nuclear ambitions and the scope of their programs.

Morton A. Kaplan

# The Unit-Veto System Reconsidered

I have argued previously that the condition that makes possible a unit-veto system is "the possession by all actors of weapons of such character that any actor is capable of destroying any other actor that attacks it, even though it cannot prevent its own destruction."[1] At the asymptotic extreme, the system has a tendency to approximate Hobbes's state of nature. Alliances are neither necessary nor helpful. They do not serve to ward off attacks and invite dangers stemming from the possible irrational decisions of alliance partners. From a security standpoint, they reduce or eliminate the need for international organization.

There has been some speculation (especially by Thomas C. Schelling) since the writing of *System and Process* that such a system is unstable except at the number of three actors. It is speculated that, if there were four or more actors, the reduction to three actors would be stabilizing. The elimination of one of the four actors would not trigger an attack on the aggressor. If one of the other two nuclear actors were to attack the aggressor, his action would make him very vulnerable to the only remaining actor with the capacity to eliminate him, and thus to obtain both security and hegemony.

The foregoing logic operates, however, only upon the hypothesis that states do not possess second-strike capabilities. If the attacked state has a second-strike capability, what will occur depends upon what kind of second-strike capability it has. If the second-strike capability is a capability against weapons, then the attacked state can disarm the attacker or at least reduce his nuclear complement to the point where he is so vulnerable that one of the two remaining states is capable both of eliminating his remaining nuclear arsenal and of largely disarming the remaining neutral nuclear power. If this is the situation, the preemptive attack itself both partially disarms the attacking state and subjects it to further

[1]Morton A. Kaplan, *System and Process in International Politics* (New York: Wiley, 1957), p. 50. This essay modifies the conclusions reached in the earlier work.

49

disarmament. Moreover, since there is little to gain from the preemptive attack except reducing the size of the system, the risks seem clearly to outweigh the gains. If it were possible for the attack to be exploited in order to gain nuclear predominance through acquisition of the resources of the attacked state, then the attack itself would provide an incentive for an alliance within the system by the two neutral nuclear states.

If, on the other hand, the second-strike capability is only a countervalue capability, then the response might invoke mutual suicide. If the attacked state is not capable of destroying the attacker—a retreat from the asymptotic condition—it might be deterred from a countervalue response on the assumption that the attacker retains the capability, provided he has not shot off too many rockets, to utterly destroy him. Again, however, it is difficult to see what the potential gain is from the initial preemptive attack.

Let us assume for a moment that the attack is anonymous. This is perhaps permissible in a pure model, although it is difficult to think of actual historical attacks that have occurred in the absence of political crisis. For instance, the Japanese attack on Pearl Harbor was a surprise only in terms of the locale of the attack. Moreover, the very anonymity of an attack would make it extremely difficult to secure any significant political advantage. Such an attack could not be used to make other states terrified of the attacker, for they would not know the identity of the attacker. In this case, such attacks can be deterred by appropriate firing doctrine. For instance, one public firing doctrine might involve small attacks by surviving nuclear weapons on each of the remaining nuclear forces in the system. This would be likely to make each force more vulnerable to first strike, and could therefore serve as a deterrent to any actor's attacking any of the others. Another public doctrine might involve a decision to attack one city in each of the remaining states. Although there would probably be an effective counterdeterrent—namely, a public doctrine by every state in the system to respond to such an attack by one of double size—again it is difficult to see what political or military advantage could be gained from an attack that would be sufficient to invoke even a small possibility of such a penalty.

No state can assume that its attack will remain anonymous. Apart from the problem of nuclear signatures, there are other methods for monitoring attacks. If we assume the attack is a large one—for there seems little to be gained in a small anonymous attack, except the creation of a situation of uncertainty and terror that might well backfire on its initiator because of induced external irrationality and public fear at home—then obviously it can be easily monitored. Suppose, however, the attack were to come from submarines. The *New York Times*, which distrusts the Pentagon on almost every other ground, assumes for some strange reason that the self-interested United States Navy is speaking gospel truth when it argues that there is no way to bring down or to incapacitate nuclear submarines. If that is true, then no attack can destroy the nuclear force of any other side. If, as a consequence, the preemptive attack is a counter-value attack, designed merely to decrease the number of nuclear powers, a public doctrine of general countervalue response would seem sufficient to deter any but a mad ruler. Even if one did not really believe the public doctrine, the smallest probability that it would be used would seem sufficient for deterrence in these circumstances. Indeed, mere public speculation concerning such a doctrine, let alone its adoption, would seem sufficient for deterrence. If, on the other hand, as I believe for reasons that will not be stated here, it is possible to develop ingenious devices that would permit monitoring of underwater fleets, then an attack is possible but it could not remain anonymous.

Is it possible that a small anonymous attack during an unpopular activity—for example, a foreign intervention—might be associated with that activity and deter it? For instance, suppose nuclear weapons were widespread at the time of an activity analogous to the Indochinese War, and that one weapon exploded anonymously on an American city. That might work. However, there is the risk that the attack would not remain anonymous. In that case, if the attacker had an unstable nuclear force, a preemptive attack by the United States would then be not unlikely. Thus, although there is some prospect that the anonymous attack would work, the risks would seem to outweigh the gains. If the anonymous attacker had a stable nuclear force—a real unit-veto-type system—this strategy might support a norm of nonintervention, a norm that would probably be consistent with the stability of a unit-veto system in any event. But this measure would be dangerous, and it is difficult to believe that it would commend itself to a prudent political leadership.

Thus, even if each nuclear state could do significant damage either to the nuclear capability or to the values of the attacking state alone, and not to additional states, the system is likely to be a stable one in its pure form. This stability would exist for any reasonable number of states. If the attacked state were capable of retaliating against any two other states, or even more strongly against all other states, then this conclusion would only be reinforced, but it would not be changed in any significant way.

It must be stated, however, that the conclusion that the unit-veto system is stable is based upon the asymptotic form of the pure system. It does not take into account qualitative changes in weaponry or asymmetries in the qualitative arms race. For instance, if ballistic-missile defenses achieve the superiority over offensive missilry that Professor Freeman Dyson forecasts for the intermediate future, we may return to systems in which conventional military threats can be employed under the umbrella of nuclear defenses. This is not to say that nuclear threats would not operate in such a world, but only that they would operate in a much different fashion. Clandestine transport of nuclear weapons to the cities of an opponent could sneak them in under the defense umbrella. In this case, the state that is least ingenious, or that has the poorest internal security, or that is most highly urbanized, or that is most easily susceptible to disorganization, might find itself in an extremely disadvantageous position. With these considerations, however, we move from the pure model to the extended model. And there are difficulties with the stability of a unit-veto system, even apart from qualitative changes or asymmetries in the arms race, once we begin to consider the internal structure of the actor.

It is certainly not obvious that a unit-veto world would be hostile to liberal and humane values and to fully rational decision making. Yet that intuition is one that appeals to my judgment. The Hobbesian state is one in which life is nasty, short, and brutal. Human beings thrust back upon themselves tend to be suspicious. Although I do not view the state as an individual writ large, I think many of the destructive social-psychological motivations of the Hobbesian state of nature would be operative. The absence of a need to associate in alliances would tend to produce a corrupting isolation. It would tend to feed back upon national decision making, to produce paranoia concerning the motivations of other states, and to produce political illiberality at home. Perhaps these consequences could be mitigated by other needs that would bring states together—the need to solve the population problem, the pollution problem, the problem of control of the seas' resources, the problem of food supply and of utilization of natural resources. On the other hand, if these problems should prove largely insoluble, and if they should produce circumstances of extreme conflict, then they would reinforce the conclusion we reached as to the social-psychological instability of a unit-veto system.

Let us extend the model a bit further. Let us consider two variants of nuclear-diffusion systems, which I have previously labeled respectively "the unstable-bloc system" and "the incomplete nuclear-diffusion system." To visualize the unstable-bloc system consider a world in which both the United States and the Soviet Union have secure second-strike forces. Four or five other states have nuclear systems, but these are good for minimum deterrence only.

Such a world would be potentially unstable. The motivation for alliances would continue to exist in this world, but the dangers posed by alliances would also increase greatly. The small nuclear systems belonging to alliance members would be much more vulnerable to attack than the larger systems and, to the extent that they were vulnerable, they would be provocative. During a period of intense international crisis, the existence of such forces within an alliance might be seen as a danger by the leader of the alliance. As the tension rose, the possibility that the rival bloc leader would preempt this force would rise. As this probability rose, the dangers of being included in this alliance would rise with it.

In the incomplete nuclear-diffusion system, small nuclear forces have spread to fifteen or twenty other nations. These forces would, in fact, deter most attacks against the homeland of each nuclear power, but not all, particularly in extremely provocative situations. Despite the argument that such minimum-deterrence systems would possess a triggering capability for the major nuclear power, this is unlikely.

Had the Czechoslovaks possessed even a few nuclear weapons, the Russians might have considered much more carefully their decision to intervene. However, not all crises arise as a consequence of carefully planned policy. The crises that we need to fear would arise out of uncontrollable escalating events. In such crises, the possession of a poor nuclear system serves not to deter a major nuclear power but to provoke it. Possession of such a nuclear system would not increase the bargaining power of the state that holds it; rather, the state's bargaining power would be reduced and pressure upon it by its bloc leader or by other alliance partners that fear being dragged into a nuclear holocaust would be increased. The very fact that the state possessing such a system knows that it might provoke a strong enemy but that its nuclear system cannot be used to attack him preemptively without inviting obliteration would serve to weaken the will of the possessing nation and to introduce political instabilities into the international system.

A further distinction needs to be made between the kinds of countries possessing nuclear systems. It is one thing for a United States, a Russia, a France, an England, or even a China to possess such weapons. It is another thing for a Castro, an Nkrumah, a Ben Bella, or a Nasser to possess them. The developed states are reasonably satisfied with their lot in life. They are pragmatic about their approach to world politics. They are calculating about their international decisions. Decisions are usually made as a consequence of a complicated decision-making process in which alternative points of view are brought to bear upon a subject. Even Hitler was not able to enforce the gassing of the German people, despite his claim that they had "betrayed" him.

If, however, nuclear weapons are possessed by states with oversimple ideologies, by states that think they have nothing to lose, by underdeveloped political systems in which decisions can be made by an extremely small number of disorganized and romantic individuals, then even though we do not have to believe that there is a high or even moderate probability that nuclear weapons will be used, any small rise in probability would make us more uncomfortable than we would like to be. Even if we do not believe that the use of nuclear weapons by such a state would bring Armageddon, it is not unlikely that to use them at all, and the need to control the user, would introduce changes in the international political system that we can hardly even speculate about and that we almost surely would detest.

To summarize: To the extent that the pure model holds, the rationale for threats and attacks would be minimized by a unit-veto system. The search for hegemony would not be a useful one in such a system. The more the model is relaxed for internal considerations, and the greater the extent to which the decision making of the participating states is open to view (as in democracies) the lower is the extent of suspicion in the system. Conversely, the greater the degree to which military dispositions, technological advances, and political decisions are covert and capable of changing the strategic balance, and the greater the extent to which decisions are made by a small body of unaccountable men, the greater are the tensions within the system. As these tensions build, the tendency rises to attempt to exploit threats against other states in order to acquire political leverage. As we relax the system even more and introduce, for instance, a danger of a qualitative change in the arms race that might create a temporary instability, the likelihood of preemption becomes greater.

Suppose we relax the model still more, and consider a situation in which the Soviet Union acquires a first-strike capability against the United States—the kind of capability that the Soviet Union might have after 1975. This situation could be made effective in any of several ways. During a very intense international crisis, the real—or alleged—superiority of the Soviet Union might be used to force the United States to accept a political defeat in Europe. Such a defeat might involve a relinquishment of West Berlin, or it might involve a change of the status quo—for instance, a Soviet invasion of Yugoslavia during a post-Tito-regime crisis. Success by the Soviet Union in a venture of this type might lead to pressures on Western Europe that would be only slightly less serious than the pressures that led to the Czechoslovak coup of 1948.

Alternatively, there might be an actual preemption by the Soviet Union against the United States. Since it is extremely unlikely that the Soviet Union could knock out all American weapons or could guarantee itself against all reprisals by the United States, I assume it would demand neither an American surrender nor that America destroy its own remaining nuclear forces—nor even some guarantee that America would not rebuild its nuclear systems. On the other hand, if the United States faced obliteration, it might not seek the satisfaction of destroying Moscow, Leningrad, and a few other Soviet cities, despite the enormous damage such attacks might do to the Soviet system. The Soviet Union, however, might demand the Finlandizing of Europe. The United States would not be entirely unwise in these circumstances to grant it, despite the enormous change that would occur in the world situation.

If, on the other hand, the United States were to supply a united Western Europe with sufficient "know-how" for the acquisition of at least a semistable nuclear force, the Soviet Union would be extremely unlikely to risk the damage that might be inflicted upon itself by this European force while it faced an intact American nuclear system. To attack the United States first, while the European nuclear forces were intact, would not be an inviting prospect either, for the European forces are the ones immediately threatened by a Soviet advance. The acquisition by West Germany, Communist China, and Japan of even semiadequate nuclear forces would probably deter a preemptive attack on the United States.

These projections lead me to suggest, with respect to the bargaining that occurs in this nuclear age, that the Soviet pressure against nuclear armament for West Germany stems not so much from a fear that the West Germans would use those nuclear weapons against Russia—I believe that the Russians think that they are manipulating us with this argument, not that they fear such an attack—but from an attempt to avoid a situation in which they cannot develop a Czech-type pressure against either China or Western Europe. In short, even though I do not claim that the Soviet Union is actively seeking world hegemony, I do think they wish to protect the possibility of a situation in which they can make such a choice. I believe that it is difficult to account for their weapons-acquisition choices in the absence of this hypothesis. However, if we can reduce the provocative quality of the independent nuclear forces by providing adequate command and control, and by reducing the probability that they can be entirely knocked out, then we will thereby reduce the incentive for the Soviet Union to seek a first-strike capability against the United States, or to seek a Czech-type of advantage. If we allow multiple nuclear forces to develop into highly unstable forces, then we increase the destructive pressures within Western alliances, increase the self-deterrent characteristics of these forces, increase their provocative nature, increase the potential for Soviet threats that will be seen as legitimate, and set the stage for political demands.

CHAPTER 4

George H. Quester

# The Politics of
# Twenty Nuclear Powers

An attempt will be made in this chapter to examine the politics of a world of twenty or more nuclear-weapons states, a world in which nuclear proliferation will have gone much further than we all hope is likely. In no sense is this intended as a prediction that such proliferation will occur; indeed the author regards such a growth in the number of nuclear-weapons states as possible but very unlikely. Rather, this chapter will be a contemplative exercise in predicting what the consequences *would be* if NPT and all other inhibitions to the spread of nuclear weapons failed.

## WHAT KINDS OF WEAPONS?

Should proliferation occur, a basic question will concern the kinds of nuclear-weapons capabilities involved. Will they be counterforce or only countercity? Will they depend on being the first to attack?

It seems very probable that such nuclear forces would amount to at least first-strike countercity forces. When we deprecate the mere acquisition or production of nuclear warheads, we often cite "delivery systems" as an especially crucial and difficult barrier to be overcome. Yet if the bombs are produced, it is likely that they will always be delivered easily enough. A coastal city can be doused with deadly radioactive fallout by bombs exploded in the sea upwind from it. Bombs can be delivered by the international jet airliners that almost every nation purchases, seemingly to show the flag. They can be delivered by rockets, which will be generally more available as offshoots of various space-research programs. In addition to the plutonium now coming into circulation, the processing of uranium for various purposes will become commercially appropriate, making enriched uranium readily available. Uranium lends itself more easily than plutonium to hydrogen bombs, and there will thus be no barrier to "$n^{th}$" explosives becoming H-bombs, if an A-bomb were not itself convincingly destructive.

It is true that in order to really threaten a first-strike assault on any nation's cities, such *n*th weapons systems must still overcome some defensive barriers. ABM systems will have been purchased by a number of the current great powers, but however good such systems may be, they will probably not be perfect. For some means of delivery, air defense systems will have to be bypassed, but these too will show signs of imperfection, especially since the brunt of *greatpower* attacks would no longer come by aircraft. Thus, there is hardly even a guarantee against bombs being delivered by aircraft seemingly making normal passenger runs. Improved antisubmarine (ASW) techniques as well as tightened Coast Guard patrols and controls might help to head off attacks from submarine or other means of delivery by sea. Yet the institution of obtrusive and visible coastal controls is unlikely, at least until some city has actually been attacked in this manner.

Will such *n*th nuclear-weapons states also be able to execute attacks against cities on a second strike, even after a superpower's strategic missiles and aircraft have done everything possible to preempt and head off such attacks? Again, the answer will have to be "yes" rather than "no." Nations new to the nuclear-weapons business may find it too expensive to purchase missile-carrying submarines or to build secure and deep concrete silos for land-based missiles. Yet it is still plausible that dispersible and therefore invulnerable delivery systems will become cheaply available in the coming decades—for example, the vertical-takeoff (VTOL) or short-takeoff (STOL) airplanes being developed now in Britain and Sweden. If the Swedish Air Force had only 10 atomic bombs, and dispersed some 200 Viggen STOL aircraft to 200 road intersections across Sweden, could the USSR really be assured that it could launch a successful preemptive attack on Sweden and be sure that the Swedes could not hit Leningrad in retaliation?

Other second-strike delivery methods, apart from dispersible aircraft, will remain plausible. As suggested above, controls on border crossing and movement would have to be far more rigorous than they are at present to prevent the simple clandestine delivery of nuclear warheads into the cities marked for retaliation. A Chinese explosion at sea off San Francisco might be preventable only if every tramp steamer were subject to controls, but to institute such controls is a very formidable task. The short-lived inspections of Communist-flag ships for nuclear warheads in the later 1940s (only the *Batory* had to be searched) were admittedly inconclusive, and were the object of some ridicule; geiger counters alone cannot certify whether or not the contents of a large crate are nuclear explosives. Smaller countries may not have whatever technical ingenuity or managerial competence is required for such grand retaliations, but one must suspect that itinerant bands of technicians may be offering their services from country to country. Even if controls can be placed on the dissemination of materials and hardware, it will be more difficult to control the movement of men who know how to organize a bombing attack.

Our next question is whether any of the newest nuclear powers will have acquired a first-strike counterforce capability sufficient to plausibly threaten to disarm one or more of the great powers, thus preventing any retaliation against themselves. Here the answer is indeed very likely to be negative. It would be costly and difficult to perfect guidance systems accurate enough to menace the missiles implanted in underground silos in Siberia or Montana. The sheer numbers of great-power missiles will keep nth countries from accumulating enough for a preemptive strike in which one missile has to be fired at each silo.

The trend will be for the United States and the Soviet Union to toughen up their retaliatory forces against each other, and thus against everyone else, leaving a new strategic force scarcely any attractive opportunities at all. ABM protection may be purchased for the missile silos themselves, and it would be extremely expensive for a smaller nation to develop the penetration aids required to bypass such protection. Over time, the bulk of the U.S. and Russian retaliatory force will also have been shifted to the underwater environment. It will be virtually impossible for smaller states to develop the technology required to locate and destroy such missile-launching submarines.

Will nth nuclear forces typically be "all-azimuth" forces, that is, forces capable of striking at every major foreign country? If not, one must speculate on how much difference this will make. It is indeed probable that new nuclear forces will be very uneven in their destructive capabilities. Targets that are nearer the attacker can be more easily destroyed; cities on seacoasts might be more vulnerable. Yet this unevenness may decrease as ordinary commercial aircraft increase in range, and as militarily usable rockets become more generally and cheaply available. In any event, the political consequences of any geographic limitations on destructive capabilities will be less than is sometimes imagined. The indirect consequences of a plausible threat of nuclear strikes can draw in the whole world, even if that world for the moment is not directly within firing range.

If such forecasts as to the military capabilities to be proliferated are correct, one must turn toward the political future of the international scene. Will war be more or less likely as proliferation continues, and will it normally be nuclear war? Will the distribution of political power as we know it remain largely the same, or will it be drastically altered?

## THE LIKELIHOOD OF INTERNATIONAL WAR

There is a plausible argument that nuclear proliferation will lessen the likelihood of superpower preemptive first strikes against each other; if nothing else, proliferation will gravely complicate any effort by one nation to become the sole possessor of nuclear weapons by destroying those of all others. Even today, as American government spokesmen speculate about Russian missiles, which might under extreme circumstances make possible successful attacks on U.S. missile silos, this Russian first strike would have to be effective against British, French, and Chinese missiles as well. By the time Russian SS-9 missiles are available in sufficient quantities, Israeli, Indian, or other nuclear forces might also have to be targeted if a monopoly were being sought. The mere number of discrete military-weapons systems to be targeted may thus decisively deter all such moves for a grand monopoly. It is argued above that $n$th systems typically will have a crude survivability. An inferior retaliatory system plus a first-rate one may even constitute a better deterrent than an expanded homogenous first-rate system alone, since increasing the number of separate terms in the calculus the aggressor must work through can be more inhibiting than increasing the actual values of each term. If this were true, twenty different nuclear powers might all deter grand preemptive strikes by any one, since each, in order to gain monopoly, would have to contemplate at least nineteen different targets.

The superpowers may be less prone to counterforce offensives after further proliferation, but might $n$th powers not contemplate such offensives among themselves, in efforts to reestablish local monopolies? Perhaps such attacks would come when it was thought that bombs had not yet been assembled; a plutonium enrichment plant just put into operation would seem an attractive target before it has begun to deliver a stream of nuclear warheads.

"Surgical attacks" might be used in hopes of keeping others from joining the nuclear club, or of expelling them quickly after they first reveal their readiness to enter. Having a vulnerable nuclear force, a new candidate may in turn desire quick action if he is to inflict any damage at all on the cities of a club member; if he should wait to shoot off his first cruise missiles, they may be destroyed before they can be lofted against any of their hostages. The mere prospect of nuclear warheads could thus stimulate totally preemptive wars, where each side strikes only because it fears that the other is launching a strike. The likelihood of stampedes into mutually unwanted wars increases generally as speed in military decisions comes to have a greater effect on who will win, or on whose population will escape suffering in a war. If, therefore, one's radar suggests a neighbor may be attacking, one may feel driven to launch an attack of one's own, for fear of being preempted.

An argument for preemption might thus make sense for any side that can really hope to wipe out the other's strategic force. A typical $n$th nuclear power might only be vulnerable to preemption, however, and not capable of it (for example, when confronted by the $n$-4th); it is not inevitable that "preemptive nervousness" will exacerbate the probabilities of nuclear war here. For instance, my hold on your main cities may indeed be continually threatened by your preemption; yet what do I gain by firing off my rudimentary projectiles in a doubtful case? It was similarly contended that either the Soviet or American sides would be nervous in the early 1960s as soon as the other had sufficient missiles to threaten a preemptive strike. Unless both can simultaneously threaten a counterforce attack, the weaker side would probably still rest easy in a crisis, and this indeed seems to have held true during the U.S. superiority. I accomplish nothing by destroying cities for the sake of destroying simply because I might soon lose the ability to do so.

Moreover, much of this instability may not materialize. Rudimentary plutonium plants can be established clandestinely, and (as suggested above) $n$th delivery systems may typically not be vulnerable. Any scenario which would be unstable in local terms must also be considered in the context of the existing superpowers. Whether or not the weapons of the preempted state had been supplied from outside, one of the nuclear great powers might well be tempted to replace any weapons destroyed in such a counterforce attack. It would no longer be clear that the weapons had been supplied rather than indigenous; whatever stigma had been attached to furthering proliferation to "one more country" would be ambiguous when the $n$th state was already almost within the club. The great powers, however opposed they might have been to further proliferation to an $n$th, might be just as opposed to preemptive wars launched by $n$-4ths; resupplying nuclear weapons to anyone who loses them in preemptive counterforce attacks might thus be plausible simply as policy intended to deter such attacks. In effect, we might have the nuclear equivalent of what seems to be the current Soviet arrangement with the United Arab Republic—that whatever military equipment the Israelis destroy is speedily replaced.

Some years ago, strategic writers were prone to speculate on noncounterforce "limited strategic wars," wars in which nuclear weapons would be used against the homelands of the great powers, but in ways carefully circumscribed so as to retain restraints on the side being attacked. Perhaps only conventional military bases would be hit, or just a few cities, or only "prestige items" such as national parks or large dams. It was often asserted that increasing invulnerability and stability of the retaliatory forces on each side would make such wars more possible, since in such a case a superpower could afford to experiment in a crisis without automatically stampeding the other side into all-out war. Despite the increase in the relative invulnerability of strategic forces among the great powers, speculation on such limited strategic war has subsided, perhaps because

the option has, on reflection, come to seem more dangerous a[
sible than had first been imagined. One then wonders whether
of nuclear weapons to many more states would again make th.
war more probable. Will proliferation make nuclear weapons every-
where seem more "conventional," so that an implicit precedent will have
been set for their use?

More probably, the opposite effect will be seen as the spread of such
weapons makes the great powers extremely reluctant to set the specific
precedent of *use*. An American bomb on an empty Soviet national park
would legitimate the use of many $n$th bombs on many other targets. If nuclear weapons had not been used in anger since Nagasaki, the great powers
would probably wish to maintain that tradition. In general, a demonstra-
tive use of nuclear weapons by the great powers will probably become less
likely as nuclear weapons spread. These states have much to lose; they
have had a great deal of experience in handling such weapons, and they
are unlikely to be intoxicated by the novelty of nuclears.

Even if the superpowers are averse to experimenting with "limited
strategic wars," similar caution might not be shown among the $n$th states.
Such states might have leaders less responsible than in the current five, or
they may simply suffer from the novelty of possessing nuclear weapons.
Threatening another state that has not yet procured its nuclears, or even
one of the superpowers, may seem attractive if only to redeem whatever
investment went into the weapons program. An argument may thus reap-
pear for preemptive counterforce attacks by one of the superpowers to
keep some apparent madman from touching the nuclear trigger. This
counterforce offensive would hardly have the goal of simply reducing the
nuclear club from $n + 1$ to 1. Rather, it would reduce the club again to $n$.

As the nuclear club approaches twenty members, therefore, the world
might see someone's membership forcibly vetoed as an object lesson to all
other members. Yet veto by a preemptive use of nuclear weapons would
have to be applied very early, and the charter members may never quite
muster up the initiative. The mere prospect of this veto power may instead
suffice to inhibit any new nuclear-weapons state from discussing its new
arsenal irresponsibly. Such nations might thus emulate Communist China
when it was entering the club, with moderate statements disclaiming any
intention of using nuclears except in retaliation. In 1964 there was indeed
speculation about American or Russian preemptive strikes against the
Chinese; in 1970 it is too late for such preemptive strikes to be credible,
and it is also too late for Peking to be led into great irresponsibilities simply by the novelty of atomic weapons.

With regard to the tactical use of nuclear weapons, one can speculate
on the possible military scenarios that might occasion their use, and which

side they might therefore benefit. The weapons would of course play a
significant role if actually detonated, but they also effect a threat by their
mere existence. Does the tactical nuclear weapon help the larger or the
smaller force? Does it help the offensive or the defensive? Presumably the
answers depend on whether we are discussing warfare in the air, on land,
or at sea.

Taking first the air versus air case, the introduction of tactical nuclear
weapons probably tends to favor the offensive, and the smaller air force.
Such weapons presumably allow a single bomber to destroy all the opposing airplanes at any particular airdrome. The weapons thus tend to be
an "equalizer," and to help the air force that gets its planes into the air
first, and over into the opposing air space.

Turning to ground warfare, it has sometimes been conjectured that nuclear weapons will help the defensive, in that offensive breakthroughs
normally require a large concentration of troops and armored vehicles at
the point of attack. Such concentrations might thus be very inviting targets
for tactical nuclear weapons; again, these weapons seemingly act as an
equalizer, seemingly assisting the side with fewer troops. If the attack
clearly has to come through some narrow mountain pass, tactical nuclears might favor the defense all the more clearly, used conceivably as
preemplaced nuclear land mines. Perhaps the ideal defensive weapon would
be a bomb too large to be mobile. Yet typically one must have a pretty thick
wall of defending troops to force the offensive side to concentrate. The attacker might possibly be able to use tactical nuclears against this thick
defensive wall, since the defense almost by definition gives away its location
more clearly than the offense. If attractive targets for tactical nuclear
weapons should appear in both armies, the ensuing high casualties might
favor the army with the more extensive reinforcements. In the net, the
impact of tactical nuclears on ground warfare can thus often be of help to
the offensive and the larger armies.

Turning finally to sea warfare, it might again seem that nuclear weapons act as an equalizer, in that one bomb fired from one ship can destroy
many. Yet the net impact might well be to aid the defensive, since the offensive exploitation of seapower has often involved the well-organized assembly of numerical superiorities. Lanchester Square Laws and conventional wisdom have admonished us never to "divide the fleet," but the
threat of nuclear attack will put an end to most of the great naval maneu-
vers of formation, as well as to any serious and massive amphibious operations.

In summarizing the impact of nuclear weaponry on the likelihood of
tactical war, one sees several effects. Since the weapon sometimes favors
the offensive, it threatens to induce wars that might otherwise never have

occurred. At the same time, wars may be discouraged because the equalizing effects of the weapon make any normal "military superiority" less certain. Finally, nuclear weapons can always threaten "strategic retaliation" against the winner's cities if the loser faces substantial or total defeat; this would necessarily deter either side from pushing for a total victory, and perhaps even from initiating a war.

Hence, the spread of nuclear weapons may make even conventional tactical wars less likely. Lest we extoll this point too highly as a beneficial aspect of proliferation, we must note that the probabilities of conventional war have already been limited, apart from this hypothetical spread of nuclear weapons. While slightly increasing the impediment to limited war, the spread of nuclear weapons might mainly change the source of the impediment; but the cost of limited war would probably be increased.

Focusing only on nations as we know them, it is thus not easy to predict whether proliferation will generally make nuclear war much more likely. The world now has five nuclear powers with many thousands of warheads, but only two warheads have ever been used (and by one power) in combat. As proliferation goes on, the record of the international system may not remain this good; but the ambivalence of so many nations as to the halting of proliferation suggests that they do not expect the record to be drastically worsened either.

## SHIFTS IN POLITICAL POWER

The impact of nuclear weapons on the likelihood of today's conventional wars brings us to our second major concern regarding proliferation, the distribution of political power among the states we know.

There has long been debate on whether the existing world of five nuclear powers has actually been bipolar. One semantic resolution of this argument has been to stipulate that the *source* of political power has indeed been bipolar, in that only the U.S. and Soviet industrial and military establishments really amount to anything substantial. When referring to which *preferences* get satisfied and which get frustrated, however, the conclusion would instead be that the world is multipolar. In terms of freeing nations to do as they will, the second nuclear force thus balances out and neutralizes the first. In this view, two nuclear powers have the same impact on the distribution of influence as would five or twenty. Everyone benefits, but the first and the second were the only ones that mattered causally.

A close examination of the policies of France, Britain, and China might result in the conclusion that these states have indeed gained (or retained) a little prestige from being "nuclear powers" over what would have been available to them otherwise. In the case of Communist China, nuclear weapons may even have added some real strategic independence. Yet it is not easy to demonstrate that these states are substantially more able to ignore and frustrate the great powers than nonnuclear states (for example Japan), or that they would have lost much of their freedom of action had they not gone nuclear. Acquisition of nuclear weapons will not give the next fifteen club members much political influence beyond what they already have.

Where nonnuclear states are explicitly covered by a great power's nuclear umbrella, some needs might be created for "alliance coordination" of the possible use of such weapons. Yet most of these needs are eliminated by the changed rationale for nuclear targeting. When one nuclear power contemplated limited counterforce wars aiming nuclear weapons at particular military targets on the aggressing side, it was necessary for the military, and indeed the political, planning of the various states to be more closely coordinated. But once the umbrella had simply become an understanding that weapons would be fired at the cities of the aggressor in a retaliatory countervalue (rather than precise counterforce) fashion, needs for coordination were substantially diminished, together with any political spinoffs therefrom.

In general, the nuclear umbrella refers to the likelihood that a nuclear or conventional attack on a state will bring into play some superpower's nuclear weapons intervening on its behalf. We can speculate on whether the spread of national forces would intensify or weaken political commitments to such intervention. There is a standard argument that acquiring one's own nuclear weapons enhances the coverage of a great power's nuclear umbrella. The French, so the argument runs, could force American commitment to French defense by destroying Moscow in the event of a Russian attack. With Moscow destroyed, the Russians would have no reason to exempt New York from attack, with the counterresult that the American strategic forces would destroy all the rest of Soviet cities. Hence, the French Force de Frappe would only have to be large enough to act as a catalyst and become a trigger. With this trigger, France could deter attack just as if it had the full weight of the American Strategic Air Command in its hands.

This argument depends on some assumptions which might be challenged. If the Russians indeed valued all those other cities that only the United States could destroy, would they really destroy New York when the French Air Force had expended its entire punch in destroying Moscow? Either the French threat against Moscow would be sufficient to deter, without an extension of the United States nuclear umbrella, or the Russians would have some incentive to discriminate between antagonists after they had been attacked.

There is, indeed, the counterargument that acquisition of an indigenous nuclear force might terminate the coverage of a great power's nuclear umbrella. While India has not yet gone nuclear, some coverage from both the United States and the Soviet Union seems to exist. In part it exists because each side feels that India needs reassurance, and because each side preemptively fears that the other might rush in to offer such reassurance, deriving great benefits to its political position in India. Once New Delhi had acquired its own nuclear weapons, however, each side might wash its hands of the matter, secure in the assumption that New Delhi will not have to rush to the other for political and military support against the Chinese.

Leaving aside nuclear umbrellas, the current possessors of nuclear weapons might no longer commit their own forces to the defense of anyone else after proliferation, but instead substantially relax their restrictions on the sale and transfer of such weapons to other nations. As the absolute number of weapons holders rose, it might become a matter of relative indifference to the United States or the Soviet Union as to whether proliferation went any further. Indeed, foreign exchange could be earned by such sales; alternatively, the intention might be to assure that such weapons sold to various other countries would be more fool-proof, controllable, and secure than those produced indigenously. In this analysis, if Japan insisted on manufacturing missiles which might be vulnerable, the United States would consider selling Tokyo a Polaris force instead.

One might thus predict that further nuclear proliferation would not much change the present multipolar distribution of real political influence, but might alter the extent to which the two superpowers in particular are causally relevant to all this. One could argue, in addition, that the halting of proliferation would indeed entail a shifting of political influence from the various states towards the bipolar superpowers. When talking of a change, one has to keep his baseline clearly in view. Proliferation might stabilize the existing distribution of influence, while bans to proliferation could upset this distribution.

The reasoning on this point has been spelled out by a number of states resisting the Nuclear Non-Proliferation Treaty. A halt to proliferation will probably now indeed require the general acceptance and ratification of the NPT. But NPT in several ways legally enshrines the existing five nuclear powers, subjecting all other states to IAEA inspection, acknowledging the birthright to these weapons in five cases and eliminating it in all others. Italians, for example, have argued that true European unification will be impossible once the NPT has endorsed France and Britain as nuclear states and relegated Germany and Italy permanently to non-weapons status. Prestige is a real part of the substance of political influence—if the sovereignty of nations must be compromised tomorrow to avoid proliferation next week, the distribution of political influence may be altered tomorrow rather than next week, and in the opposite direction.

The prestige of weapons options can cause problems for the halting of proliferation if national leaders desire such prestige for its own sake, or if it really amounts to political power. Yet prestige can also solve some problems. Nations acquiring nuclear weapons might be pressed with hostile questions as to whom they had intended to attack; the simple answer can now be offered that the national honor demanded that their fighting men be equipped with the very newest and best of weapons.

## THE THREAT TO FEDERAL SOVEREIGNTY

Yet there is indeed another impact of nuclear proliferation on international politics as we understand them today. The peculiar process by which one nation invades and totally occupies another country, including its capital city, may have to be terminated if the smaller nation now possesses warheads for retaliation against the cities of the larger. How many $n$th countries would continue to be "responsible" in their use of nuclear weapons when they were being overrun?

The territorial integrity of the Dominican Republic, or Czechoslovakia, or even of Nazi Germany, might thus have to be respected, where in other times such countries would be totally occupied. So might also the independence and territorial integrity of Biafra, Nagaland, or Quebec. There would always be some doubt as to whether the nuclear-armed secessionists would be so rash as to destroy Lagos or Ottawa because their independence was not being respected. Yet the uncertain prospect of such fierce retaliation might still be enough to deter a federal military advance in the first place.

The federal forces (for example, the Russians entering Czechoslovakia) might respond by "Salami tactics," designed to reduce the risks of retaliation without giving up the conquest. As the resisting secessionists (Prague) made their threats, the invading forces each day would encroach just a little, making the counterthreat that the destruction of Moscow would mean the destruction of as-yet-untouched Prague. Despite their sense of territorial unity, the Czechs might then have difficulty in establishing some clear line, the crossing of which would certainly bring death to Moscow. Yet if Czechoslovakia were to choose to submit rather than resist, even when resistance could escalate to nuclear destruction, it is not so clear that nuclear-armed Biafrans would choose to spare Lagos, or that other independence movements would not act with great ferocity.

It is assumed here that proliferation *to* twenty countries will amount to proliferation *within* twenty countries; had Nigeria obtained the bomb in 1962, both Nigeria and Biafra might *ipso facto* have had it in 1968. Even if ordinary $n$th countries were to be inhibited in their brandishing of nuclear weapons, it is still assumed that movements whose independence is questioned or threatened would be less inhibited.

Deterring an invasion where independence is already established would thus be one phenomenon clearly aided by the spread of nuclear-weapons technology. Forcing a grant of independence where it had not been granted before might be another. Thomas Schelling has distinguished the latter situation as "compellance," not quite the same as the former "deterrence," and it may indeed be somewhat more difficult to force a change in an opponent's policy, rather than to simply prevent a change. Yet the secessionist movement could still plausibly plant bombs in an ascending scale of cities, destroying the smallest town first, then a larger one, then another, with the warning that this would continue until independence were granted. French Canadians who were fanatic enough about Quebec's independence might work through the list of all Canadian cities in descending order of English-speaking population.

If such applications of nuclear proliferation to coerce independence are at all plausible, they could incidentally spell the definitive end of all hopes for world government. Even if the two superpowers and 98 percent of the world had decided somehow to submit their military power to the control of an international organization, could not some small power with nuclear warheads of its own refuse to submit, using threats against Moscow and Washington to validate its threat? The segment need not even have been an independent state before the establishment of world government— South Carolina, for example, might at such a time secede not just from the United States, but from the world.

Rather than altering the macroscopic distribution of power in international affairs, the major impact of substantial nuclear proliferation might thus show up at the microscopic level, seriously challenging the ability of central governments to coerce and hold sovereignty over peripheral areas. Small states seeking to break away from the absolute control of larger states might then be able to do so; it would no longer be possible for Soviet troops to intervene in Czechoslovakia as easily as they did. Provinces may be encouraged in their attempts to secede, since the threat of nuclear bombardment on the central or federal capital would suffice as the ultimate deterrent to any efforts to quash such independence. In the summer of 1968, commentators in a number of countries regarded the invasion of Czechoslovakia as a significant argument against the Nuclear Non-Proliferation Treaty: If Prague had the bomb, would the USSR have dared to invade?

Historically, civil wars have been more severe and inhuman than wars between sovereign nations, in part because more is at stake. If the spread of nuclear technology were no longer hemmed in by national boundaries, would it be limited to central-government auspices? Indeed, would it be kept within governmental auspices at all, when the world has twenty "legal" weapons owners? We have already seen several reports of sloppy controls on the disposition of nuclear materials. Assuming that there will be no shortage of physicists who know how to assemble fissionable materials into explosive charges, relatively small groups of willful men will be able to explode atomic bombs whenever they wish.

The opportunities for such microproliferation might even be exploited by ordinary criminals. One can imagine a nuclear warhead being planted in a city with the threat that it will be detonated unless some large amount of money is delivered to an anonymous Swiss bank account, or perhaps left offshore aboard an empty motorboat. One does not have to accept Ian Fleming's *Thunderball* scenario and James Bond to admit that this form of million- or billion-dollar blackmail is at least plausible. Criminal operations (that is, operations with no discernible political purpose) have several times exploded dynamite bombs in police stations and public buildings merely as a diversion to mask a bank robbery. More seriously, we have had attempts to blow up bridges and sabotage railways in Zambia, allegedly merely to drive up the price of copper futures in Europe and America. If these projects are feasible, can we really discount the human psychology required to take on the bigger project of holding a city for ransom?

The possibility of criminal theft of the necessary nuclear materials can not so easily be dismissed. There has been at least one case in the United Kingdom of materials being stolen for their cash resale value, happily not—on that occasion—with a view to bomb production. Tighter materials controls must be instituted to ensure against such thefts, as well as to prevent wastage (or simple misplacement) of materials which can be highly toxic even if never assembled into explosives. Controls have been tightened up within the United States, and the acceptance of the Nuclear Non-Proliferation Treaty will be most important in inducing other nations to act similarly lest IAEA inspection show them to be careless and inefficient.

Yet our assumption that there may be twenty nuclear powers by the year 2000 means, if nothing else, that the NPT will have failed by then. Failure of the NPT may induce a reaction against all of its features and influences, with a setback to national control systems which otherwise would have been beefed up in anticipation of its successful NPT operation.

The feasibility of nuclear strikes on such a small scale might also depend on the miniaturization of nuclear warheads. States with substantial nuclear-weapons establishments have indeed been able to compress the mechanisms of bombs to very small sizes, reputedly as small as a bazooka shell. However, the more mischievous political movements or criminal plots may not yet have at their disposal the technology required for such miniaturization; thus, crude bombs might always have to be about the size of a truck, making clandestine emplacement or delivery a little more difficult. Closed societies with relatively few private vehicles in circulation, for example Eastern Europe, would thus find it easier, relative to larger societies, to prevent and frustrate the emplacement of nuclear weapons for the purposes of such blackmail. Still, time is not on our side here either. If ordinary nuclear weapons should become available to secessionists, fanatics, and mobsters in the year 2000, very small, easily portable bombs could be in their hands by 2020.

But purely criminal motives will probably not account for most of this "nuclear blackmail." Such an operation would more typically combine criminal and political elements—the greed and ruthlessness of the individual criminal with the higher purpose and social justification of an alienated political movement. To kill as many as fifty thousand persons at one blow may require more than the monetary lust of the Mafia. There is some honor among thieves, and there are many thieves in every city. The underworld information network usually betrays any criminal who has killed for no good reason; thus it would probably also betray a criminal who had killed (or contemplated killing) so many people for purely selfish reasons.

Nevertheless, there should be no difficulty in finding political window dressing which would allow such atomic bombers to capture a certain underworld legitimacy. Becoming a political fanatic covers one's tracks in several ways; fanaticism supplies accomplices where needed, accomplices less likely to betray the bomb planter. Fanaticism also wins the toleration or approval of neutrals who might have been appalled at nuclear-bombing threats simply for the purposes of personal gain. It is not hard to imagine the causes that might thus legitimate micronuclear blackmail. Breton independence, Black Power, Italian-American rights (the Mafia reverting to its old format?) one man/one vote in Rhodesia or South Africa, Trotskyism—all these might suffice to make acceptable the threat (and perhaps even the carrying out of the threat) to destroy a city with a nuclear explosive.

All this may seem like madness, which either dismisses it or forces us to contemplate the likelihood of madness. Apart from criminality blended into political fanaticism, could not a "mad scientist" elect to destroy New York or Los Angeles because he had decided that they had become evil places, or threaten to destroy them if some special reforms were not immediately introduced? One might be tempted to look to our experience with troublemakers using other destructive techniques. We have seen Arab political groups placing bombs on airliners bound for Israel with callous disregard for the lives of the persons on board the planes. The scenarios we are contemplating for the future also require relatively little prior backing for the procurement and use of nuclear weapons. If the deaths of airline passengers were plausibly calculated as being instrumental in winning otherwise unavailable political returns in 1970, would not the detonation of a nuclear explosion seem as plausible a venture in 2000?

People now leave dynamite bombs about American cities from time to time. To date, no chemist has poisoned a city's water supply by adding chemical or biological agents to it. The bypassing of the safeguards built into a reservoir system would require considerable ingenuity and scientific competence, but have we any guarantee that such competence is incompatible with what we might style as madness?

Even though CBR (chemical, biological, and radiological warfare) as yet has shown us no troublesome previews of the twenty-first century, one should note that atomic bombs have already been manipulated as vehicles of internal political arrest in two of the existing nuclear powers. The last military insurrection in Algeria occurred just before a scheduled detonation of a French atomic device. To avoid the possibility of the bomb falling intact into the hands of the rebelling generals, the French government ordered that it be exploded several days early. At the height of the Great Cultural Revolution in Communist China, a PLA general in a western province was reported to have threatened to use his nuclear weapons if the revolution's threat to his position was not moderated. Thus, when considering the international political impact of nuclear proliferation, we must take into account the internal political record of the various states, rather than generalizing about abstract redistributions of political status.

The first five nuclear-weapons arsenals emerged in countries that had reasonably strong traditions of military subordination to civilian authority. France and China, to be sure, have seen military revolts at various points in history, and closer examination might even find flaws in the patterns of the Soviet Union, United Kingdom, and United States. Yet compared to all the states that may someday acquire nuclear weapons, the current members of the nuclear club show more effective civilian control than average. Similarly, with regard to the "irrational" in politics, the current five look better than the average we might expect. Perhaps great power breeds a strong sense of responsibility and restraint; if it does not, we can expect the world to get worse more easily than it gets better.

### CONFRONTING NUCLEAR BLACKMAIL

A society confronting threats of nuclear attack on its cities might try to "toughen up" in various ways, so as not to have to give in to such blackmail. An effort to discourage urbanization, designed to disperse the population and thereby avoid presenting credible targets, might seem appropriate. Indeed, writers in the late 1940s sometimes speculated that this would be a necessary and appropriate policy for the United States and the USSR in face of each other's nuclear threat. Perhaps urbanization should be discouraged for other reasons as well. In this respect, subsidies might be channeled to encourage citizens to locate away from urban centers; higher taxes on city dwellers might provide further incentives.

To date, all efforts to discourage urbanization seem to have been ineffective, however. Even in societies as tightly controlled as the USSR, cities grow more rapidly and extensively than the social optimum would have it. It is thus unlikely that this approach will effectively reduce the vulnerability of twenty-first-century societies to private nuclear blackmail. Perhaps this will remain so only until the first city has been destroyed by a nuclear explosion. Yet Hamburg and Tokyo were almost as totally destroyed in World War II as Hiroshima and Nagasaki, and people still crowded back into these cities as soon as they had been rebuilt. If city dwellers are willing to risk the air pollution of the urban centers, they may just as readily decide to risk urban nuclear explosions.

As a partial measure, states may strive to train their urban dwellers in the techniques of rapid evacuation of cities. But past efforts in this direction have also been discouraging. Civil-defense efforts have sometimes been mocked and scoffed at; sometimes they have been implemented in great panic, as in Paris at the time of the Munich crisis. Even when such evacuations have been well executed, as in London in the fall of 1939, the evacuees have quickly become restless in their countryside refuges, sneaking back to their vulnerable urban homes. If such evacuation schemes ever did become very effective, they might be a new cause of tension between the superpowers. If Moscow and New York could both be cleared on several hours notice, might there not again be reason to fear a sudden launching of World War III?

More active forms of defense may be installed, especially after the first bomb. Old-fashioned air-defense systems could be renovated and strengthened to prevent attacks by private plane. ABM systems could be purchased or maintained where otherwise they would have been rejected. Controls could be imposed on surface entry into urban areas. Even diplomatic immunity might be abridged so that nuclear warheads could not be introduced piecemeal by diplomatic pouch. If this kind of tampering with diplomatic usage seems improbable, one need only cite Communist China as an example of how far it can go—who would dare to smuggle a bomb into the embassy grounds in Peking today, hoping that the attempt would go undetected? Yet the feasibility of such steps may remain limited to the really closed societies of our globe; other countries would probably be averse to imposing such controls, even if the threat had been reified by explosions in several cities.

Instead of physically shielding its population, a state might attempt to fend off blackmail by feigning an irrational indifference. If carried off properly, the message might be established that states would rather risk nuclear explosions than give in to such threats. Yet such a policy does not seem very credible. One might reflect on some analogous situations today, specifically hijackings of airliners and bombscares in public buildings. In most parts of the world today, persons threatening the safety of airplane passengers or the airplane itself are given virtually total leeway in dictating its destination. It is likely that this decision by airline managements not to resist has encouraged would-be hijackers, but it has also drastically reduced risks of injury to innocent passengers and of loss of valuable aircraft. One exception has been in Latin America, where hijackings have several times been resisted, even at the risk of bullet damage.

Capitulation also seems to be the rule in response to telephoned threats of bombs placed in buildings, at least when such threats are not recurrent. Typically, buildings are emptied to avoid risk to life, and to facilitate a search. Presumably, the officer responsible is reluctant to assume responsibility for any deaths that might follow. After threats have been repeated for several days, and no bombs have been found or detonated, the same official would probably begin to ignore them; who could blame him if a bomb really exploded after six false alarms?

If one assumes that most nuclear threats will still be specifically political, one further approach to protecting cities remains, already applied in a number of countries. This involves the placing of hostages from the potentially attacking groups in the cities that might be attacked. Thus, a Black insurrection in the United States would kill many of its ethnic brothers by using nuclear detonations in American cities. An Arab nuclear attack on Israel today would kill many Arabs in Jerusalem or Haifa. A nuclear attack on any South African city would kill many more Blacks than Whites. It might thus behoove some Canadian government to count the number of French-speaking citizens in cities of the western provinces, lest it be faced with the threat of nuclear rather than conventional explosions emerging from the Quebec separatist movement.

"Political" movements are here defined as those which specify a large number of people as the beneficiary of the concessions sought. To label the people served by one's cause is to expose them to possible retaliation. In the cases cited above, retaliation comes automatically because the cities are shared by the threateners and threatened; but what if they were not?

It might be difficult for a government to commit itself to deliberate retaliation, particularly when its own citizens would be among the victims. The hostages might be innocent persons, disinterested in the independence that the movement was trying to win for them, not ready or willing to inflict nuclear destruction for such a cause. The parallel in international politics suggests how drastically the domestic environment could be altered. In international politics, the country that brandishes nuclear weapons places its population on the line as hostages for its own good behavior. So also may any intranational political cause. If the Soviet leadership were to kill a great number of Americans in a nuclear attack, we would kill a great number of innocent Russians in retaliation, Russians who were probably indeed opposed to the launching of World War III. It is thus imaginable that French Canadian terrorist nuclear attacks on cities like Vancouver would force the Canadian central government to retaliate murderously against innocent French-speaking towns.

But the likelihood that a sense of nationhood could survive such hostility seems very small. By driving the central government to such measures, the separatists would win their independence by default. One could more readily imagine brutal retaliation against a resident population already seen as "alien"; would Israelis not be tempted to retaliate murderously against Arabs in Palestine, or South Africans against Blacks?

## ANONYMITY AND POLITICS

There are some general points to be made about anonymity in the handling of all these nuclear weapons. Secrecy and anonymity may at times be crucial to the acquisition process, lest some state preempt a clandestine bomb project before it comes forth with any useable bombs. Such secrecy is indeed likely to become more possible as more men learn how to handle plutonium and more plutonium shows up to be handled. Secrecy may be a function of the closed or open nature of particular societies, but even open countries may have mastered the arts of pluralistic ignorance, whereby the whole of society never really knows what its individual parts are doing.

It used to be argued that an actual test detonation was required to make sure an atomic bomb would work. This is likely to change in the future, since computer-simulation techniques already make tests much less necessary. As for the necessity of verifying simulation data, it has sometimes been reported that the United States has never had an actual dud in its test program; bombs have had larger or smaller explosive yields than predicted, but they have never failed to explode. In any event, if tests were deemed necessary it would be possible to arrange an anonymous test detonation, in which a tramp steamer dropped a nuclear charge off in some unfrequented part of the ocean, with months passing before a radio signal detonated the charge. All the world would know that the bomb worked, but only its producers would know whose prototype it was.

We now turn to the most critical possibility: the anonymous delivery and use of nuclear weapons. Here we could again imagine merchant ships or submarines dropping their charges offshore. As bombs become smaller, delivery by suitcase or light airplane would become feasible. As long as national boundary controls are not tightened to some extreme degree, the clandestine delivery of a bomb will remain possible. Identifying the source of such an explosion might become a very difficult task if the victims have no political clues as to where to assign the blame. The "fingerprint" of the isotope pattern of a bomb's fallout tends to vary with the peculiarities of national bomb designs, but a comprehensive knowledge of such fingerprints will often be impossible.

Considerable speculation has been devoted to the risks of catalytic war—war begun by anonymous token nuclear strikes against one of the major powers by an $n$th country intending to provoke retaliatory strikes against the other major powers, and hence causing World War III. In effect, one would be applying the mechanism of the Lavon Affair, but on a much grander and more horrendous scale: In that case Israeli saboteurs allegedly destroyed an American government building in Cairo with a view to alienating the United States from Egypt. The catalytic use of nuclear weapons would involve the anonymous destruction of one city with a view to provoking the retaliatory destruction of a great number of the assumed attacker's cities.

Such anonymous catalytic uses of nuclear weapons might be discouraged by various declaratory strategies, if such strategies could be made credible. The potentially aggrieved nation might announce that it would in such cases strike with nuclear weapons at all other nations, thus surely punishing the unknown culprit. Alternatively, the policy in such cases might be to retaliate against the weakest known nuclear power, or to strike in proportion to the remaining nuclear threat on the premise that an attempt at counterforce damage-limitation is still appropriate when a clandestine catalytic strike has increased the risk of general war.

The problem is, of course, that all such announced policies would be close to unbelievable as actual responses to the destruction of a single great-power city, and so would hardly serve to deter such attacks. Yet it is equally incredible that the United States would immediately level all Soviet cities if an unidentified missile had destroyed a single American city. It would be far more likely that no U.S. nuclear-missile strikes at all would take place until a careful and deliberate examination had made some progress in identifying the probable assailant.

One could ask rhetorically whether there could ever be a need for retaliation after a nuclear strike, much less *speedy* retaliation. Even after a full Soviet strike on all the cities of the United States, would it not be far more rational to sue for peace, rather than destroying the one probable source of relief supplies? After a *limited* infliction of nuclear damage the rationality of retaliation might be much clearer. How could you make your threats on behalf of Baltimore credible if you did not retaliate against Moscow for its attacks on Minneapolis? The establishment of announced retaliatory responses can, in any event, be justified in terms of deterrence: Even if it were not rational to retaliate after the fact, it might be helpful before the fact to be considered capable of such irrationality.

Thus, *speedy* retaliation does not seem advisable, and speed in retaliatory mechanisms is necessary to the success of the catalytic war scenario. For encouraging evidence of U.S. propensities for slower deliberation, we can look to the official reactions to two very serious political assassinations: of President John Kennedy and presidential candidate Robert Kennedy. In either case, the preliminary evidence could easily have lent itself to an interpretation of murder directed from abroad. In neither case did the idea of quick retaliation against any outside state become salient. The loss of a city may be far more horrible than the loss of a president, but still it would probably not occasion the immediate use of U.S. or Soviet retaliatory nuclear weapons.

A state or political movement that exploded a single warhead without identifying itself might also have difficulty in convincing the victim that more bombs were primed for detonation. In effect, such a situation parallels the U.S. problem with Japan in 1945, when the American stockpile was indeed exhausted after the second bomb had been dropped on Nagasaki. The bomb on Hiroshima had not been sufficient to instill any visible move toward surrender; the second bomb presumably conveyed the impression that continued and repeated punishment would ensue if resistance continued. Since a clandestine attacker could not invite an inspection of his stockpile, would two or more cities have to be destroyed to produce concessions? And would this tactic, as in the case of Japan in 1945, in effect be forcing concession to what was after all a short-term bluff?

Leaving aside catalytic wars, the political use of anonymous nuclear strikes may prove rather limited. In phrasing political demands one essentially sheds a large part of one's anonymity, hence exposing a target for reprisal. Anonymous nuclear blackmail might thus emerge mainly from a purely criminal basis, but the criminal approach raises difficulties of payment. Political payment can be delivered easily enough without requiring further activity by the threatener himself, as by withdrawals of troops, distribution of food, opening voting booths to Black Africans, and the like. But criminal returns would more typically be on a cash basis, which raises delivery and pickup problems for the blackmailer.

One can visualize a secret rendezvous at sea in which billions of dollars in unmarked bills change hands, but the surveillance technology of the twenty-first century may leave any such criminal operation quite insecure. If the blackmailers had no identifiable political purposes, the law-enforcement apparatus of the entire world would probably cooperate in seeking to apprehend and punish them. If money were indeed the only form of ransom demanded in a nonpolitical blackmail scheme, pressure would probably be brought to bear against institutions, such as the Swiss bank, that facilitated clandestine transfers of assets. It is impossible for blackmailers to collect if it is impossible for victims to pay. It is hard to see how the world could leave the current financial practices of Zurich untouched if they facilitated plots based on nuclear threats against Miami or Kiev.

## CONCLUSION

One could review much of the above argument by simply listing the possible uses of nuclear weapons. There is always a danger that by focusing on some particular use we forget or deemphasize others.

One obvious factor that is often forgotten is, very simply, that nuclear weapons can be used to kill larger numbers of people than any other means is capable of. Historically there have indeed been individuals who wished to perform such genocide; if Hitler were alive and came into the possession of nuclear weapons, would he not choose directly to destroy Tel Aviv?

The use of limited stockpiles of nuclear weapons as a catalytic device to induce much greater destruction has also been discussed. Instead of destroying Tel Aviv directly with his limited stockpile, Hitler (or Mao) might provoke a much larger impact by tricking other nuclear forces into action. The first "killer" approach pays no attention at all to motivation; the second is based on a theory of rational behavior. If a hypothetical state preferred a world in which the United States and Soviet Union no longer held a material preponderance, a small nuclear strike at both superpowers, based on the assumption that they would complete each other's destruction, would not be implausible.

Leaving motivation aside again, nuclear weapons could be used simply to avert the use of other nuclear weapons. If our bombers or missiles carry off their "counterforce" preemptive strike with the proper degree of surprise, we can hope to keep you from damaging us, and thus put aside all complicated theories on how to deter you.

Returning to the world with which we are more familiar and to policies we more clearly approve, nuclear weapons today are typically harnessed to deter obnoxious behavior by other states. If you use nuclear weapons against my cities, I will use them against yours. What is more, if you try to occupy my cities even without using nuclear weapons, I will drop nuclear bombs on your cities.

Attempts to force concessions—to practice "compellence" rather than deterrence, in Schelling's terms—would be much trickier to execute. Examples include U.S. pressure on the USSR to remove its missiles from Cuba, as well as a number of the intrastate nuclear blackmail schemes that were suggested above. The concessions to be extracted could be monetary as well as political, although nothing of this kind has yet occurred.

Finally, in a pernicious blend of the above arguments, nuclear weapons could be used to destroy a city, not out of pure hate for its occupants, but to restore and enhance the credibility of any of the threats made as part of deterrence and compellence. A state might fail to grant some faction's demands when no city had been destroyed since Nagasaki, but it might be much more "responsive" after the first explosion.

There is thus little new in contending that the world will be less pleasant if nuclear weapons spread to many more countries. What has been argued here is that this unpleasantness will take forms somewhat different from those normally assumed: as threats to the authority of governments themselves, emerging from movements with little to lose. If one agrees that proliferation among states will probably facilitate proliferation within states, then the domestic-arena problems suggested above are little more than logical extensions of our familiar international scenarios.

PART **II**

# *Modular Analysis*

## CHAPTER 5

Kenneth E. Boulding

# The Weapon as an Element in the Social System

## THE ROLE OF WEAPONS IN SOCIAL SYSTEMS

Before discussing the problems of a multinuclear world I would like to develop a more general topic—the role of weapons in social systems. A weapon must be defined as a material object, the significance of which arises out of the fact that it occupies a role in the social system, the role being that of a potential producer of "bads" or disutilities. A material object is not a weapon unless it occupies such a role, and a great many things, like tableknives, may be weapons under some circumstances but not under others. The nature of weapons is complicated by the fact that they occupy different roles in a number of different social systems. In particular, they occupy two very different roles—one when they are used in the actual production of "bads," such as in killing somebody out of anger or revenge, and another when they are used as part of a threat system, in which what is significant is the credibility of the threat to produce "bads" and its effect on the behavior of the threatened persons, rather than the actual production of "bads."

The same physical weapon may have strikingly different significance and occupy a very different role depending upon two considerations—first, the kind of interdependence among interest or utility functions; second, the type of threat system prevailing. These principles apply both to the interaction of individuals and to the interaction of nations. For an individual we postulate a utility function which simply allocates to all relevant states of the world an ordinal number—1st, 2nd, 3rd and so on—so that the $n$th state of the world is regarded as preferable to the $(n + 1)th$, $(n + 2)th$ and so on. Similarly, for nations we can postulate a national-interest function which likewise puts an ordinal number on all the relevant states of the world, especially states of the international system. Neither utility functions nor national-interest functions should be taken as given, except in a very first approximation, as they are essentially learned; that is, they are the result of previous experience. The important point here is that the field which is ordered consists of perceptions of the orderer, whether this is a person or a nation. In other words, both utility and national interest are essentially subjective, although the subjective field is limited in some degree by objective considerations.

Within this perceptual field we have the perceptions of the welfare, and changes in the welfare, of others, either other individuals or other nations. This means that utilities or national interests are interdependent, in the sense that individual or nation $A$ includes in its perceptual field its perception of the welfare of individual or nation $B$. There are basically three types of this kind of interdependence:

(1) *Benevolence. A* is benevolent towards $B$ if $A$ feels that its utility is increased or its interest advanced when it perceives that $B$ is better off.

(2) *Indifference. A* is indifferent to $B$ if $A$'s perception that $B$ is better off makes no difference to $A$'s perception of its own utility or interest. This is the classical economic assumption of selfishness.

(3) *Malevolence. A* is malevolent towards $B$ if $A$ prefers a position in which it perceives that $B$ is worse off to one in which it is better off.

These relationships may be measured by a "rate of benevolence." The rate of benevolence of $A$ towards $B$ is how much $A$ would be willing to sacrifice in order to perceive that $B$ is better off by a dollar. If the rate of benevolence is zero, we have indifference; if it is negative, we have malevolence. We thus see that indifference is actually a very unlikely case, being merely the zero point on the scale of benevolence-malevolence.

The probability of the use of weapons increases as we move down the scale from benevolence to malevolence. Weapons may be used in a malevolent system when $A$ wishes to damage $B$ without getting any benefit for himself, apart from the satisfaction that he feels at the diminution of $B$'s utility. The converse of this, benevolence, produces the creation and transfer of goods rather than the creation and transfer of bads. Weapons may theoretically be used even in the case of benevolence, as when a parent whips a child supposedly for the child's own good. The higher the degree of benevolence, however, the less likely are weapons to be applied, since the bads that are created lower the utility of the user of the weapons. Economists usually suppose exchange to be characterized by indifference, that is, independence of utilities. If $A$ gives something to $B$ and $B$ gives something to $A$, this could take place in the absence of either benevolence or malevolence. In practice, however, it looks as if a small degree of benevolence is necessary in order to legitimate exchange, in spite of the fact that both parties benefit from it.

## THREAT RELATIONSHIPS

Weapons are most likely to be used in threat relationships. Threats, again, are more likely to be used as we move down the scale from benevolence towards malevolence. Furthermore, the use of threats is likely to move us down the scale towards malevolence, so that we may easily run into deviation-amplifying feedback systems here. Even if we start off with a relationship between *A* and *B* of mutual indifference, if *A* threatens *B* in order to get some goods out of him, even without feeling any malevolence towards him, *B* is likely to feel malevolent towards *A* which may in turn induce a feeling of malevolence in *A* towards *B*.

There are five threat systems: (1) threat-submission, (2) threat-counterthreat, (3) threat-defiance, (4) threat-escape, and (5) threat-control. Weapons may be used in threat-submission systems in which *A* threatens to create bads for *B* and *B* transfers values to *A* in order to prevent *A* from creating bads. In such systems *B* is usually unable or unwilling to create bads for *A*. Threat-counterthreat systems exist when both *A* and *B* have weapons and threaten each other. The difference between threat-submission and threat-counterthreat is that in threat-submission it is clear who suffers and who gains if the threat is actually carried out, whereas in threat-counterthreat this is no longer clear. In threat-counterthreat systems considerations of retaliation, credibility, and bluffing come to be important. A threat-defiance system is one in which either *A*'s or *B*'s threats are ignored. Threat-defiance systems often lead to the actual production of disutilities. A threat-escape system is one in which, if *A* threatens *B*, *B* simply moves away from *A;* that is, puts distance of some kind, either physical or social, between him and the threatener, so that the threat capability of *A* is diminished to the point where it does not affect *B*'s behavior. This kind of system is frequently possible because of the principle that threat capability is a function of the distance from the threatener. This is the principle which I have called "the law of the further, the weaker." Threat-control occurs when there is multilateral agreement to forego or to control the use of threats in a "social contract." This arrangement, of course, is the foundation of civil government. It may involve an agreement to monopolize the use of threats in legitimated government, or it may happen by informal agreement, or even by a reaction process by which *A*'s behavior influences *B* and *B*'s influences *A* and so on.

In international relations, in revolution and internal war, there is frequently a movement from tribute to deterrence and malevolence. Some nation or group will attempt to get goods by threatening bads to others. If the threat results in submission, there is usually some form of tribute—that is, one-way transfers of goods under threat. This system is legitimated in many institutions—the legal system, taxes, universities, and the Church (the threat of Hell or excommunication has been a particularly successful threat). If the legitimacy of tribute breaks down, the system may degenerate into deterrence or threat-counterthreat. Threat-counterthreat, in turn, usually breaks down also—although it may degenerate into either threat-defiance (brinkmanship), threat-escape (emigration), or threat-control (disarmament or arms limitation). The degeneration of threat-counterthreat systems is largely dependent on the national-interest functions. Threat-defiance may be associated with malevolence while threat-control may be associated with indifference or benevolence. Thus, threat systems and national-interest functions interact in a cyclical process as in the Figure 1.

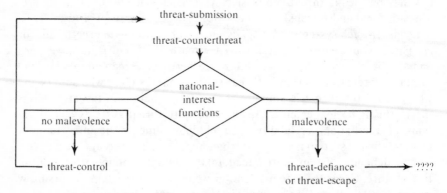

FIGURE 1. The interaction of threat systems and national-interest functions.

In United States-Russian relations, where malevolence is not very high, nobody expects to get goods out of anybody else by means of threat, but there is nevertheless a very costly and dangerous system of deterrence. Deterrence cannot ultimately be stable because of the high cost of maintaining it and because if the probability of its breaking down were zero or near zero, the system would cease to deter.

## AFFECTIVE CLUSTERING

One of the great unsolved problems of social science is that of the dynamics of benevolence and malevolence, especially the clusterings of benevolence into communities and malevolence into enmities. The problem can be illustrated by a matrix analysis. Consider a matrix $A$ with $n$ columns and $n(\Sigma m_i)$ rows where $n$ is the number of nations in the world and $m_i$ is the number of people in nation $i$. Each element of the matrix—say $a_{ij}$— represents the affective orientation of each individual toward all nations including his own. Affective orientation is not exactly the same as benevolence or malevolence but it may be considered to be closely related. An "affective community" may be defined by clusters of positive affect, and an "affective enmity" by clusters of negative affect. For example, in that part of the matrix corresponding to the United States and the Soviet Union one would expect the citizens of each country to have positive affect for their own country but negative or neutral affect for the other country (see Figure 2).

*AFFECT TOWARD*

|  |  | S.U. | U.S. |
|---|---|---|---|
| S.U. | 1 | + | − |
|  | 2 | + | 0 |
|  | : | + | − |
|  | : |  |  |
|  | ᵐS.U. | + | 0 |
| U.S. | 1 | 0 | + |
|  | 2 | − | + |
|  | : | − | + |
|  | : |  |  |
|  | ᵐU.S. | − | + |

*CITIZENS OF*

FIGURE 2. Affective orientation of Soviet Union and United States citizens toward each nation.

Affective clusterings may be the result of the legitimization of a preexisting community (as is the case above with two nation-states). On the other hand they may influence the formation of new communities such as alliances or regional organizations, as in Western Europe where the hypothetical matrix in Figure 3 may be seen as explaining the exclusion of Britain from the European Economic Community. (The matrix elements in Figure 3 are summary measures of affect for the entire population—henceforth to be called $\bar{a}_{ij}$.)

Karl Deutsch has suggested that community formation means that positive affect for the community increases while positive affect for the noncom-

*AFFECT TOWARD*

|  |  | Br | Fr | It | Ge | Ne | Bel |
|---|---|---|---|---|---|---|---|
|  | Britain | + | − | − | 0 | + | 0 |
|  | France | − | + | + | + | + | + |
|  | Italy | − | + | 0 | + | + | + |
| *CITIZENS OF* | Germany | − | + | + | + | + | + |
|  | Netherlands | 0 | 0 | 0 | + | + | + |
|  | Belgium | 0 | + | 0 | + | + | + |

FIGURE 3. Hypothetical matrix of citizens' affective orientation toward the countries of Western Europe.

munity decreases (self-closure).[1] Although Deutsch's hypothesis clearly does not exhaust the possibilities of theorizing about the dynamics of affective clustering, it may be verified or falsified by empirical evidence. This line of inquiry, therefore, may be a fruitful one.

It is suggested here that affective clustering may be related to the existence of malevolence, indifference, or benevolence, and therefore related to threat systems. One of the problems with identifying a threat-submission system empirically is that it is difficult to distinguish between a one-way transfer made as a result of amity (a gift) and a one-way transfer made as a result of threat or coercion (tribute). If $\bar{a}_{ij}$ is positive or neutral, then a one-way transfer from $i$ to $j$ may be considered a gift. If $\bar{a}_{ij}$ is negative, then a one-way transfer from $i$ to $j$ may be considered tribute. If a deterrence system exists in a cluster of positive affect or indifference it will probably degenerate into a threat-control system. Where deterrence exists in a negative affect cluster, it is much more likely to degenerate into threat-defiance and system break-up. Thus, it is not wise to expect deterrence to prevent conflict where malevolence predominates (as in the Middle East) or to prevent conflict merely by manipulating the threat system. It is probably much more reasonable to isolate clusters of negative affect or malevolence from

[1]Karl Deutsch, *et al.*, *Political Community and the North Atlantic Area* (Princeton, N.J.: Princeton University Press, 1957).

the rest of the world in terms of access to weapons, and to manipulate the reward systems so that malevolence is decreased.

## DETERRENCE SYSTEMS

Several mathematical frameworks are useful for the discussion of threat-counterthreat, or deterrence systems: Hotelling models, reactivity curves, and Richardson models. *Hotelling models* require knowledge about three parameters for each member of the system (see Figure 4): *threat capability* (the height of the vertical lines in Figure 4); the *loss of threat gradient* (the slope of the lines extending horizontally from the top of the threat capability lines); and the *distance* of each nation from all the other nations in the sys-

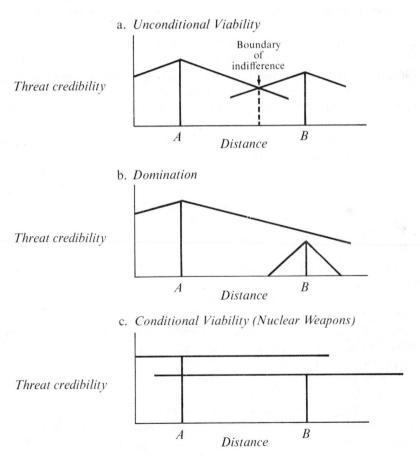

FIGURE 4. Hotelling models of threat systems.

tem. A two-country threat system is a system of *domination* if, as in Figure 4b country $A$ may threaten country $B$ without fear of any credible counter-threat. Necessary and sufficient conditions for domination are that the loss of threat gradients do not intersect in the interval between $A$ and $B$ and that the gradient of either $A$ or $B$ intersects the abscissa before it intersects the other's threat-capability line. Domination coincides with threat-submission in the discussion above. A two-country system is a system of *unconditional viability* if, as in Figure 4a, both countries may threaten each other but neither is able to threaten the other without fear of great loss or defeat in carrying out the threat. The necessary and sufficient conditions for this system are that the loss of threat gradients intersect somewhere between $A$ and $B$. The intersection point is called the boundary of indifference—where an "I-dare-you-to-cross-that-line" stalemate would be reached. Unconditional viability corresponds to a stable deterrence system. The loss of threat gradient is based on an assumption, true for most weapons, that the cost of transporting bads increases with distance. This assumption may not be true for nuclear weapons delivered by ballistic missiles where the cost of delivery is virtually constant for any place on the globe (see Figure 4c). Thus, the best that can be expected from a nuclear deterrence system is *conditional* rather than unconditional viability—where no state can dominate another but there is never a boundary of indifference.

A very fruitful line of development is the possibility of creating artificial or conventional boundaries of indifference by the process of mutual agreement in order to take the problem of national boundaries off everybody's agenda. This is probably the secret of the establishment of stable peace in North America and Scandinavia. This arrangement, of course, requires a certain minimum of benevolence, but fortunately not very much. It would involve a change in the national-interest function, such that country $A$'s perception of its own welfare would take a sharp dip if it ever invaded country $B$, and vice versa. This is one of the possible avenues to threat control.

In *models of reactivity curves* we take the national war industry as a measure of the threat system and postulate an ecological system in which the size of the war industry of every nation is a function of that of every other. In Figure 5, the size of the war industry in $A$ is a linear function of the size of the war industry in $B$, and vice versa. If the two curves intersect at $E$, then some stable equilibrium point exists—if not, the system will be unstable. The linear model requires knowledge about two parameters for each nation—the initial hostility ($OA_0$ and $OB_0$) and the slope of the reactivity curve ($m_A$ and $m_B$)—in order to predict (and the stable equilibrium point) or instability. The minimal condition in the linear model for intersection is that $m_A m_B < 1$. In the three-country case, the reactivity co-

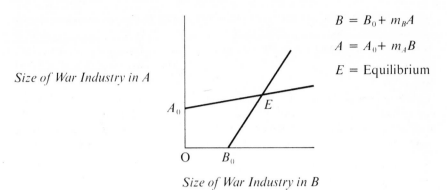

$$B = B_0 + m_B A$$
$$A = A_0 + m_A B$$
$$E = \text{Equilibrium}$$

*Size of War Industry in A*

*Size of War Industry in B*

FIGURE 5. A two-country linear reactivity curve model.

efficients must all be less than about 0.7.[2] Thus, the effect of adding to the number of countries in the system is to increase the possibility of instability. It is possible, of course, to consider reactivity curves which are not linear. Lewis Richardson suggested that reactivity curves might resemble curves of diminishing returns in economics, as in Figure 6.

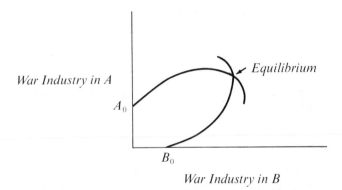

*War Industry in A*

*Equilibrium*

*War Industry in B*

FIGURE 6. A nonlinear reactivity curve model.

In nonlinear models the conditions for stability become more complex. Richardson's discussion of such models is quite complete.[3] Some nonlinear models are similar to ecological models of animal populations in that unless reactivity and initial hostilities lie within a certain range, the system may be either completely unstable or metastable and subject to continual oscil-

[2]See Kenneth E. Boulding, "The Parameters of Politics," *University of Illinois Bulletin*, 63: 139 (July 15, 1966), 1–21.
[3]Lewis F. Richardson, *Arms and Insecurity* (Chicago: Quadrangle, 1960).

lation between rapid arms races and rapid disarmament. The lesson to be learned from reactivity curves is that industries, under certain conditions such as insistence upon parity in weapons production, may create arms races which increase the danger and cost of deterrence and the likelihood of malevolence.

Both Hotelling and reactivity-curve models can easily be extended to the likely case of discontinuous functions. An example of a discontinuous loss of strength gradient is that connected with a bow-and-arrow attack on a stockaded fort, as in Figure 7. Discontinuous reactivity curves are also pos-

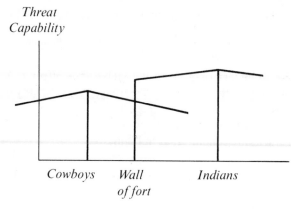

FIGURE 7. Cowboys and Indians.

sible since war industries may have full employment or maximum-capacity limits or step-level reactivity functions.

## CONCLUSIONS

In general, my reaction to the deterrence debate is that there is too much reliance upon the stabilizing nature of deterrence taken by itself. Both historical and logico-mathematical analysis lead me to believe that deterrence is associated with malevolence and is likely to be unstable in the long run. Given the nature of nuclear weapons and the national war industries, it is unlikely that alternatives to deterrence ("Love your enemy for he has created you") will be seriously considered. There is some hope for change in that two factors will help to stabilize international politics for the next few decades—stability in the rank-ordering of nations and the global interdependencies which will accompany the process of ecological problem solving.

There is a much lower probability of a change in the international peck-

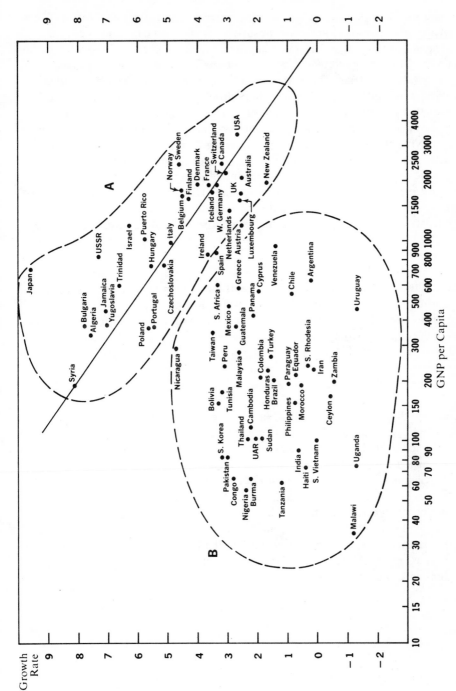

FIGURE 8. Percent per annum rate of growth in the early 1960s.

ing order than there ever was before—at least in terms of GNP ranks. The theory of exponential growth is absurd—a fact which can easily be demonstrated with a simple bivariate scatterplot (see Figure 8). Growth rates are negatively correlated with GNP per capita for countries in group $A$ in Figure 8—countries which are generally considered to be industrialized. What this plot demonstrates is that development is a process in which growth rates decrease as GNP per capita increases, so that while it is quite likely that countries in the upper part of $A$ will eventually catch up in GNP per capita with those in the lower part, it is unlikely that there will be rapid reversals in anyone's position due to rapid growth.

The problems of global air and water pollution are clearly going to necessitate regional and global problem solving. This should help to keep channels of communication open and may result in the creation of institutional infrastructures capable of transforming deterrence into threat-control. The problem here is how to turn a system with deteriorating dynamic feedback into a system with appreciating dynamic feedback, which would take us from bad to better rather than from bad to worse. In quantitative terms the difference between these two systems may be very small. This difference is what I have sometimes called the "watershed principle." There is a kind of watershed in the $n$-dimensional parametric social space on one side of which things go from bad to worse and on the other side of which they go from bad to better. Obviously, if one is close to the watershed and on the wrong side of it, a little effort produces an enormous result, and the world may very well be in this position today. To climb up to the watershed indeed is often a kind of labor of Sisyphus. We roll the stone of human learning up the hill toward peace and it continually breaks away from us and rolls down again. If there is a watershed, however, the hill has a top, and once over the top, the world is very different indeed. The climb to the watershed goes on two feet—one is the development of a learning process of individual behavior and national behavior towards long views, realistic images of the world, and an appreciation of the remarkable payoffs of mutual benevolence. The other is the development of institutions, in this case essentially world political institutions of various kinds which can change the payoffs of the system and encourage the learning process. Fortunately there is no nonexistence theorem about a process of this kind, so at least one can end the analysis on a note of modest optimism.

John C. Harsanyi

# *A Simple Probabilistic Model of Nuclear Multipolarity*

In the mathematical model that follows nuclear stability depends on the ratio of nuclear weapons (on whether this ratio exceeds a certain critical ratio, $c$), on the number of countries possessing nuclear weapons, and on the presence or absence of alliances. This model is not meant to be taken too seriously. It is based on rather drastic simplifying assumptions, though it does seem to illustrate some important aspects of the problem of nuclear stability. Later in the chapter it will be argued that such simplistic models are inadequate and should be replaced by more sophisticated models based on game-theoretical considerations.

## THE MODEL

Let $x_i$ denote the number of nuclear weapons stockpiled by country $i$ ($i = 1, 2, \ldots, n$). Suppose that $x_i$ cannot exceed $A$ for any country $i$ so that

$$0 \leqq x_i \leqq A \text{ for } i = 1, 2, \ldots, n. \tag{1}$$

Assume also that the numbering of the countries is such that

$$x_1 \geqq x_i \text{ for } i = 2, 3, \ldots, n. \tag{2}$$

Thus, $x_1$ is the strongest country. In addition, assume that the $x_i$ have uniform probability distributions on the interval $[0, A]$, so that

$$\text{Prob } (x_i \leqq a) = \frac{a}{A} \text{ where } a \in [0, A]. \tag{3}$$

In Figure 1, the whole rectangle between 0 and $A$ has an area of one unit. The shaded area represents Prob $(x_i \leqq a)$.

It will be assumed that any country $i$ will always refrain from attacking another country $j$ so long as

$$x_i < cx_j, \tag{4}$$

where $c$ is called the *critical ratio*. If, for example, no country $i$ would ever attack country $j$ unless it were at least twice as strong as country $j$,

93

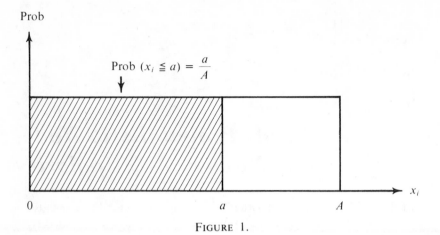

Prob

$$\text{Prob } (x_i \leq a) = \frac{a}{A}$$

FIGURE 1.

then $c = 2$. It will be assumed that this critical ratio is the same for all countries in the system. Therefore, a system consisting of $n$ countries will be stable if even the strongest country satisfies (4) with respect to any other country, so that

$$x_1 < cx_i \text{ for } i = .2, 3, \ldots, n. \tag{5}$$

The above inequality will be called the *stability condition*.

We shall now consider some simple cases. The two-country case is illustrated in Figure 2. Since both countries' stockpiles must be less than $A$, it is necessary only to consider the area within the square $OBCD$. Indeed, since $x_1 = x_2$ by (2), it is necessary only to consider the area within the triangle $OCD$. Let the distance $ED = \frac{A}{c}$. Then the probability that the point $(x_1, x_2)$ will lie in the shaded area of Figure 2 will be equal to the ratio of the triangular area $OCE$ to the triangular area $OCD$. Therefore, the probability of stability in the two-country case will be

$$p_2 = \frac{\text{Area } OCE}{\text{Area } OCD} = \frac{\frac{1}{2} A(A - A/c)}{\frac{1}{2} A^2} = 1 - \frac{1}{c}.$$

If the point $(x_1, x_2)$ lies in the unshaded area $OED$, then there will be stability. The probability of instability is therefore $1 - p_2 = \frac{1}{c}$.

In the three-country case, we have stability only if *both* of the following two conditions are satisfied:

$$x_1 < cx_2 \tag{6}$$

and

$$x_1 < cx_3. \tag{7}$$

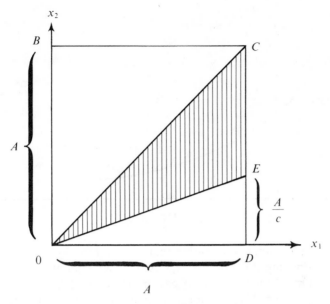

Figure 2.

But either condition will be satisfied with probability $p_2 = 1 - \dfrac{1}{c}$. Since the two conditions are statistically independent, the probability that condition (5) will be satisfied is

$$P_3 = (P_2)^2 = \left(1 - \frac{1}{c}\right)^2. \tag{8}$$

In the $n$-country case we obtain

$$p_n = (p_2)^{n-1} = \left(1 - \frac{1}{c}\right)^{n-1}. \tag{9}$$

Thus the probability of stability in the $n$-country case is given by this mathematical expression.

The meaning of this result is fairly obvious. Given a fixed critical ratio $c$, the probability of stability, $p_n$, decreases as $n$, the number of countries, increases (see Figure 3). Indeed, as $n$ becomes very large, $p_n$ tends to zero, and instability becomes a virtual certainty.

**Stability for States with Different Nuclear Strengths**

Next, let us relax the assumption that all $x_i$'s have the same upper bound $A$. Instead, we shall assume that each country $i$ may have a different upper bound $A_i$ for its nuclear strength $x_i$, so that condition (1) is replaced by

$$0 \leq x_i \leq A_i \quad \text{for } i = 1, 2, \ldots, n. \tag{10}$$

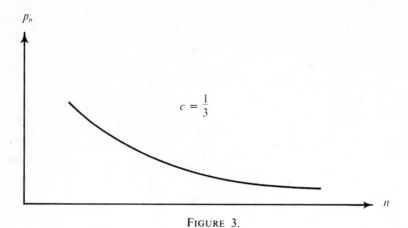

FIGURE 3.

But we shall retain the assumption that each $x_i$ has a uniform probability distribution within this range $(0, A_i)$. At first we shall also retain assumption (2), which in the two-country case means that $x_1 \geqq x_2$. (But later we shall have to relax this assumption because now our results will crucially depend on whether $x_1 > x_2$ or $x_2 > x_1$.) Now we have to distinguish three cases, depending on whether $A_1 > A_2$ or $A_2 \geqq A_1$, and on whether $A_1 > cA_2$ or $cA_2 \geqq A_1$.

*Case* $\alpha$: $A_1 \leqq A_2$ (see Figure 4). In this case, the probability of stability, now to be denoted as $p_\alpha$, can be computed in the same way as before:

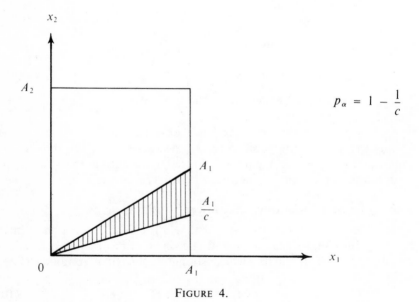

FIGURE 4.

*Case β*: $A_2 < A_1 \leqq cA_2$ (see Figure 5). In this case, the probability of stability, to be denoted as $p_\beta$, will be given by a different formula:

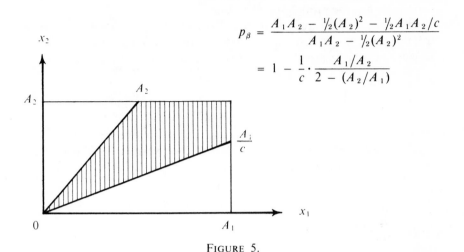

$$p_\beta = \frac{A_1 A_2 - \frac{1}{2}(A_2)^2 - \frac{1}{2}A_1 A_2 / c}{A_1 A_2 - \frac{1}{2}(A_2)^2}$$

$$= 1 - \frac{1}{c} \cdot \frac{A_1 / A_2}{2 - (A_2 / A_1)}$$

FIGURE 5.

*Case γ*: $A_2 < cA_2 < A_1$ (see Figure 6). In this case, the probability of stability, to be denoted by $P_\gamma$, will be given by still another formula:

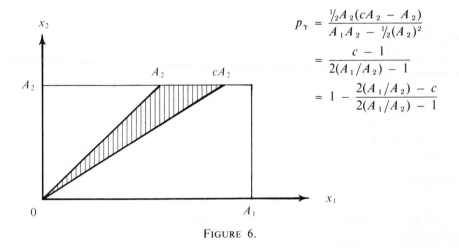

$$p_\gamma = \frac{\frac{1}{2}A_2(cA_2 - A_2)}{A_1 A_2 - \frac{1}{2}(A_2)^2}$$

$$= \frac{c - 1}{2(A_1 / A_2) - 1}$$

$$= 1 - \frac{2(A_1 / A_2) - c}{2(A_1 / A_2) - 1}$$

FIGURE 6.

It is easy to verify that, for any given value of $c$, $p_\beta$ and $p_\gamma$ are smaller than $\left(1 - \frac{1}{c}\right)$. This means that when we relax the assumption of a common upper bound $A$ for all the $x_i$'s, the probability of stability will tend to *decrease* (at least in cases $\beta$ and $\gamma$—in case $\alpha$ it will remain unchanged).

By a similar computation, we can also verify the following fact. Instead of computing $p$, the probability of stability, in each of the three cases by a different formula, we can also proceed like this. We compute $p$ by all three formulae and then choose the *smallest* $p$ value obtained in this manner; this will be the correct $p$ value. That is, we can write

$$p = f(c, A_1, A_2) = \min(p_\alpha, p_\beta, p_\gamma) \tag{11}$$

$$= \min\left[\left(1 - \frac{1}{c}\right), \left(1 - \frac{1}{c} \cdot \frac{A_1/A_2}{2 - (A_2/A_1)}\right), \left(\frac{c - 1}{2(A_1/A_2) - 1}\right)\right].$$

However, this formula is valid only under the restrictive assumption that $x_1 \geq x_2$. In order to obtain a generally valid formula, we shall first of all assume that the numbering of the two countries is such that

$$A_1 \geq A_2. \tag{12}$$

Under this assumption, the probability that in fact $x_1 \geq x_2$ is $1 - \frac{1}{2}(A_2/A_1)$ (see Figure 7).

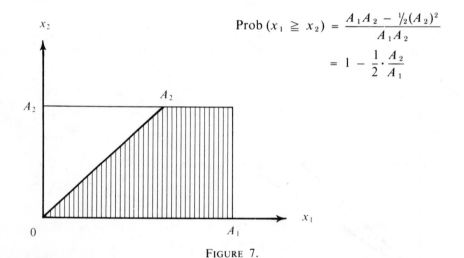

$$\text{Prob}(x_1 \geq x_2) = \frac{A_1 A_2 - \frac{1}{2}(A_2)^2}{A_1 A_2}$$

$$= 1 - \frac{1}{2} \cdot \frac{A_2}{A_1}$$

Figure 7.

On the other hand, $\text{Prob}(x_1 \geq x_2) = \frac{1}{2}(A_2/A_1)$. Consequently, the general formula for computing the probability of stability is

$$p = \left(1 - \frac{1}{2}\frac{A_2}{A_1}\right) f(c, A_1, A_2) + \frac{1}{2}\frac{A_2}{A_1} f(c, A_2, A_1). \tag{13}$$

In the $n$-country case, let us assume that

$$A_1 \geqq A_2 \geqq \cdots \geqq A_n. \tag{14}$$

Then the probability that $x_j$ is the largest of all the $x_i$'s is given by

$$q_j = \prod_{i=1}^{j-1}\left(1 - \frac{A_j}{A_i}\right) \cdot \prod_{i=j+1}^{n}\frac{A_i}{A_j}. \tag{15}$$

Assuming that $x_j$ is in fact the largest of all $x_i$'s, the probability of stability is

$$\prod_{\substack{i \neq j \\ i=1}}^{n} f(c, A_j, A_i). \tag{16}$$

Therefore, if we do not want to make any restrictive assumption about which quantity $x_i$ is the largest, the formula for computing the probability of stability in the case of $n$ countries is

$$p_n = \sum_{j=1}^{n} q_j \prod_{\substack{i \neq j \\ i=1}}^{n} f(c, A_j, A_i), \tag{17}$$

where $q_j$ and $f$ are the quantities defined by equations (15) and (11).

### Stability in the Presence of Alliances

The problem of stability in the presence of alliances can be subsumed under our discussion of stability in case of unequal upper bounds. Suppose the $n$ countries are divided into $k$ disjoint alliances (that is, no country can belong to two different alliances at the same time). Let $y_j(j = 1, 2, \ldots, k)$ be the total number of nuclear weapons possessed by alliance $j$. Even if we assume that the number of weapons, $x_i$, owned by each individual country $i$ is subject to the *same* upper bound $A$, this would not be true for alliances. For example, if a given alliance $j$ consisted of $m$ different countries, then the upper bound for its nuclear stockpile $y_j$ would be not $A$, but rather $A_j = m \cdot A$. Thus, we can assume that

$$0 \leqq y_j \leqq A_j \qquad \text{for } j = 1, \ldots, k. \tag{18}$$

For the sake of simplicity, we shall again assume that $y_j$ has a uniform probability distribution within this interval $(0, A_j)$. This last assumption is not quite consistent with our basic model, because if each individual country's nuclear stockpile, $x_i$, has a uniform probability distribution, then the quantities $y_j$, representing the sum of two or more $x_i$'s, will *not* have a uniform probability distribution. However, this assumption of a uniform distribution considerably simplifies the computations required, and does not essentially affect our basic conclusions, and therefore we shall make use of it.

Under this assumption, the probability that the system will be stable is still given by equation (17), except that if the $n$ countries form $k$ disjoint alliances, then $n$ must be replaced by $k$ in the formula. As $k < n$, and as the probability of stability *increases* as the number of independent political units decreases, the existence of alliances will tend to *increase* the stability of the system. For instance, if the system consists of 10 independent countries, then the probability of stability is

$$p_{10} = \left(1 - \frac{1}{c}\right)^{10-1} = \left(1 - \frac{1}{c}\right)^{9}.$$

On the other hand, if the 10 isolated countries are replaced by 5 two-country alliances, then the probability of stability increases to

$$p_5 = \left(1 - \frac{1}{c}\right)^{5-1} = \left(1 - \frac{1}{c}\right)^{4}.$$

If $c = 2$, then $p_{10} = 1/512 = .002$, while $p_5 = 1/16 = .063$. Thus $p_5$ is $512/16 = 32$ times larger than $p_{10}$.

However, this conclusion is valid only if the different alliances are *not very unequal* in size. In contrast, if some alliances are much larger than others, then the existence of these alliances will *increase* instability because it will increase the probability that the nuclear stockpile of the largest alliance will be more than $c$ times larger than the stockpiles of some small alliances (or those of some isolated countries outside all alliances).

## OBJECTIONS TO THE MODEL

In my opinion, a basic objection to the model is that the very concept of a critical ratio $c$ is of rather doubtful validity. It may be true that no country will engage in a nuclear attack against another country if it does not have a sufficient degree of nuclear superiority. But it does not follow that if it does possess such superiority, then it will in fact start a nuclear war against the weaker country. (Indeed, if this were the case, then by now all nonnuclear countries would have been annihilated by the nuclear powers.)

However, even if there were to be such a thing as a critical ratio $c$, it is not a satisfactory procedure to *assume* it as a basic datum in our model; rather, the value of $c$ should have been *derived* from some more fundamental assumptions, and in particular, from a game-theoretical analysis of the whole international system. In fact, why does not country 1 necessarily attack country 2, even if it does have a sufficient degree of nuclear superiority over the latter, and even if it does regard it as an undesirable rival in many respects? One reason is that even a weaker country may be able to retaliate and impose unacceptable losses on the stronger country. Another reason may be the expectation of unfavorable reactions by third parties against a country guilty of an unprovoked nuclear attack. In the case of small nuclear powers, a third reason may be that a nuclear attack would significantly deplete their nuclear arsenal, and therefore weaken their own deterrent ability against other nuclear powers. The effect of these and similar considerations cannot be properly assessed without a thorough game-theoretical analysis of the situation.

Game theory is based on the assumption of *rational* behavior, which is essentially the same thing as *goal-directed* behavior. It is behavior pursuing some fairly well-defined policy objectives in a reasonably consistent manner. From an analytical point of view, the great advantage of the rationality assumption is that it enables us to explain and, in principle, even to predict, human behavior in terms of its goals or objectives. If I know that a given person wants to get from San Francisco to New York in a hurry, then I can predict that (assuming he has the money, and so on) he will go by a jet—and I can predict this without knowing very much about his individual psychology.

The main thing that game theory adds to this commonsense concept of rationality is the requirement to look at *both sides* (or all sides) of a given situation *at the same time.* It does not simply ask, What will be a rational strategy for player 1 against player 2? Rather it asks, What strategies will both of them follow if both of them are acting in a rational manner? What represents a rational strategy for player 1 cannot be decided at all without asking what a rational strategy is for player 2, since any strategy of player 1 can be rational only if it is rational *against* the strategy player 2 is likely to follow, and conversely.

Of course, the game-theoretical approach also has its limitations. For example, in any game-theoretical analysis of problems of nuclear stability, the concepts of deterrence and retaliation play a fundamental role. Yet these concepts themselves cannot be fully analyzed purely in terms of rational behavior. For even though a *threat* of retaliation may represent a very rational action, since it may deter a nuclear attack, once a nuclear attack has been made, it presumably would no longer be rational to retaliate. Thus, if everybody always acted in a perfectly rational manner, then threats of retaliation would have no credibility, and therefore would have no deterrent effect. What makes such threats credible is the fact that after an attack, people are likely to feel an emotional impulse to retaliate, even if this no longer serves any pragmatic end. Both the feeling of revenge and the feeling of gratitude (or loyalty) are emotional factors which cannot be derived from any rationality assumptions. Yet both of them may play important roles in stabilizing certain social situations, by serving as rewards for socially desirable actions or as deterrents from socially undesirable ones. Game-theoretical analysis can achieve a realistic understanding of human behavior only if it makes allowances for emotional factors of this kind.

CHAPTER 7

Reinhard Selten and Reinhard Tietz

# *Security Equilibria*

In this paper we shall investigate a modification of Scarf's deterrence model.[1] Scarf's model is in the form of a game, where the players are $n$ countries, each having a stockpile of atomic weapons which can be used against the other countries. The utility of a country depends on the damage that has been done to that country, and it may also depend on the damage that has been done to other countries.

In Scarf's model, only the result of the use of atomic weapons determines these utilities, but in our modified version who has attacked whom is also important. Thus it becomes possible to explicitly take into account the motive of retaliation. If a country $i$ has been attacked by a country $j$, $i$ will be motivated to retaliate. Therefore, an attack of country $j$ against country $i$ will influence country $i$'s utility evaluation of damage suffered by country $j$.

In order to analyze our version of Scarf's model, we have developed a new theory which we call "the theory of security equilibria." This solution concept can be applied to a class of games which we call "irreversible games." The use of atomic weapons is irreversible in the sense that bombs cannot be taken back once they have been used. Our theory is based on this simple fact.

[1] Herbert Scarf, "Exploration of a Stability Concept for Armed Nations by Means of a Game Theoretical Model." In the *Final Report on Contract No. ACDA/ST-116, Models of Gradual Reduction of Arms*, submitted by MATHEMATICA, Princeton, New Jersey, September 1967, pp. 469–497.

This study was initially prepared for the Arms Control and Disarmament Agency as part of the *Final Report on Contract No. ACDA/ST-116, Models of Gradual Reduction of Arms*, submitted by MATHEMATICA, Princeton, New Jersey, September 1967. We are grateful to the Arms Control and Disarmament Agency for permission to use this publication. We are also indebted to Professor Richard Rosecrance, who contributed valuable suggestions which induced us to incorporate some changes from the original ACDA report into this paper.
[The mathematical portions of Professor Selten's and Professor Tietz's paper appear in the Appendix.—Ed.]

Our solution concept has the form of an algorithm which computes "security equilibria." A computer program has been written and the set of security equilibria has been computed for a systematic sample of cases of the model described in the following section. Our assumptions on the countries' preferences are explained in Section 2. A nonrigorous introduction to our solution concept is given in Section 3, where an illustrative example will be used. The computational results are discussed in Sections 4 and 5. The appendix to this volume contains a more formal development of the theory of security equilibria for irreversible games and its application to deterrence models.

# 1. A CLASS OF SIMPLE DETERRENCE GAMES

The players are $n$ countries, with country $i$ having a *stockpile* of $b_i$ atomic bombs. For the sake of simplicity, we assume that any country can be completely destroyed by one bomb. The destruction of a country does not involve the destruction of its bombs (for example, rockets may be installed in submarines). Clearly, there is no point in having more than $n - 1$ bombs, because a country cannot do more than destroy all the other countries. Therefore we can assume without loss of generality that $b_i$ is an integer with $0 \leq b_i \leq n - 1$.

A "state of the world" which is reached after a sequence of nuclear attacks may be described by a vector

$$x = (x_1, \ldots, x_n)$$

whose components are defined as follows: $x_i = 0$, if country $i$ has not been bombed; $x_i = j$, if country $i$ has been bombed by country $j$. We always exclude the possibility that a country might bomb itself; we also assume that no country will be bombed twice. (It is unnecessary to destroy a country which has already been destroyed.) Obviously, we always must have $x_i \neq i$. We exclude the possibility of production of new bombs. This exclusion is justified if our theory is understood as an analysis of short-range stability. Accordingly, the stockpile $b_i$ is the upper limit of the number of bombs which country $i$ can use against other countries. Hence, the number $i$ can occur at most $b_i$ times as a component of $x$.

A vector $x$ that satisfies the conditions implied by the preceding paragraph is called a *state*. The set $X$ of all states will be referred to as the *state set*. Obviously, $X$ is finite.

A state $y$ is called attainable from a state $x$ for a coalition $C$, if the members of $C$ are able to cause a transition from $x$ to $y$ by attacking other countries; this is expressed more precisely by the following formal definition: a state $y = (y_1, \ldots, y_n)$ is *attainable* from a state $x = (x_1, \ldots, x_n)$

for a coalition $C$, if $x \neq y$ and if for $x_i \neq y_i$ we always have $x_i = 0$ and $y_i = j$ with $i \in N - C$ and $j \in C$. (This definition excludes attacks of members of $C$ against other members of $C$.) Further, $y$ is attainable from a state $x$, if it is attainable from $x$ for at least one coalition $C$.

The state $o = (0, \ldots, 0)$ which has only zero-components is called the *initial state*. Those states from which no other states are attainable will be referred to as *technical end states*. A technical end state is reached if all countries are destroyed, or if all stockpiles are depleted, or if there is only one undestroyed country which is also the only one still possessing a positive number of bombs.[2]

Each country $i$ is assumed to have a *utility function* $u_i$, which assigns a utility $u_i(x)$ to every state $x \in X$. The vector

$$u(x) = [u_1(x), \ldots, u_n(x)]$$

will be called the *utility vector* of $x$. The utility function $u_i$ expresses the preferences which country $i$ would have for the states $x \in X$, if all states could be considered to be equally stable. If it is to be expected that a state $x$ will be changed after a short time, it has no value in itself. A state $x$ which is unstable in this sense must be judged in the light of the utility attached to the stable states that eventually might be reached from $x$. Our theory will elaborate this idea in more detail.

Scarf has interpreted his model in terms of a game in normal form. Our interpretation of the model described here is more akin to the extensive form. At any state $x$, the situation is similar to that of a characteristic function game. A set of players may unite to form a coalition $C$ in order to achieve a transition to a state $y$ which is attainable for $C$ from $x$. If two mutually exclusive coalitions $C_1$ and $C_2$ are formed at the same time, it cannot be said which coalition will have the opportunity to act first. In this respect, our model is less specific than the extensive form. The rules about the move sequence are incomplete. This condition is justified by the assumption that the players do not know the rules which are not given by our model. The countries are supposed to have only limited commitment power; it is sufficient to secure coordinated actions of a coalition $C$ that wants to achieve a transition from a state $x$ to a state $y$, attainable for $C$ from $x$; but it is not sufficient for the enforcement of agreements which go beyond such temporary coalitions for immediate coordinated actions. As we shall see, this limitation does not completely exclude some kinds of commitments, as for example the commitment not to bomb a friend, or the commitment to retaliate against an aggressor. Such general commitments can be incorporated into the utility functions.

[2]In the case of friendship groups, which will be explained in Section 2, technical end states which are not covered by this explanation are possible.

## 2. SPECIAL UTILITY FUNCTIONS

In this section we shall describe some special utility functions which are based on plausible assumptions about the preferences a country might have in a deterrence situation described by the model in the preceding section.

A country may look at a state $x$ from different points of view that are of unequal importance. Clearly, it is most important for country $i$ whether or not country $i$ has been destroyed. Therefore, we shall only consider utility functions which have the following property:

(a) *Motive of self-preservation:* If for two states $x = (x_1, \ldots, x_n)$ and $y = (y_1, \ldots, y_n)$, we have $x_i = 0$ and $y_i \neq 0$, then $u_i(x) > u_i(y)$ holds for the utility function $u_i$ of that country $i$.

A country $i$ which has been destroyed by a country $j$ is motivated to retaliate. This motive for retaliation is very important for any theory of deterrence because without such a motive deterrence would not be reliable. A country that has been destroyed would have no reason to strike back. We shall incorporate the motive of retaliation into all utility functions defined in this section. This is done by the following assumption:

(b) *Motive of retaliation:* If for $x = (x_1, \ldots, x_n)$ and $y = (y_1, \ldots, y_n)$ we have $x_i = y_i = j$, and if $y_j = 0$ and $x_j \neq 0$, then $u_i(x) > u_i(y)$ holds for the utility function of country $i$.

The first utility function defined in this section is based on assumptions (a) and (b) alone. We shall call it the *indifference utility function* because a country which has this kind of preference structure is indifferent between any two states $x$ and $y$, which do not have different utilities by the assumptions (a) or (b). The indifference utility function distinguishes only three levels of utility. They may be named "destroyed, aggressor not destroyed" ($x_i = j$ and $x_j = 0$), "destroyed, aggressor destroyed" ($x_i = j$ and $x_j \neq 0$), and "not destroyed" ($x_i = 0$). We shall define two other utility functions that can be regarded as refinements of the indifference utility function. Let $d(x)$ be the number of destroyed countries at state $x$. [In other words, $d(x)$ is the number of nonzero components of $x$; this is at the same time the number of bombs which have been used.] A "motive of good will" may be defined as follows:

(c) *Motive of good will:* If $x$ and $y$ are two states, at the same utility level relative to the indifference utility function, and if $d(x) < d(y)$ is true, then $u_i(x) > u_i(y)$ holds for the utility function of country $i$.

There is an obvious antithesis to the motive of good will:

TABLE 1. UTILITIES FOR COUNTRY $i$ ACCORDING TO THE INDIFFERENCE UTILITY FUNCTION, THE GOOD WILL UTILITY FUNCTION, AND THE BAD WILL UTILITY FUNCTION.

| Type of Utility Function | Country i Destroyed | | Country i Not Destroyed |
|---|---|---|---|
| | *Aggressor Not Destroyed* | *Aggressor Destroyed* | *Not Destroyed* |
| Indifference | 1 | $n^{(n-1)} - n^{(n-2)} + 1$ | $n^n - n^{(n-1)} + 1$ |
| Good-will | $n^{(n-1)} - n^{(n-2)} + 1 - d(x)$ | $n^n - n^{(n-1)} + 2 - d(x)$ | $n^n - d(x)$ |
| Bad-will | $d(x)$ | $n^{(n-1)} - n^{(n-2)} - 1 + d(x)$ | $n^n - n^{(n-1)} + 1 + d(x)$ |

(d) *Motive of bad will:* If $x$ and $y$ are two states at the same utility level relative to the indifference utility function, and if $d(x) < d(y)$, then $u_i(x) < u_i(y)$ holds for the utility function of country $i$.

If country $i$ is indifferent as between any two states which do not have different utilities by the assumptions (a), (b), and (c), we shall say that this country has the "good-will utility function." In the same way, another utility function, which we call the "bad-will utility function," is generated by (a), (b), and (d).

For our theory, only ordinal utility functions are needed. Therefore, it does not matter which numbers are assigned to different utility levels as long as greater numbers are assigned to higher levels. In our computer program, the three utility functions described above are computed as indicated by Table 1. Some of the special cases, for which security equilibria have been computed, are 4-country cases, where it is assumed that each of the players belongs to one of two nonintersecting "blocs" $B_1$ and $B_2$ with 2 members each. Two players belonging to the same bloc are called friends. The blocs must be understood as firm friendship groups, which may be thought of as based on common ideologies. We exclude the possibility that a country destroys a friend. Thus, if players 1 and 3 form $B_1$ and players 2 and 4 form $B_2$, only such states $x = (x_1, \ldots, x_n)$ are permitted where we do not have $x_1 = 3$ or $x_3 = 1$ or $x_2 = 4$ or $x_4 = 2$. It is interested in the welfare of its friend but, on the other hand, we cannot expect a country to value a friend's welfare more highly than its own. There are several ways to define modifications of the indifference utility function, the good-will utility function, and the bad-will utility function, based on this general idea. We have selected the possibility described by Table 2. Table 2 assumes that retaliation against an agressor will be considered as more important than the survival of a friend (in this instance the friendship is very weak). The existence of blocs offers the possibility of indirect retaliation, which damages an aggressor by destroying the aggressor's friend. We assume that the friend's survival will be valued more highly than this type of indirect retaliation. If a country has not been destroyed, it may still be motivated to retaliate on behalf of a friend that has been destroyed. This is assumed in Table 2, but we do not consider possible the motive of indirect retaliation on behalf of a friend; this motive would be directed against the friend of country $i$'s aggressor's friend.

## 3. AN ILLUSTRATIVE EXAMPLE

In this section we shall try to illustrate our approach with the help of a simple example, without going too much into technical details which are

TABLE 2. MODIFICATIONS OF THE INDIFFERENCE UTILITY FUNCTION, THE GOOD-WILL UTILITY FUNCTION, AND THE BAD-WILL UTILITY FUNCTION, FOR THE 4-COUNTRY CASES WITH FRIENDSHIP.

| Modifications of Utility Functions | Country i Destroyed | | | | | | | Country i Not Destroyed | | |
|---|---|---|---|---|---|---|---|---|---|---|
| | Aggressor of Country i Not Destroyed | | | | Aggressor of Country i Destroyed | | | Friend of Country i Destroyed | | Friend of Country i Not Destroyed |
| | Friend of Country i Destroyed | | Friend of Country i Not Destroyed | | Friend of Country i Destroyed | | Friend of Country i Not Destroyed | | | |
| | Friend of aggressor not destroyed | Friend of aggressor destroyed | Friend of aggressor not destroyed | Friend of aggressor destroyed | Friend of aggressor not destroyed | Friend of aggressor destroyed | | Aggressor of friend of country i not destroyed | Aggressor of friend of country i destroyed | |
| Indifference | 1 | 10 | 37 | 40 | 49 | 76 | 157 | 193 | 205 | 241 |
| Good-Will | $11 - d(x)$ | $39 - d(x)$ | $40 - d(x)$ | $50 - d(x)$ | $78 - d(x)$ | $160 - d(x)$ | $194 - d(x)$ | $205 - d(x)$ | $242 - d(x)$ | $256 - d(x)$ |
| Bad-Will | $-1 + d(x)$ | $7 + d(x)$ | $36 + d(x)$ | $38 + d(x)$ | $46 + d(x)$ | $72 + d(x)$ | $155 + d(x)$ | $192 + d(x)$ | $203 + d(x)$ | $241 + d(x)$ |

reserved for the Appendix. The new solution concept developed in this paper will be introduced in a nonrigorous way. A more formal definition is given in Sections 1 through 6 of the Appendix to this volume. Some of the intuitive considerations of this section will again be considered in the more formal development of our solution concept in a somewhat different manner.

Consider the case of 3 countries with $b_1 = b_2 = 1$, and $b_3 = 0$. The initial state is $0 = (0,0,0)$. All the states in Column 2, Figure 1 are attainable from the initial state by means of having one country bomb another.

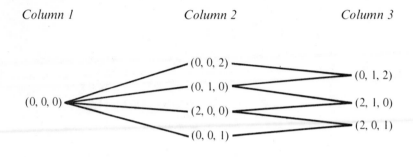

*Initial state*                                      *Technical end states*

FIGURE 1.  Attainability structure for a simple example.

All the states in column 3 are attainable from states in Column 2 (as indicated by the connecting lines). None of them is directly attainable from the initial state, since no country would enter into a coalition in which it would be attacked by another coalition member. The states in column 3 are all technical end states because all bombs have been used.

Assume that each of the 3 players has the indifference utility function, and assign the values 0, 1, and 2 to the three utility levels. (Note that we do not follow the convention of Tables 1 and 2). Then the state vectors and the corresponding utility vectors are as shown in Table 3.

The game begins at the initial state and eventually reaches an *end state*; any state is a possible end state, including the initial state, since whether the game continues depends on the behavior of the players. In order to narrow down the set of possible end states, we need assumptions about the behavior of the players.

Our theory is based on the idea that the behavior of the players is guided by security-level considerations. For every state $x$, each player $i$ forms an expectation about the worst possible utility level $u_i(y)$ connected

TABLE 3. UTILITY VECTORS
FOR THE EXAMPLE OF
FIGURE 1.

| Column | $x$ | $u(x)$ |
|---|---|---|
| 1 | $(0, 0, 0)$ | $(2, 2, 2)$ |
| 2 | $(0, 0, 2)$ | $(2, 2, 0)$ |
| | $(0, 1, 0)$ | $(2, 0, 2)$ |
| | $(2, 0, 0)$ | $(0, 2, 2)$ |
| | $(0, 0, 1)$ | $(2, 2, 0)$ |
| 3 | $(0, 1, 2)$ | $(2, 0, 1)$ |
| | $(2, 1, 0)$ | $(1, 1, 2)$ |
| | $(2, 0, 1)$ | $(0, 2, 1)$ |

to an end state $y$, which may be reached against his will from $x$ if the players do not behave irrationally. This level is called the *equilibrium security level* $v_i(x)$ of player $i$ at $x$. Obviously, the meaning of the concept of equilibrium security levels depends on what is meant by the words "irrational behavior." In our theory, this question is answered by the following rationality assumption:

*Principle of security-level maintenance:* No player will do anything which lowers his equilibrium security level.

Anything which contradicts the principle of security-level maintenance is excluded as irrational behavior. Note that on the one hand our explanation of the concept of equilibrium security levels refers to the definition of irrational behavior, while on the other hand our definition of irrational behavior makes use of the concept of equilibrium-security levels. This kind of circularity is typical for game-theoretic solution concepts.

Let us investigate what happens if we apply this theory to our example. In order to do this, in Figure 2 we repeat Figure 1 with utility vectors instead of states. The numbers at the connecting lines indicate which player achieves the corresponding transition.

How can we determine the equilibrium security levels of our example? The answer is not difficult: we must begin at the technical end states. Obviously, for the technical end states the equilibrium-security-level vectors $v(x) = [v_1(x), \ldots, v_n(x)]$ coincide with the utility vectors $u(x) = [u_1(x), \ldots, u_n(x)]$.

Let us now look at the first state in Column 2. The equilibrium-security level of player 1 is 2; nothing worse can happen to him. What is the equilibrium security level of player 2? His utility is 2, but he must fear that player 1 will bomb him and thereby reduce his utility to 0. It is true that

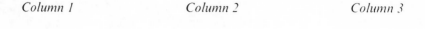

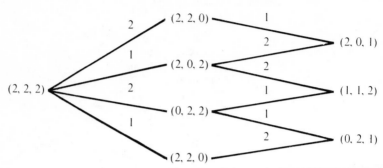

FIGURE 2. Attainability structure of Figure 1 with utility vectors instead of state vectors.

player 1 has no reason to do this because his utility remains the same, but it is also true that he has no reason not to do this. The transition does not lower the equilibrium security level of player 1. Therefore, player 2 cannot exclude this possibility. The equilibrium security level of player 3 is 0, since he cannot exclude the possibility that player 1 will not bomb player 2. The vector of equilibrium-security levels is $(2, 0, 0)$.

We now look at the second state of Column 2. The second player can move to a technical end state where he has the utility 1. Therefore, an end state where he gets less than 1 cannot be reached *against his will*. His equilibrium security level is 1. (Note that we do not assume that the players maximize utility.) The principle of security-level maintenance does not require that player 2 move to the technical end state which gives him 1. He might just as well fail to do so, and stay where he is. The other players cannot exclude this possibility, but they can exclude the possibility that player 2 moves to the first technical end state in Column 3, since this would lower player 2's equilibrium security level. Therefore the security level vector is $(1, 1, 2)$.

In the same way one can continue with the remaining states of Column 2 and finally look at the initial state. For reasons which will be explained, we assign equilibrium security levels $(2, 2, 2)$ to the initial state. The final result is given in Figure 3. It can be easily seen that the assignment of equilibrium security levels $(2, 2, 2)$ to the initial state is in harmony with the principle of security-level maintenance. If these levels are the security levels, then no player can do anything that would not lower his equilibrium security level. This means that the game stops at the initial state, where the utility vector is $(2, 2, 2)$.

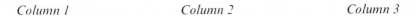

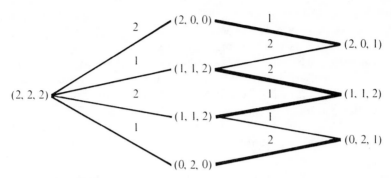

FIGURE 3. Attainability structure with equilibrium-security-level vectors instead of state vectors. (Thick lines indicate labilities.)

Unfortunately, $(2,2,2)$ is not the only assignment of equilibrium security levels to the initial states which is in harmony with the principle of security-level maintenance. As far as this principle is concerned, we might just as well assign $(1,1,2)$. Intuitively, this would mean that each of both players 1 and 2 forms his expectations on the basis of the idea that the other will definitely bomb him, and that therefore there is no reason not to bomb first. It is reasonable to assume that rational players can avoid this unfavorable coordination of expectations and instead come to the conclusion that none of them has reason to bomb the other. This opinion is advantageous and self-stabilizing and therefore should be accepted by both players. At first glance, it may seem strange that cooperation in the formation of expectations is possible and may even become necessary in certain cases, but the strangeness is due to the fact that one does not ordinarily realize that the formation of expectations is a social process that involves interactions between decision makers. Therefore, it is not unreasonable to assume that a voluntary quasi-cooperative element enters the considerations governing rational expectations about the rational behavior of the players.

In Section 4 of the Appendix we shall make this kind of reasoning more precise by incorporating a "maximum property" into our formal definition of equilibrium security levels. There we shall see, with the help of a simple example, that this property is necessary for the principle of deterrence to work.

A state $x$ is called *stable* if, for no coalition $C$, a state $y$ with $v_i(y) \geq v_i(x)$ for all players $i$ in $C$ is attainable. In our example the initial state is stable. The technical end states are stable too, since nothing can be reached from them. But the technical end states cannot be reached if the players behave rationally, since rational players must stay at the initial state. Those stable states which can be reached by rational players are called *rationally expectable*. A deterrence game is called *stable* if the initial state is stable; otherwise the game is called *labile*.

Those states which are not stable are called *labile*. In this connection we avoid the word unstable, since we do not want to indicate that a game cannot end at a labile state if the players behave rationally. If a state is stable, then rational players must remain there once they have reached it; but it is also possible for the players to remain in a labile state. Lability means that there is a latent danger of instability which need not come about.

If a state $x$ is labile, then some other states $y$ can be reached from this state $x$ without any contradiction of the principle of security-level maintenance. In this case, we say that $x$ is *labile against* the other states $y$. In Figure 3 labilities of this kind are indicated by thick connecting lines.

## 4. RESULTS OF NUMERICAL COMPUTATIONS

A Fortran program has been written that allows the computation of numerical cases.[3] With the help of this program, examples with $n = 3$ and $n = 4$ can be computed easily, but by $n = 5$ the limits of the IBM 7094 core-storage capacity have been reached. We hope to be able to write a more efficient program, based on the theorem in Section 6 of the Appendix and other theoretical results which might be helpful in eliminating unnecessary computational work.

The main results of the computation are given in Tables 4, 5, 6, and 7. Our program computes two variables, named EXNUBO and IRNUBO.[4] These variables are rough numerical measures of two different kinds of instability. EXNUBO is the average number of destroyed countries at rationally expectable stable states. For stable games, EXNUBO is zero. Therefore in our table EXNUBO is given only for labile games. EXNUBO could be interpreted as a degree of lability against rational actions.

The rational use of atomic weapons is not the only danger inherent in their existence. Perhaps our present world situation corresponds to a stable deterrence game, in which the rational use of atomic weapons is im-

---

[3]The computation was done at Deutsches Rechenzentrum, Darmstadt, Germany. The program follows the Flow Chart in Figure 1 of the Appendix which will be explained in Section 3 of the Appendix.

[4]EXNUBO for "expected number of bombs," and IRNUBO for "irrational number of bombs."

possible. If this conjecture is true, then irrational use of atomic weapons is the most dangerous aspect of the problem of proliferation. To get a rough quantitative measure of this danger, we have computed the variable IRNUBO, which is defined for stable games only. IRNUBO is the average number of destroyed countries at those stable states which are rationally expectable in the subgames at states $x$, attainable from the initial state $o$ by the "irrational" destruction of one country by another. Here a stable state is counted only once if it occurs in several subgames after "irrational actions."

In order to assess the danger of irrational actions, we may assume that the probability of an irrational action is the same for all countries that have bombs. Let $p$ be this probability, and let $m$ be the number of countries that have at least one bomb at the initial state $o$. Then the probability for an irrational action by at least one country is $1 - (1 - p)^m$, which is very near to $mp$ if $p$ is sufficiently small. If we assume that after an irrational action a stable state will be reached by a chain of rational actions, and if we assign the same probability to every stable state that might be reached in this way, then IRNUBO times $m$ is proportional to the expected number of countries destroyed after an irrational action.

It seems reasonable to conjecture that our theory does not differentiate between the indifference utility function and the bad-will utility function. At least this is true for the examples we have computed. Therefore, in our tables we give no results for bad-will utility functions.

Table 4 contains 3-player cases, where either all players have the indifference utility function or all players have the good-will utility function. All possible bomb distributions are covered under these two alternative assumptions about the utilities. Tables 5 and 6 contain the same kind of sample of 4-player cases. Table 7 shows the results of all possible bomb distributions for 4-player cases with two friendship groups. Here we need not consider cases where a player has more than 2 bombs, since we exclude the possibility that a country destroys its friend. Countries 1 and 2 form one friendship group and countries 3 and 4 form the other.

Among those games with $n = 3$ and $n = 4$ where all players have the indifference utility function (Table 4, Numbers 1 through 10; Table 5, Numbers 21 through 55), there are many labile cases. Those games where all countries have bombs are all stable; but games where some players have bombs and others have none are almost always labile. The only counterexample is game 4, which, apart from the numbering of the players, is the same as the example in Section 3.

All the games with $n = 3$ and $n = 4$, where all players have the good-will utility function, are stable (Table 4, Numbers 11 through 20; Table 6, Numbers 56 through 90). In the same way, the 4-country cases with

TABLE 6. GOOD-WILL UTILITY FUNCTIONS ($n = 4$).

| Game Number | Stockpiles | | | | EXNUBO | IRNUBO |
|---|---|---|---|---|---|---|
| | $b_1$ | $b_2$ | $b_3$ | $b_4$ | | |
| 56. | 0 | 0 | 0 | 0 | stable | 0 |
| 57. | 0 | 0 | 0 | 1 | stable | 1 |
| 58. | 0 | 0 | 0 | 2 | stable | 1 |
| 59. | 0 | 0 | 0 | 3 | stable | 1 |
| 60. | 0 | 0 | 1 | 1 | stable | 1.2 |
| 61. | 0 | 0 | 1 | 2 | stable | 1.2 |
| 62. | 0 | 0 | 1 | 3 | stable | 1.2 |
| 63. | 0 | 0 | 2 | 2 | stable | 1.2 |
| 64. | 0 | 0 | 2 | 3 | stable | 1.2 |
| 65. | 0 | 0 | 3 | 3 | stable | 1.2 |
| 66. | 0 | 1 | 1 | 1 | stable | 1.75 |
| 67. | 0 | 1 | 1 | 2 | stable | 1.700 |
| 68. | 0 | 1 | 1 | 3 | stable | 1.700 |
| 69. | 0 | 1 | 2 | 2 | stable | 1.625 |
| 70. | 0 | 1 | 2 | 3 | stable | 1.625 |
| 71. | 0 | 1 | 3 | 3 | stable | 1.625 |
| 72. | 0 | 2 | 2 | 2 | stable | 1.50 |
| 73. | 0 | 2 | 2 | 3 | stable | 1.50 |
| 74. | 0 | 2 | 3 | 3 | stable | 1.50 |
| 75. | 0 | 3 | 3 | 3 | stable | 1.50 |
| 76. | 1 | 1 | 1 | 1 | stable | 2 |
| 77. | 1 | 1 | 1 | 2 | stable | 2 |
| 78. | 1 | 1 | 1 | 3 | stable | 2 |
| 79. | 1 | 1 | 2 | 2 | stable | 2 |
| 80. | 1 | 1 | 2 | 3 | stable | 2 |
| 81. | 1 | 1 | 3 | 3 | stable | 2 |
| 82. | 1 | 2 | 2 | 2 | stable | 2 |
| 83. | 1 | 2 | 2 | 3 | stable | 2 |
| 84. | 1 | 2 | 3 | 3 | stable | 2 |
| 85. | 1 | 3 | 3 | 3 | stable | 2 |
| 86. | 2 | 2 | 2 | 2 | stable | 2 |
| 87. | 2 | 2 | 2 | 3 | stable | 2 |
| 88. | 2 | 2 | 3 | 3 | stable | 2 |
| 89. | 2 | 3 | 3 | 3 | stable | 2 |
| 90. | 3 | 3 | 3 | 3 | stable | 2 |

that horizontal proliferation has a very undesirable effect on IRNUBO. If $m$ remains constant and the number of bombs is increased, we may speak of "vertical proliferation." Intuitively one would expect vertical proliferation to increase IRNUBO. Some of our results confirm this expectation (Table 4, Numbers 7 through 10; Table 5, Numbers 41 through 55); but

TABLE 7. FRIENDSHIP GROUPS (1, 2) AND (3, 4) ($n = 4$).

| Game Number | Stockpiles | | | | | EXNUBO | IRNUBO |
|---|---|---|---|---|---|---|---|
| | $b_1$ | $b_2$ | $b_3$ | $b_4$ | | | |
| *Indifference Utility Functions* | | | | | | | |
| 91. | 0 | 0 | 0 | 0 | stable | | 0 |
| 92. | 0 | 0 | 0 | 1 | labile | 1 | |
| 93. | 0 | 0 | 0 | 2 | labile | 2 | |
| 94. | 0 | 0 | 1 | 1 | labile | 2 | |
| 95. | 0 | 0 | 1 | 2 | labile | 2 | |
| 96. | 0 | 0 | 2 | 2 | labile | 2 | |
| 97. | 0 | 1 | 0 | 1 | stable | | 2 |
| 98. | 0 | 1 | 0 | 2 | labile | 1 | |
| 99. | 0 | 1 | 1 | 1 | labile | 1 | |
| 100. | 0 | 1 | 1 | 2 | labile | 1 | |
| 101. | 0 | 1 | 2 | 2 | labile | 1 | |
| 102. | 0 | 2 | 0 | 2 | stable | | 2 |
| 103. | 0 | 2 | 1 | 1 | stable | | 2 |
| 104. | 0 | 2 | 1 | 2 | labile | 1 | |
| 105. | 0 | 2 | 2 | 2 | labile | 1 | |
| 106. | 1 | 1 | 1 | 1 | stable | | 2 |
| 107. | 1 | 1 | 1 | 2 | stable | | 2 |
| 108. | 1 | 1 | 2 | 2 | stable | | 2 |
| 109. | 1 | 2 | 1 | 2 | stable | | 2 |
| 110. | 1 | 2 | 2 | 2 | stable | | 2 |
| 111. | 2 | 2 | 2 | 2 | stable | | 2 |
| *Good-Will Utility Functions* | | | | | | | |
| 112. | 0 | 0 | 0 | 0 | stable | | 0 |
| 113. | 0 | 0 | 0 | 1 | stable | | 1 |
| 114. | 0 | 0 | 0 | 2 | stable | | 1 |
| 115. | 0 | 0 | 1 | 1 | stable | | 1 |
| 116. | 0 | 0 | 1 | 2 | stable | | 1 |
| 117. | 0 | 0 | 2 | 2 | stable | | 1 |
| 118. | 0 | 1 | 0 | 1 | stable | | 2 |
| 119. | 0 | 1 | 0 | 2 | stable | | 1.67 |
| 120. | 0 | 1 | 1 | 1 | stable | | 1.67 |
| 121. | 0 | 1 | 1 | 2 | stable | | 1.67 |
| 122. | 0 | 1 | 2 | 2 | stable | | 1.67 |
| 123. | 0 | 2 | 0 | 2 | stable | | 1.33 |
| 124. | 0 | 2 | 1 | 1 | stable | | 2 |
| 125. | 0 | 2 | 1 | 2 | stable | | 1.75 |
| 126. | 0 | 2 | 2 | 2 | stable | | 1.50 |
| 127. | 1 | 1 | 1 | 1 | stable | | 2 |
| 128. | 1 | 1 | 1 | 2 | stable | | 2 |
| 129. | 1 | 1 | 2 | 2 | stable | | 2 |
| 130. | 1 | 2 | 1 | 2 | stable | | 2 |
| 131. | 1 | 2 | 2 | 2 | stable | | 2 |
| 132. | 2 | 2 | 2 | 2 | stable | | 2 |

the 4-country cases with good-will utility functions and $m = 3$ show that sometimes IRNUBO is decreased by vertical proliferation (Table 6, Numbers 66 through 75).

## 5. SOURCES OF STABILITY AND INSTABILITY

Despite the simplicity of our deterrence models, the result of the analysis gives some interesting insights into the sources of stability and instability. However, we must be cautious in interpreting our results, since we did not take into account some of the features of real deterrence situations which may be of importance. For example, we did not consider the possibility that atomic weapons might be used in order to destroy other atomic weapons. Nevertheless, we think that our results do contribute something to a careful evaluation of the arguments in favor of non-proliferation agreements.

There follows a discussion of four different sources of stability that can be seen in the results of our computations:

*Stability by Proliferation.* In our tables all games where all countries have bombs are stable. In Section 6 of the Appendix we shall prove that this condition is a consequence of a general theorem. The intuitive reason for this phenomenon is very simple. Because of the motive for retaliation, no country can bomb another country with impunity if all countries have bombs.

*Stability by Scarcity of Bombs.* It is trivially true that a situation in which no country has bombs is stable. But this trivial case is not the only one where scarcity of bombs is a source of stability. Consider the 3-country case in which all players have the indifference utility function, and where we have $b_1 = b_2 = 1$ and $b_3 = 0$. This is the case in the example of Section 3. Here we have stability because of a scarcity of bombs. Countries 1 and 2 do not attack country 3 because they would lose their means of defense by doing so. The game becomes labile if country 1 is given an additional bomb (see Table 4, Numbers 4 and 5).

*Stability by Good Will.* In our tables, games with good-will utility functions are always stable. It can be shown that every deterrence game with good-will utility functions for all players is stable (see Section 7 of the Appendix). The intuitive reason for this is simple: A country that has this kind of utility function cannot attack another country without decreasing its own utility. Since this is true for every country, no country needs to fear an attack by another.

*Stability by Friendship.* Consider the 4-country case with two friendship groups $(1, 2)$ and $(3, 4)$ and modified indifference utility functions where the stockpiles are $b_1 = b_3 = 0$ and $b_2 = b_4 = 2$ (Table 7, Number 102). The game is stable, but it would not be stable without friendship groups (see Table 5, Number 28). Clearly the friendship element is the source of stability. (The same is true for games 97 and 103 in Table 7). In Section 4 we have seen that among the friendship-group games with modified indifference utility functions where some players do not have bombs, it is precisely those games where both groups have the same number of bombs which are stable. In this connection we may speak of a *balance of armament*. Our computational results suggest that stability by friendship works if and only if the balance of armament is exactly right, but we cannot say whether this result can be generalized to describe cases with more than 4 players.

As we have seen, all-out proliferation has a stabilizing effect, at least as far as the consequences of rational behavior are concerned. On the other hand, proliferation can destabilize situations in which not all countries have bombs. A game the stability of which is due to scarcity of bombs may become labile should a player receive an additional bomb (see Table 4, Numbers 4 and 5).

Scarcity of bombs is not the only reason why proliferation might destabilize a game. If, in the 4-country case with friendship groups (1,2) and $(3, 4)$ and modified indifference utility functions, where the stockpiles are $b_1 = b_3 = 0$ and $b_2 = b_4 = 2$, player 3 receives a bomb, the game loses its stability (Table 7, Numbers 102 and 104). This result is due to the fact that the additional bomb disturbs the balance of armament. Intuitively, the situation is as follows: In the example with $b_1 = b_3 = 0$ and $b_2 = b_4 = 2$, the big powers 2 and 4 cannot bomb each other because they fear retaliation. If country 4 bombs the weak country 1, it thereby brings the play to a state which is labile against a state where country 3 is bombed by country 2. This threat against its friend deters country 4 from attacking country 1. If country 3 receives a bomb, this threat becomes ineffective, because now country 2 would have to fear retaliation from country 3. Therefore, after country 3 has received a bomb, country 1 is no longer protected against attack by country 4.

Note that, in a situation with friendship groups where an additional bomb destabilizes the game, stability can be restored by reestablishing the balance of armament through equal increase in the stockpile of the other friendship group, a phenomenon reminiscent of an armament race (see, for example, Table 7, Numbers 97, 99, and 103).

If we speak of sources of stability and instability, we must not forget the danger of irrational use of atomic weapons. This source of instability is measured by the variable IRNUBO, which tends to be increased by horizontal proliferation. The undesirable effect of horizontal proliferation on IRNUBO is a strong argument in favor of nonproliferation agreements.

In spite of the fact that the real world is much more complex than our simple cases, we may speculate as to whether the same sources of stability are effective in the present world situation. If we tentatively accept the hypothesis that the present world situation corresponds to a stable deterrence game, we can exclude the possibility that the stability is due to all-out proliferation, since many powers do not have atomic weapons. The fact that we observe friendship groups suggests that stability by friendship is an effective source of stability. Since both the United States and the Soviet Union have very big stockpiles, we may say that, between the friendship groups centered around these superpowers, we observe a balance of armament. But how can we explain the fact that many neutrals outside the protective shield of the friendship groups do not have bombs and nevertheless survive? Our results about games with good-will utility functions suggest a possible answer: As long as two powers have no conflict of interest, it is reasonable to assume that they will have good will toward each other, in the sense that each of them attaches at least some value to the survival of the other. This means that a country without any serious conflict of interest with atomic powers can stay neutral even if it does not have any atomic weapons, since it can rely on the good will of potential aggressors. Even if this kind of good will is selective rather than universal, we may conjecture that it is capable of producing the same kind of stabilizing effect as the universal good will of our special utility functions.

One may ask whether it is true that only those countries without atomic weapons and which do not have serious conflicts with atomic powers can stay neutral. The case of India and China seems to indicate that, at least in some instances, this explanation is not satisfactory. But in this case perhaps an element of scarcity comes in. Since China's stockpile is probably quite small, an atomic attack against India would seriously reduce her means of defense against Russia. In this light, it is understandable that some Indian politicians think that India should become an atomic power in order to be able to preserve her neutrality in the face of China's growing stockpile of atomic weapons.

# PART III

# Deterrence and Reward

CHAPTER 8

Richard Rosecrance

# Deterrence in Dyadic and Multipolar Environments

It is typical of strategic threats that the punitive action—if the threat fails and has to be carried out—is painful or costly to both sides. The purpose is deterrence *ex ante*, not revenge *ex post*. Making a credible threat involves proving that one would have to carry out the threat, creating incentives for oneself or incurring penalties that would make one evidently want to.

—Thomas Schelling
*The Strategy of Conflict*

In one sense the problem of strategic stability is novel. In years past, at least before the onset of the nuclear age and prior to the development of strategic delivery systems, the problems which Schelling portrays did not exist. In previous ages, when there was no distinction between deterrence and defense, there was also no difference between *ex ante* and *ex post* incentives. If one was attacked, he would defend against the attack. Resistance to attack was then his best alternative (the one providing the greatest utility under the circumstances). If a national leader decided not to resist, he opened his population to harm by the invading power and subjected himself to control by a foreign head of state. In addition, the threat to resist offered a measure of *ex ante* deterrence. Since a potential aggressor knew that it would be in the defender's interest to resist with the power at his command, the aggressor would not be tempted to attack unless he believed he could overcome that resistance.[1]

At some point, however, deterrence was no longer equal to defense. It was no longer possible to mount a defense against strategic attack; therefore one could not deter by denying success to an aggressor, by making an attack costly and unprofitable in terms of territory gained and men and re-

---

[1] This does not, of course, suggest that wars do not occur under such circumstances. Nations have not always been deterred even when rational calculation should have led them to avoid war.

sources expended. One had rather to threaten counteraggression (retaliation) upon an enemy's homeland. This posed in much starker terms the distinction between *ex ante* and *ex post* incentives.

## DETERRENCE IN DYADIC ENVIRONMENTS

In speaking of a two-party deterrence relationship we want the deterree (the potential aggressor) to face an expectation matrix[2] comparable to the following:

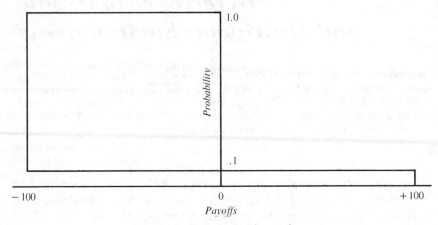

FIGURE 1. Deterree's Alternatives.

In this instance the potential aggressor (the deterree) has a very good chance of getting large negative payoffs and only a small chance of getting large positive payoffs if he decides to attack. If the potential aggressor starts from a position of 0 utility, he will scarcely be tempted to attack, for his expectation is negative. [His expectation in this case equals $(+100 \times .1) + (-100 \times .9)$ or $(+10) + (-90) = (-80)$.]

But while these are the payoffs we wish to offer a potential aggressor where deterrence is not equal to defense, they are not easy to arrange. Indeed, in such circumstances there is a central contradiction in dyadic- (two-party) deterrence theory. For, on the one hand, *ex ante*, one must assure high probabilities of a devastating response to any aggression in case hostile action takes place. On the other hand, *ex post*, one may *or may not* want to make a devastating response if hostile action *does* take place. There is thus a major difference between *ex ante* and *ex post* incentives.[3]

[2]I am indebted to David Singer for this formulation.
[3]See Harsanyi's piece in this volume, p. 101.

To see why this distinction exists, let us take a few examples. It has been the policy of the United States and NATO to refuse to rule out the use of nuclear weapons in Europe if the Soviets turn their conventional might against Berlin or Western Germany. Indeed, given their conventional predominance, there is no other strategy which could make an aggressor hesitate. To assure deterrence of an attack on the central front or of an absorption of Berlin one may even want to *pledge* that one will retaliate with all the force at one's command upon an enemy making such an attack. These are the *ex ante* incentives.

If an attack actually does take place, on the other hand, one may very well not want to carry out one's declared policy. If the United States hits the Soviet Union massively with nuclear weapons, it presumably will not be able to prevent a Soviet nuclear retaliation against American and European cities. Thus, the automatic recourse to the *ex ante* policy would bring about a chain of events in which perhaps 200 million people would be killed by strategic weapons. What one says one would do before the event is not what one actually wants to do if the event occurs.

Somewhat similar quandaries are involved in assuring reliable deterrence of an attack on the United States. To reinforce deterrence of such an attack, one may well want to pledge in advance that United States' forces will wreak the most terrible vengeance upon the homeland of an attacker. These are the *ex ante* incentives. On the other hand, in most instances of possible Soviet attacks on the United States, the United States would *not* want to retaliate in unlimited fashion upon Soviet cities and population. Probable Soviet aggressive attacks would concentrate on hitting American strategic forces, missile and bomber bases. If United States policy makers were then to decide to retaliate massively on Soviet cities, they might merely be inviting Soviet forces to stage second-wave massive attacks on American cities, attacks which to that point were by no means inevitable. Once again *ex post* incentives are very different from *ex ante* incentives. In this instance, the carrying out of the deterrent threat actually harms the attacked as much as it does the attacker.

Even in the case where an initial Soviet nuclear attack had been directed primarily at United States cities, it is by no means certain that the revenge motive would lead to a spasm retaliation upon Soviet urban populations. Whether United States planners would be tempted to indulge in this retaliation or not would depend upon their perceptions of the best means of war termination. If it were presumed that the final political shape of the world would be determined in negotiations with the USSR, America might decide to retain its large unimpaired strategic nuclear capability (presuming it could do so) to prevent further attacks and to influence the course of the bargaining. In this process, ratios of surviving missile stocks could be of great significance.[4] Once again *ex ante* and *ex post* incentives are in conflict. Thus, one may even make this statement: *The success of deterrence as a prewar policy may depend upon convincing the enemy that one would do things that it would not be in one's interest to do if an attack actually occurred.* This has been the toughest problem to solve with regard to deterrence theory, and, as we shall see later, it has not been solved.

Various attempts at solution have nonetheless been made. Thomas Schelling has suggested a variety of commitment strategies in which a state would either verbally or in some measure physically commit itself to a military response. Verbal commitments have included pledging one's honor to defend a particular area or ally, committing oneself to go to war over Berlin, signing defense pacts with some forty other nations. Verbal commitments also include alliance declaratory policy in which it is asserted that military arrangements provide for well nigh automatic escalation to nuclear warfare should an aggressor attack. In October, 1962, President Kennedy told the Russians that "it shall be the policy of this nation to regard any nuclear missile launched from Cuba against any nation in the Western Hemisphere as an attack by the Soviet Union on the United States, requiring a full retaliatory response upon the Soviet Union."[5] If the Soviets believed this declaration, it did not matter whether such a step would be rational for the United States or not. The Soviets would have every incentive to make sure that no missile was launched from Cuba.

But verbal commitment can be supplemented with physical commitments of forces in place. In Europe, the United States has sent an American garrison to West Berlin and five divisions for service on the central front in Germany. If the Soviets were to launch an attack, American soldiers would be among the first to be killed. This in turn would aggrieve sentiment in the United States and cause demands for retribution. If the troops in place are inadequate to defend in conventional terms, and one anticipates strident demands for revenge, a potential aggressor may come to the conclusion that the United States has adopted a strategy of mandatory nuclear escalation. The troops are merely a "trip wire" or "plate-glass window" to trigger United States nuclear retaliation. To reinforce one's determination to escalate, one might give authority to use nuclear weapons to commanders in the field. At the extreme, a nation might even consider enhancing its credibility by giving control over its nuclear weapons to electronic barrier networks. If the barrier were passed, the weapons would fire automatically. Mr. Herman Kahn once discussed the notion of an unreprogrammable doomsday machine located in the center of

[4]See M. D. Intriligator, *Strategy in a Missile War: Targets and Rates of Fire,* Los Angeles: University of California Securities Studies Paper 10, 1967.
[5]Quoted in Elie Abel, *Missile Crisis* (Philadelphia: Lippincott, 1966), p. 123.

the earth and triggered electronically by the hostile crossing of any salient political-military frontier. Whereas each of these devices and stratagems has been discussed and some actually applied, statesmen have been very reluctant to use mechanisms which would involve an automatic commitment. Decision makers want to retain the power of decision even in the advanced stages of a crisis. In the case of electronic detonation, moreover, there is always the possibility of malfunction or failure. Radar systems sometimes give erroneous indications, as both DEW line and BMEWS radar have done. In the instance of a doomsday machine, while it might be an ideal (?) deterrent weapon, there are other values besides the maximum insurance of deterrent credibility. No matter what one does, one probably cannot reduce the probability of war to zero by manipulating deterrent mechanisms. There will be irrational, unauthorized, or accidental events which could trigger the extinction of mankind, given the existence of doomsday machines. Thus, no power has seen fit to emplace them or to seriously consider developing them.

A somewhat less provocative position which yet offers some deterrent credibility is what Schelling has called "the threat which leaves something to chance." It is essentially the position that "we may or may not retaliate, but even we do not know for sure." A power would then arrange to conduct a limited war so that the probability of further escalation was not zero. It could not be sure that escalation would take place, but neither could it guarantee that there would be no escalation. If one fights limited war in a risky enough fashion, both in terms of the targets involved and the level of destruction, one can raise the probability of escalation significantly.[6] In strategic planning, one could adopt a "launch-on-warning" posture, in which missiles, to be invulnerable, must be fired off before the aggressor's missiles strike. There would be no electronic automaticity to this, but policy makers would know that if they did not get their missiles in the air, they would not survive.

One might also devise less than satisfactory command and control arrangements, so that after a crisis in which a series of national leaders are killed there would be unauthorized firings by some units. Whether this system might or might not be implemented would be a function of the lengths to which we had gone with the "fail-safe" system and the installation of "permissive-action links" on our warheads. It is possible that the United States has proceeded so far with electronic locks designed to prevent unauthorized firing that, even if the national command authority were to be eliminated, missiles could not be fired.

A more direct way of providing full credibility for the use of deterrent

[6]See Bernard Brodie, *Escalation and the Nuclear Option* (Princeton, N.J.: Princeton University Press, 1966).

forces is to mount what Kahn has called "a splendid first strike capability."[7] If a nation builds larger or more accurate forces conjoined with a city-oriented ABM, perhaps it can hope to knock out most of the enemy's missiles on land and to intercept those launched from the sea with its ABM. In this way a state might hope to cancel the effect of retaliation, leaving it free to respond to any enemy threat anywhere in the world. Then one could be sure of making credible his guarantee to Europe, for a potential aggressor would know that U.S. preemption in response to an attack on Europe would not cause devastating retaliation on the United States.

When Robert S. McNamara first became Secretary of Defense he placed great stress on the doctrine of "damage-limitation." This condition would be considerably short of a first-strike capability against the Soviet Union, but it would be a capability good enough to hold down damage in the United States should a missile war take place with Moscow. It would mean, therefore, if its technical preconditions were met, that the United States could respond strategically to a Soviet aggressive move in Europe without risking the destruction of the American population. In order to have such a capability the United States would have to be able to limit the number of arriving Soviet warheads in somewhat the fashion shown in Figure 2. If

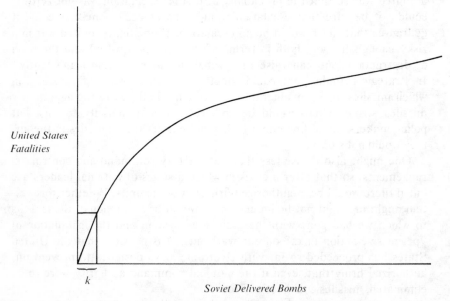

*United States Fatalities*

*k*

*Soviet Delivered Bombs*

Figure 2. Conditions necessary for damage limitation.

[7]Herman Kahn, *On Thermonuclear War* (Princeton, N.J.: Princeton University Press, 1961), p. 36.

one could hold down the number of arriving Soviet warheads to some small number, $k$, then the damage to the United States, while large, still might be acceptable. If incoming Soviet warheads could not be held down to some small number, however, the United States would not be able to minimize damage to its population. If the number of Soviet delivered weapons could not be reduced, a nation might consider civil defense or a city-oriented ABM as a means of shifting the curve to the right and coping with a large number of warheads.

There are, however, two problems with these various solutions to the problem of reconciling *ex ante* and *ex post* incentives: First, there is a serious question as to whether it is desirable for us to limit our responses in such a way as to make *ex ante* deterrence credible. Second, there is a real question as to whether, even if it were desirable to do so, it would be in our power to do so. If we were to make a major and sustained attempt to reinforce deterrent credibility, we would be acting against most of the innovations in strategic doctrine that have arisen in the past ten years.

Let me refer generally to the difficulties in enhancing deterrent credibilities. First, the entire policy of Mr. McNamara in his last years as Secretary of Defense was to renounce both first-strike and damage-limiting capabilities. Since 1965, at the very latest, the Soviets have had a secure second-strike capacity, an assured destruction capability against the United States. We do not now have, nor are we likely to have, a capability which precludes or reduces to negligible proportions the Soviets' ability to retaliate.

Second, the whole tendency of our policy since 1961 has been to reserve a complete range of strategic options for the President in order to avoid advance commitment to any single option. We have sought to prevent unauthorized behavior, to prevent accidental detonation. We have planned to conduct a limited war in ways that do not raise the spectre of immediate escalation. Certainly, there has been no tendency to accept or even to consider doomsday machines governed by electronic barriers. As far as Europe is concerned, Secretary McNamara labored hard and long to try to raise sufficient forces so that any Soviet attack could be contained on the ground, without recourse to nuclear weapons.

This policy has now been changed. The Nixon Administration is not pressing for a conventional force in Europe large enough to defend against Soviet attack without employment of nuclears. It is not clear, however, that the net effect of this change strengthens the credibility of our guarantee. We are now seeking to reduce our forces in Germany. Other nations will also cut back on troops. This would appear to suggest that we now rely more on nuclear escalation than we did previously. In the context in which these reductions appear, however—growing pressure on the defense

budgets of major powers, the need to spend more on domestic programs—
the result is not to enhance NATO solidarity. This policy suggests a weak-
ening rather than a strengthening of our commitment. In this sense it de-
tracts from our deterrent credibility.

The insistence upon reserving options for the United States President,
moreover, also affects our relations with allies. To the degree that the
President preserves his range of choices even in circumstances of crisis,
there cannot be agreement on preprogrammed strategies to resist in
tandem with Europe. Thus, our very alliance commitments have been
affected, and our undertakings have been deprived of the force they had
under Eisenhower and Norstad.

Third, just as the Defense Department has tried to preserve the President's options in the event of an attack on Europe, it has labored to give
him a full range of choices in the event of an attack on the United States.
The first-generation ICBMs would have had to be launched on warning.
The Minuteman was supposed to avoid this difficulty. It was designed so
as to be able to "ride out" an attack and still be capable of retaliation. Today it appears that technological developments and Soviet SS-9s will make
Minuteman vulnerable to attack. One should note, however, that the response to this recognition of vulnerability has not been to return to the
"launch-on-warning" notions of 1960–1961. Rather it has been to try to
find some means—in this case ABM protection—to permit some significant portion of the force to survive. This would obviate the necessity of
launching on radar indication.

Fourth, from the standpoint of deterrent credibility, it might have been
useful to put strategic missiles in urban areas. To attack these missiles an
aggressor would have to hit our cities. The revenge motive would reinforce
retaliation on the enemy's urban population. But we did nothing of the
sort. Planners tried to separate base areas and urban areas. This meant
that an enemy, bent on attacking our strategic installations, did not have
to strike our cities as well. But it also meant that we would then have fewer
incentives to respond on this urban population. Not only might we have no
incentives to respond upon the enemy's cities, we might have positive
reasons for hitting his launching sites. Some of his missiles might be more
accurate than others, the less accurate ones being withheld for later
strikes against cities. Some of his missiles might fail on the counterforce
launch, but be readied later for attacks on cities. Some of his missiles
might have a refire capability. Thus, if we retaliated on his cities (and not
his sites), the enemy would be able to launch a second-wave attack directed against our cities, and he would certainly have the incentive to do so
if our response had been directed at his urban areas. With such a strategy

we leave the enemy's second-wave capability unimpaired while giving him a major motive to employ it against our population.

It therefore became necessary to find other targets for our retaliation. Counterforce retaliatory targeting was one alternative. Nonpopulous industrial installations were another. We might even consider the notion of limited strategic war in which a tit-for-tat strategy was adopted: hitting ships, port facilities, or even individual cities until the war could be brought to a close.

Like the strategy of city retaliation, however, these strategems were also available to an opponent. There could be a series of exchanges on strategic sites. Limited strategic attacks could be employed by both sides. While such patterns of retaliation could do damage on both sides, it was not clear that the aggressor would suffer more than the defender. It was not even clear that the defender would not be affected more grievously, since the aggressor would have the advantage of planning and executing a well-prepared first strike. When the original versions of these strategies were announced by Secretary McNamara, there was an outcry in Europe that our retaliatory strategies had become so relatively nonpunitive that they no longer offered a sufficient deterrent sanction. Credibility of some kind of response would be high, but the response itself might be inadequate.

Finally, if one wants to make sure that there will be a response to nuclear aggression, one must be willing to let the missiles and bombers go if something happens to the President or to the constitutional chain of command. On the other hand, if one wants to make sure that there is absolutely no danger of unauthorized firing, one must not delegate nuclear-release authority, at any stage, to a military officer. One may even introduce electronic or other devices that make unauthorized action extremely difficult, even impossible. To the degree that we have placed much greater emphasis upon positive command and control at all times to avoid the danger of accidental or unauthorized behavior, we obviously make it less certain that our strategic weapons will be fired in a real contingency. Again, credibility declines.

Now it is of course true that any of these policies might be reversed, thus placing great emphasis on quick release and high deterrent credibility. It would even be possible to return to the strategy of "massive retaliation," guaranteeing a spasm retaliation upon enemy cities. But the reasons for avoiding resorting to such measures are overwhelming. Deterrence is only one possible foreign-policy value. While it might theoretically be possible to reduce the probabilities of war to some low figure by means of deterrent processes, it would never be possible to lower them to zero. Thus a nation must think about the need to mitigate the consequences of war, should it occur. It is therefore not at all surprising that nations have begun to think more and more about what they would do in the event of war, and less and less about placing all stress on deterring it—which is another way of saying that nations quite logically are coming to recognize the ineluctable difference between *ex ante* and *ex post* incentives.

It would be possible to reconcile these incentives if a state developed a first-strike capability—a capability so overpowering that its possessor could strike the enemy and get off scot free. But such a capability would still not meet the minimum requirement for mutual deterrence, for the opponent could not deter the possessor's military initiative. The attempt to achieve such a capability, moreover, would be certain to provoke a major arms race. Since it would be obvious that one's goal was a successful first-strike capability, the opponent would sacrifice other values to make sure that such a capability was not attained.

A critic of this analysis might be tempted to claim that a basic deterrence could even be found in a case where a nation was committed to a withholding strategy in response to attack. An aggressor, one might assert, would still not be tempted to attack because he would be faced with possible strategic-military inferiority in the peace negotiations. Thus one would not attack because one did not want to diminish his bargaining counters. But suppose an aggressor had already attacked and had already secured the desired gains—part of Western Europe or Berlin. How credible would be the defender's strategy from that point on? The defender would have to threaten retaliation in order to force the aggressor to give up his gains. In one sense this problem is more difficult than that of deterrence; it is a compellance problem. The defender has to compel the aggressor to do something. If the defender has not demonstrated his credibility by retaliating, his credence may be low, and his antagonist may not believe him. In any event, deterrence by bargaining counters bears the slightest resemblance possible to deterrence by massive retaliation.

The conclusion to be drawn, in my judgment, is that we are not now meeting and should not try to meet the minimum requirements of dyadic-deterrence theory. We have not reconciled and cannot stably reconcile the requirement for deterrent credibility with the requirement of protecting our own population. *Ex ante* rationalities, in which we pledge that we will fire if the opponent even quivers, are inconsistent with *ex post* rationalities. The logical objections to deterrence are also reinforced by the unheroic nature of the age. In 1959 Herman Kahn gathered judgments from informed observers that an American President might be willing to retaliate massively in response to an attack upon Europe even though this might mean sixty million U.S. dead.[8] I am sure analysts would offer a much lower

---

[8] Kahn, p. 30.

figure today. Deterrence theory, therefore, has crucial difficulties even in a dyadic-interaction case.

## DETERRENCE IN MULTIPOLAR ENVIRONMENTS

Deterrence, however, is even more difficult in a multipolar environment than in a dyadic one. First, the dyadic case is simpler in that there are only two central nuclear countries. Each protagonist measures itself against the other; it is relatively easy to measure the minimum requirements for necessary force. Second, there is no problem in identifying the aggressor. If there is a nuclear attack, it must have been staged by the opponent; there is no difficulty in knowing whom to retaliate against. Both of these situations, however, are greatly complicated in a multipolar order.

In the first place, it is not clear how much force one needs. Should one plan to retaliate against all members of the international strategic system, against some, or only against one? One does not know how large an assured destruction force he needs. The lack of certainty on this point is likely to accentuate the arms race. Some aspects of this problem can be seen even today. The United States maintains separate strategic capabilities for use against the Chinese and the Russians, and it must have enough left over to cope with the Chinese no matter what the Russians do. The Russians also program some of their capacities for China. But the two-power arms race between the United States and the Soviet Union may be accelerated because the capabilities reserved for use against the third power may be viewed by the principal opponent as destined for himself. Thus, in the presence of third powers, bilateral arms races may be run more rapidly.

In the second place, in strategic multipolarity the question may arise, "Retaliation against whom?" There is the possibility of spread of mobile or concealed capabilities—submarine-launched missiles or conceivably even orbital bombs. The miniaturization of weapons will make possible suitcase bombs which might be clandestinely introduced into the cities of an important power. Even fishing boats in major port cities could be used to transport and hide nuclear weapons.

Two possible problems are presented here. First, there are dangers of "anonymous delivery," in which a state merely wants to attack another state and avoid retaliation. Second there is the threat of "catalytic war," in which a state seeks to simulate an attack by some third power, inducing the victim to retaliate upon the innocent party.

It may appear that there would be no incentive to "anonymous delivery," since a state could not coerce another power with such a threat without revealing his intentions. But this presumes that the only motives for using punishment are to induce, persuade, or compel a state to do something one wants. There may be motives of retribution, revenge, or hatred which do not require specific compliant actions on the part of the target state. Various Arab nations might like to eliminate Israel as a major force in Middle East politics even if they would not thereby solve the problems of the Arab refugees, Israeli-held Arab territory, and so on. If one Arab state could anonymously attack Israel and get away with it, it might be tempted to do so. It is conceivable that some outraged nation might wish to "punish" the United States for its past behavior in Southeast Asia, or the Soviet Union for its actions in Eastern Europe. Even if Eastern European nations did acquire nuclear weapons, they might well hesitate to threaten the Soviet Union frontally or overtly in attempts to coerce Soviet behavior. They might, however, be willing to consider clandestine punishment for past transgressions. Later, and anonymously, a regime might even threaten that if Soviet behavior did not "improve," attacks on additional Russian targets might be made. It would even be possible to imagine a regime simulating the behavior of an aggrieved nationalist group, thus deflecting attention from the external to the internal arena. Presumably no foreign nations were implicated in the deaths of John and Robert Kennedy. But if a nation wished to do away with these men, its best interest would be served by picking what would appear to be a purely domestic or internal instrument on which to place the blame.

Catalytic war is more difficult than anonymous delivery, but cannot be ruled out as a multipolar strategem in a crisis. To take Donald Brennan's scenario (Chapter 1), imagine that in October of 1962 the Chinese had been able to maintain a missile-launching submarine on station off Cuba in the Caribbean. At that time, President Kennedy said that he would regard a missile launched from Cuba upon any nation in the Western Hemisphere as an attack by the Soviet Union, justifying a full retaliatory response on Russia. The Chinese might have been able to exploit that situation. It is not inconceivable that they might have simulated a Cuban missile attack on New York, Washington, or Miami. Not many Chinese weapons in this circumstance might have been needed to trigger a U.S. assault on the Soviet Union. These possibilities increase with the spread of multipolar strategic capabilities.

If, in these two respects, a multipolar order is likely to confront greater instabilities than a dyadic system, there is at least one respect in which strategic problems will be easier to solve. Multilateral strategic systems present the "dilemma of the victor's inheritance" in a way that bilateral systems do not. In a two-power strategic world, after eliminating the major opponent one does not encounter other strategic opposition. If one has solved the problem of coping with one nuclear power, one has *ipso facto* solved the problem of coping with them all. In a multipolar context this is not true. After an attack on the United States the Soviets would have to consider whether their expenditure of missiles against the United States made them vulnerable to the Chinese. If Chinese capabilities were large, Soviet unilateral aggression would be much less likely.

But if unilateral aggression is much less likely in a multipolar context, multilateral aggression is much more feasible and likely. Let us assume for a moment, with Professor Harsanyi, that there is some critical ratio $c$ which represents the ratio of superiority which an aggressive state must achieve in terms of number of missiles/warheads before he can successfully launch a preemptive blow against a particular state. In a dyadic system until the age of MIRV—multiple independently targetable reentry vehicles—$c$ ratios for land-based missiles were always greater than 1. The $c$ ratios for warheads at the present time remain above 1, and $c$ ratios for all strategic launchers are still greater than 1. Presuming states with equivalent capabilities, the criterion for stability in a system is that $c > n - 1$ (where $n$ is the number of states in the system). In the dyadic case $n = 2$, so that a $c$ ratio which is greater than 1 assures stability.

It is quite possible to imagine circumstances in a multipolar strategic environment, however, in which $c$ is not greater than $n - 1$, and in which, as a result, the other members of the strategic system may gang up on a single power. If $c = 2$ and there are three powers in the system, the system is unstable, for two can successfully attack the third. If one power now raises his arms position slightly, so as to avoid vulnerability, the other two powers will become even more vulnerable. Only if $c > 2$ would such a system be stable. The difficulty, however, of multipolar strategic systems is that probable technological and political tendencies move inversely to stability. As time goes on, more and more nations will become nuclear strategic powers; thus $n$ will rise. But the countries joining the nuclear system are not likely to have capacities as invulnerable as those possessed by the two charter members of the nuclear club. Thus, paradoxically as $n$ rises, $c$ is likely to fall. Both tendencies are destabilizing. As states fall below the minimum deterrent threshold in an expanding nuclear world, they may be tempted to use their capabilities while they still possess credibility. If states fall beneath the minimum technological deterrent threshold on an overt basis, they may have to place more stress upon covert methods. The greater the number of strategic powers, the greater the anonymity any one state can achieve. A power may not be able to successfully attack or retaliate against another power, overtly on its own. It may, however, be able to launch a clandestine attack or, greatly after the fact, make a clandestine retaliatory attack upon its foe. The second response becomes the more likely as the foe becomes embroiled in a crisis with some third power.

One is led to the rather horrific conclusion that signature retaliatory capabilities will be inadequate for quite a number of powers in a multipolar strategic world. More recourse, therefore, will probably be made to covert—anonymous or catalytic—capabilities. Preemption also appears more likely.

The problem of deterring such attacks under conditions of strategic multipolarity is complex. A state might develop the doctrine of hitting all other nuclear powers in case it is attacked by one. But such notions would not have political or internal credibility. Moreover, they might be counter-deterred by other nations' adopting a doctrine of automatically destroying an antagonist that has shot nuclear broadsides at the rest of the world. A power might employ a statistical strategy of randomly retaliating, so that the aggressor would have a .1 or .2 chance of being hit. But the innocent power which was attacked would also be likely to seek vengeance; thus there would be some doubt as to whether a statistical strategy actually would be carried out. It is possible that a nuclear victim would ask to examine the state of nuclear forces in each of his colleague's countries to see which had been recently fired. It is also possible to imagine a number of countries (even though innocent) refusing any such inspection, however, for fear of revealing the vulnerable points in their strategic armories. If clandestine devices had been detonated in the cities of the victim, moreover, how would inspection of regular strategic weapons reveal the attacker?

In sum, it appears that there is even greater difficulty in applying deterrence theory in a multipolar than in a bipolar context. The minimum technological conditions are less likely to be met, putting a premium upon unorthodox solutions, some of which are very destabilizing. The *ex ante* and *ex post* incentives jibe even less here than in dyadic systems, for there is the additional problem of "retaliation against whom?" If it is difficult enough in the United States to develop a political focus on Russia or China as the presumptive foes in order to justify massive retaliation as the sanction upon their aggressive behavior, it will be even more difficult to prime the electorate to be ready to spring upon any one of ten to twenty foes in case it should misbehave. Part of the credibility of retaliation in the two-party context was supplied by the "cold war" and public hostility to "Communism" and the Soviet Union. In a world of many nuclear powers, notions of external threat will be much more diffused; they will be analytical rather than personified. It is difficult to muster citizens' support for retaliating against or countering an "analytical" threat. Thus, the rationale for a deterrent posture based upon the threat of retaliation loses even more force in a multipolar environment.

**BEYOND DETERRENCE**

I would formally conclude, then, that there are unreconciled and irreconcilable difficulties in the dyadic nuclear-deterrence model and that these difficulties are accentuated in a multipolar environment. This does not mean that deterrent forces and mechanisms should be rejected, though they have clearly been shown to be inadequate. While there can be no certainty of deterrent retaliatory punishment in either model, there is at least *uncertainty*. A nation with weapons might use them; it might be irrational; it might not calculate its utilities correctly. An aggressor cannot be sure that he will not be struck. There are grounds for hesitation. But rational grounds for retaliation by a defender are largely nonexistent. Rational incentives would lead powers to adopt strategies on *ex post* grounds which would not offer deterrence *ex ante*. The uncertainties are biased against deterrence. Whatever advantages the wraith of deterrent thinking offers, it does not solve the problem of producing stability in the future. It may therefore be useful to have deterrents to attack, but it would be a gross mistake to rely totally upon them.

One of the strange outcomes of post-World War II strategic deliberation has been the almost exclusive concentration upon the threat of punishment as the major equilibrator of the international system. Even the most traditional learning theorists in the field of psychology argue that behavior is as direct a function of reward as it is of punishment. While an entire literature has grown up since 1945 focusing upon manipulations of the punishment structure in world politics, virtually nothing has been said or written about manipulations of the reward structure. The reasons for this are not hard to understand. Since the appeasement efforts of the nineteen-thirties mainly stressed rewards as incentives, and since they failed, states have been disposed to look elsewhere for methods of maintaining international stability. But the failure of "appeasement" is not a reason for considering rewards an inappropriate subject for investigation or employment. Appeasement does not work under conditions of the constant-sum game. If there are two major international protagonists, $A$ and $B$, and the sum of their positions is a constant $k$, reward cannot be used. Any attempt to enhance the position of $B$ only succeeds at the expense of $A$. Thus the use of reward as an instrument of international stability depends on finding relationships among states which are not strictly constant-sum, where two nations may increase their position simultaneously. Increasing, or variable-sum, games are ideal subjects for reward-structure manipulation. Economic realms clearly show variable-sum outcomes, even if territorial ones do not. Most important for the future, therefore, would be the definition of realms in which constant-sum results did not hold. If it were possible to enhance the positions of two potential adversary states simultaneously, both would be less likely to engage in disruptive military actions in order to alter those positions. If states experience high *status quo* utilities, they are less likely to find war an attractive alternative.

Richard N. Gardner

# *International Organization and Reward: Potentialities and Limitations*

Within the nation-state, the behavior of an individual is influenced in directions which the community considers desirable through a complex assortment of positive and negative sanctions. The citizen is rewarded with material benefits, status, or power for certain kinds of behavior, either through the competitive forces of a free economy, limited interventions of government such as tax incentives, or, in the case of state-controlled economies, direct action by government or party leadership. He is deterred from behavior which the community abhors by a system of criminal and civil penalties. He is reinforced in his obedience to community standards by being constantly reminded of them, whether by parents, teachers, the mass media, or just by traffic signs announcing a speed limit.

The attempt to construct an equally effective system of rewards, penalties, and reinforcements at the international level to prevent war and encourage cooperation among nations is the central challenge of our time. In the pursuit of this goal mankind has created, mostly in the last quarter century, an impressive array of international organizations. The failures of these agencies to influence national policies toward peaceful and constructive behavior are all too obvious. Yet there have been some successes, even if they are not well advertised or well known. We need to study both the successes and the failures if we are to appreciate the potentialities and limitations of international organizations in influencing the behavior of nation-states.

## ECONOMIC ORGANIZATIONS

The greatest success of international agencies in influencing national policies—and here one obviously uses "success" in a relative sense—has been in the economic field. Although the current crisis in international trade, finance, and development now tends to obscure the fact, the international community has come a very long way from economic anarchy toward economic order in the last quarter century. One important reason for this progress is the system of rewards, penalties, and reinforcements for good behavior built into the constitutions and operating policies of the three central world economic agencies created at the end of the Second World War: The General Agreement on Tariffs and Trade (GATT), The International Monetary Fund (IMF), and the International Bank for Reconstruction and Development (IBRD).

This is not the place to undertake a comprehensive review of the achievements of these agencies—a task I have attempted elsewhere.[1] Rather, a brief summary may be in order of how they have attempted to "manipulate the reward structure" to encourage nations to follow desired economic policies.

GATT offers rewards for the removal of trade restrictions by sponsoring periodic negotiations to reduce these restrictions on a reciprocal and multilateral basis. It provides penalties for violations of its rules through procedures which require compensation by offending countries or, in the alternative, authorize retaliation by those adversely affected. It offers continual reinforcements to good behavior through the rules laid down in its charter and the decisions of the contracting parties—rules and decisions which may be, and often are, cited by government leaders in resisting domestic protectionist pressures. GATT's brilliant Director-General, Eric Wyndham White, demonstrated the potentialities of international agencies by skillfully nursing to a successful conclusion the Kennedy round of tariff negotiations. If GATT's star is presently in decline, it may be less the fault of its structural limitations (though these are real and need to be remedied) than the failure of its members to utilize its still considerable potentialities for trade expansion.

In the case of the IMF and the IBRD, it is the power to grant or refuse access to financial resources rather than the GATT system of reciprocity and reprisal that constitutes the principle means of influencing national policy. There is no doubt that in a number of cases this power has been used to good effect. Nevertheless, it must be admitted that the influence of the Fund and Bank has been limited. The financial resources disposed of by these institutions have been relatively small. (This limitation may be overcome as the quotas of the IMF and the resources of the International Development Association (IDA), the Bank's soft-loan affiliate, are substantially increased.) The other limitation inherent in Fund and Bank resources as a means of influence is more difficult to overcome—the leverage operates only against countries in need of those resources.

[1]"A Twenty-Five Year Perspective," *Sterling-Dollar Diplomacy*, rev. ed. (New York: McGraw-Hill, 1969).

The IMF has been much less successful in influencing the policy of creditor countries than recipient ones, and the IBRD has not yet found satisfactory means of coaxing a sufficiently large volume of development aid from donor countries.

## THE UNITED NATIONS

The success of the United Nations in stimulating cooperative behavior from its members has been a good deal more limited than that of the economic agencies mentioned above. But the UN does deploy its own set of rewards, penalties, and reinforcements which can sometimes be decisive in influencing even the great powers. These rewards, penalties, and reinforcements operate in much more subtle and less explicit ways than in the economic agencies. Two case histories, drawn from the author's experience, may serve as illustrations.

The first example is the UN program of outer-space cooperation. In 1961, when President Kennedy took office, no program of multilateral cooperation in outer space existed or was envisaged. Indeed, powerful interests within the United States and Soviet governments opposed a multilateral approach, and were hostile to any significant UN involvement.

Nevertheless, the UN exercises a strong attraction, particularly in the United States simply because, as George Leigh Mallory said of Mount Everest, it is there. This is particularly true in an administration which is sensitive to the domestic and international political advantages of certain kinds of initiatives in the UN. In the late spring and early summer of 1961, the White House made clear that President Kennedy would address the General Assembly in September provided he had something important to say. The President's General Assembly speech in 1961 thus stimulated a search for "new initiatives" which the President could announce to the UN. The search for these initiatives was vigorously undertaken by the State Department's Bureau of International Organization Affairs in collaboration with sympathetic allies in other parts of the government. The search produced three major "initiatives"—the U.S. program for General and Complete Disarmament, the UN Development Decade, and the program of outer-space cooperation.

The U.S. space "initiative" was embodied in resolution 1721 of the 16th General Assembly. It called for the development of a legal regime for outer space, of practical programs of information exchange and technical assistance, of a global program to make use of satellites and earth equipment for weather forecasting and weather research, and of international arrangements to use satellites for space communications. The initial resistance of the National Aeronautics and Space Administration to this initiative was gradually overcome within the United States government by the argument that NASA's negotiations for foreign tracking facilities and other kinds of foreign cooperation would be assisted by a UN program which offered other countries a greater opportunity to benefit from the U.S. space effort. The Pentagon and the CIA which resisted any UN initiative on the ground that it might risk General Assembly condemnation of the newly emerging "Samos" program of space reconnaissance, were finally moved by the argument that such a negative action by the General Assembly would be much less likely if the United States filled the existing UN vacuum on space cooperation with a convincing program in the common interest. In any event, resolution 1721, by declaring outer space freely available for all activities in conformity with the UN Charter, and by endorsing the use of satellites for weather observation under multilateral auspices, went far to provide the desired legitimacy for the "Samos" program.

If the UN helped stimulate a constructive set of United States space proposals, it also helped to stimulate an affirmative Soviet response. As is usual in such matters, the Soviet Union moved only slowly and grudgingly. For weeks, it failed to respond to U.S suggestions that it cosponsor a draft resolution on space. It was only at the last minute, when the American draft was circulated as a UN document with broad cosponsorship from others, that the Soviet Mission to the United Nations was finally heard from. After two days of hectic negotiations, acceptable language was found to accommodate Soviet interests on a number of points (mainly concerning the role of the Secretary-General, then the object of Soviet attack in the "Troika" proposal). Unanimous General Assembly action swiftly followed.

The UN resolution provided a useful stimulus to Soviet action in the period that followed.  In Geneva, the Secretary-General of the World Meteorological Organization, David A. Davies, in response to the third section of the Assembly resolution, issued invitations to Washington and Moscow to send their top weather experts to begin drafting a plan for a World Weather Watch. The American weather expert, Dr. Harry Wexler, arrived in Geneva in a few days, but nothing was heard from the Soviet side—nothing, that is, until one day the Soviet Ambassador in Geneva came to WMO Headquarters demanding to know what Dr. Wexler was doing there. He was politely informed by Mr. Davies of both the UN resolution and of the request to Moscow for a weather expert. Taken aback, the Soviet Ambassador promised to look into the matter. A few days later, Dr. V. A. Bugaev, Director of the Soviet Central Weather Forecasting Service, arrived in Geneva. Within a matter of weeks, the plan for the World Weather Watch was completed and approved by the WMO's Executive Board.

In the years that followed, the Soviet Union launched weather satellites and exchanged cloud pictures and other information with the United States and other UN members in accordance with the WMO program. There is no doubt that the UN and WMO initiatives were helpful to those in the Soviet Union like Dr. Bugaev who wanted the Soviet leadership to give greater priority to weather satellites and to information exchange with the outside world.

Although it is difficult to measure such things with precision, it is likely that the UN space initiative also helped to contain those military leaders in the United States and the Soviet Union who wished to exploit space for military advantage. To the 1961 recommendation that there should be no claims of national sovereignty in space or on celestial bodies, a 1963 General Assembly resolution added the promise not to station weapons of mass destruction in space or on celestial bodies. By 1966 these principles were embodied in the Space Treaty, together with a number of other important commitments. While it cannot be proved that these commitments could not have been negotiated without the UN, the UN did provide an important stimulus for cooperation and a useful global cover for what was essentially a Soviet-American agreement. In the domestic political climate of the fall of 1963, President Kennedy could not have concluded a bilateral executive agreement with the Russians prohibiting the stationing of nuclear weapons in space. At the same time, it would have been difficult for the Soviet Union, already under attack from China for having entered into the test-ban treaty, to have made another bilateral arms deal with the United States. The UN helped both superpowers to deal with these political problems.

A second example of significant UN influence on national policy is in the field of population. Although population growth was having catastrophic effects on economic and social development, international support of family-planning efforts appeared to be blocked by political considerations when the UN launched its first Development Decade in the early 1960s. President Eisenhower, toward the close of his tenure as President, had strongly rejected any U.S. government role in birth-control efforts either at home or abroad. The election of John F. Kennedy, the first Catholic ever to be President of the United States, was interpreted by some as an insuperable barrier to any change in this policy. The major aid-giving countries of Western Europe, including even the United Kingdom, were reluctant to act in this area. In Latin America and French-speaking Africa, family planning was generally taboo for religious reasons. Government concern with the population problem was limited to the Scandinavian countries and certain countries of Asia, such as India and Pakistan, and this was not enough to launch an international effort. Some way had to be found to broaden the geographical base of concern and particularly to move the country which had the bulk of the financial and scientific resources needed to support meaningful programs—namely the United States.

During 1961 and the first half of 1962, a small group of officials in the Department of State repeatedly tried to reverse the negative U.S. population policy. But at the top levels of the State Department there was reluctance to urge a new policy on the White House. Some specific catalyst was needed to break the stalemate—to strengthen the hand of those middle-level U.S. officials advocating an idea whose time had obviously come. It appeared in the 1962 General Assembly from a Swedish initiative in the population field. When the Assembly finally reached the Swedish item in December 1962, the United States had to stand up and be counted. After arranging to serve as United States representative on this agenda item, I drafted a statement which emphasized U.S. concern with population growth at home and overseas, called for a more active UN role, and announced U.S. willingness to "help other countries, upon request, to find potential sources of information and assistance on ways and means of dealing with population problems." The statement was sent in draft form directly to the Secretary of State, who passed it without decision to the White House, where it was approved by President Kennedy himself.

This "end run," by-passing the usual decision-making process within the State Department, broke the log-jam. Shortly thereafter, new instructions were issued to AID missions around the world citing the UN statement as the basis for a new policy. The much-feared domestic political reaction did not materialize. After President Kennedy's death, President Johnson carried the policy forward; by the end of 1960s AID was spending close to 100 million dollars a year on family planning overseas, some of it for the purchase of contraceptive materials.

The UN played an equally important role in influencing the policy of other countries. After the adoption of the Swedish resolution in December 1962, population became a respectable subject in international forums. By the late 1960s, the General Assembly, ECOSOC, UNICEF, and even WHO, had authorized multilateral assistance for family planning. Aid-giving countries like the United Kingdom, which had shown great timidity in the 1962 UN debate, were participating in bilateral as well as multilateral family-planning efforts. More and more developing countries, even in Latin America and French-speaking Africa, were sponsoring, or at least permitting, family planning. Even the Soviet Union, which had spoken strongly against the need for family planning in the 1962 debate, gradually adopted a policy of tolerance toward UN population programs.

In the population field, as in the area of outer space, it is impossible to "prove" that this impressive beginning at international cooperation would not have taken place without the UN. Admittedly, it was only a question of time before the stark logic of population growth in relation to existing resources would have forced changes in national attitudes. But the evidence strongly suggests that because of the UN these changes occurred at least several years earlier than might otherwise have been the case. Perhaps even more important, thanks to the "legitimizing" role of the UN, these changes occurred without abrasive confrontations between religions, races, or ideologies. Moreover, the modest but growing amounts of money available through the UN Trust Fund for population, and the more significant sums available for family planning in bilateral assistance programs, are now providing significant incentives to developing countries to face their domestic population problems. Finally—and this may be the most significant of all in the long run—the World Bank, as well as some of the major aid donors—are beginning to include effective programs of population control among those critical measures of "self-help" which aid recipients must undertake to qualify for a substantial amount of foreign assistance.

## THE FUTURE

What are the future prospects for "manipulating the reward structure" through international organizations? To avoid confusion, it is necessary to answer this question under three headings—the use of economic rewards to influence economic policy, the use of economic rewards to influence political policy, and the use of political rewards to influence political policy. (The word "political" is used here in a broad sense to include military decisions.)

With respect to the use of economic rewards to influence economic policy, the utility of international organizations seems likely to grow. However, this growth may be uneven, with frequent setbacks along the path to a more satisfactory world economic order. Past experience with the economic reward structure, whether in the UN itself or in the more specialized trade and financial agencies, suggests that international agencies can influence national policies only where there is a fairly even balance within the national political system between the supporters and opponents of cooperative policies. As the present situation in the United States indicates, the reward structure in GATT may be too weak to hold back resurgent protectionist pressures, particularly where the administration is not providing strong leadership to liberal trade forces.

One important test for the economic reward structure will come in efforts to defend and improve the global environment. Most developing countries are negative or at least indifferent on this subject, and many of them fear that it will divert resources from urgent development needs. Increasing attention is now being devoted to the urgent question of how the reward structure can be strengthened to change these attitudes—and also to capitalize on the new concern with environment among those developed countries which have been responsible for most of the damage already done to the global environment. Serious consideration now needs to be given to new programs of research and information exchange on measures to protect the environment, to the training of specialists in the environmental field, to a global environmental monitoring system, to building environmental safeguards into multilateral as well as bilateral aid programs, and to conditioning tariff preferences and tariff concessions generally on the observance of environmental standards in the production of internationally traded goods. To help overcome the skepticism of many developing countries, it may be desirable to consider a substantial "sweetener" in the form of an Environmental Trust Fund administered by the UN Development Program, paralleling the Population Trust Fund established in 1967.

One attractive possibility for using economic rewards to influence economic policy could come from relations between the main world economic agencies and the Soviet Union, which remains outside of them. The Soviet Union could be offered a share of the Special Drawing Rights being created each year by the IMF, on condition that it use a portion of it for contributions to multilateral aid efforts, and another portion for trade with the non-Communist world. An arrangement of this kind would have advantages in it for everybody. Although it may be a long way off, Soviet participation in the Bretton Woods institutions and GATT is worth working for because it could profoundly influence the future of East-West political as well as economic relations.

If an acceptable way could be found to associate the Soviet Union with the work of the Fund and Bank, the path would be opened for other Eastern European countries to participate. The most satisfactory form of association is likely to be one which enables the Eastern European countries to receive Special Drawing Rights (SDRs) and participate in World Bank consortia, while remaining outside of the regular operations of the Fund and Bank. An associate membership of this kind would avoid the awkward problem of giving the Soviet Union a substantial voice in the regular operations of the Fund. It would also make it unnecessary for the Soviet Union to accept those Fund obligations which would cause it special difficulty—the disclosure of its gold reserves and the elimination of restrictions on its current transactions.

East-West financial cooperation is highly desirable; but it is cooperation within the West that is particularly urgent. Unless the balance-of-payments-adjustment process can be made to work better between the industrialized countries of the North Atlantic Community and Japan, the prospects for liberal trade and aid policies will be grim. The Fund and the OECD have not developed much leverage on the policies of the surplus countries, nor have they had much influence on the world's major deficit country—the United States. Indeed, there are ominous signs that the United States is entering a new period of monetary nationalism in which it will try to unload onto its foreign creditors whatever volume of dollars results each year from unilaterally determined domestic policies. But other countries are not likely to acquiesce indefinitely in this sort of arrangement; at some point they may refuse to create more SDRs (which were supposed to replace the United States deficit as the principal source of new liquidity) and they might well retaliate against U.S. trade and U.S. investment within their borders.

If present trends continue, the developed non-Communist world may soon be divided into two monetary blocs—a dollar bloc and an enlarged Common Market bloc—separated by discriminatory trade and financial controls. The political and economic consequences of this development would be unfortunate. If it is to be avoided, the industrialized countries will have to devote much greater energy than heretofore to strengthening the Fund and the OECD. Specifically, this would mean more meaningful consultation on national economic policies and the negotiation of effective adjustment "packages" in which surplus and deficit countries pledge themselves to mutually satisfactory measures for reducing these imbalances. A really big increase (for example, a doubling) in Fund quotas would help provide the Fund with more authority in the adjustment process. But the real incentive for giving greater authority to international agencies is the one that has been implicit in the situation all along—namely, that this is the only way to assure freedom of trade and payments and the avoidance of a mutually destructive system of adversary economic blocs.

With respect to economic rewards influencing political behavior, the prospect is much more uncertain. While examples can always be cited—such as the Indus Waters settlement, where multilateral financing assisted political agreement—our experience in the Middle East, Vietnam, and elsewhere suggests that strong animosities and conflicts of interest do not yield easily to the power of economic incentives. Of course, multilateral economic cooperation can have political payoffs in the very long run as it binds countries and their leadership groups together with increasing ties of common interest. But the payoffs may only be visible after decades, and a too-explicit statement of the political implications of economic cooperation can set back the entire enterprise. Any formal linking of political conditions to economic assistance is likely to prove counterproductive, as experience with the Soviet Union and developing countries has amply demonstrated. Indeed the fragile structure of economic cooperation in the UN system is already under great strain as a result of ill-advised efforts to inject political issues. The withholding of U.S. funds from the International Labor Organization because a Russian was appointed to a top position, the controversy over the Special Fund project in Cuba, and the argument between the General Assembly and the World Bank over the Bank's operations in South Africa are examples of the danger.

The manipulating of the political reward structure to influence political behavior is, of course, the most difficult matter of all. The power and prestige of the UN in the field of peace and security is at an all-time low. UN peacekeeping operations in Cyprus, the Middle East, the Congo, and Kashmir have been of real value, but the future potentiality of the organization to mount such operations is uncertain, particularly with the prospect of the seating of Communist China. The resolution of the Secretary Council providing "security assurances" to nonnuclear powers that accept the Non-Proliferation Treaty has little credibility in the light of these harsh realities.

Despite the obvious political roadblocks, every effort should nevertheless be made to strengthen the peacemaking and peacekeeping capacities of the UN.[2] A move toward universal membership accompanied by a restructuring of the Security Council to give permanent or semipermanent membership without veto to countries like West Germany and Japan, and possibly also India, Italy, and Brazil, might provide some political incentives to these countries to forego nuclear weapons and assume greater responsibilities for maintaining world peace. Whether UN membership and a seat on the Security Council will do much to influence the future policy of Communist China is a larger question. It is a calculated risk—but obviously one that we will have to take.

[2]For some specific proposals, see the author's "Can the United Nations Be Revived?" *Foreign Affairs*, Vol. 48, No. 4 (July, 1970), pp. 660–676.

## CHAPTER 10

Ernst B. Haas

# Multilateral Incentives for Limiting International Violence

To punish a government in order to deter its taking recourse in violence is perpetually to test the credibility of the deterrent. Moreover, it risks applying a form of therapy more destructive than the ailment to be cured. After all, why deter all wars? Some may be fought in remote corners of the world at such a low level of intensity that international intervention—whether multilateral or otherwise—would seem hardly appropriate. Nor may it seem worthwhile at all times to enforce the provisions of the nuclear Non-Proliferation Treaty (NPT) if a party chooses to violate them; might not Japan and Germany act as "responsibly" with their nuclear arsenals as do Britain and France? If so, why punish them? And if Japan and Germany, why not India, Brazil, Egypt, and Israel . . .?

This paper examines a number of possible techniques of *rewarding* non-nuclear states and of *reinforcing* their present determination not to go nuclear. Assuming that, potentially, a combination of rewards and reinforcements can be effective in limiting recourse to international violence when reliance on punishment cannot, some types of rewards and reinforcements available are examined as to their utility in buying off recourse to violence. To do this we distinguish several ways of resorting to the use of force internationally. We also examine the international systems which will probably arise in the next ten to twenty years and seek to specify the applicability of our rewards and reinforcements to them. In all cases the limiting assumptions and conditions of the projection must be kept clearly in view: the chief limiting condition being the interdependence, globally or regionally, of the major policy domains of governments. But even if we observe all these strictures, the final prognosis for the effectiveness of such techniques is not very encouraging.

## MAJOR ASSUMPTIONS APPLICABLE TO PRESENT AND FUTURE SYSTEMS

My assumptions are few and hardly calculated to startle anyone. No system is assumed to include less than five nuclear powers. A dozen other states are assumed to possess the capability of rapidly acquiring the hardware and skills to mount a catalytic or an anonymous attack, to have an imperfect first-strike capability. In the foreseeable future, nuclear lore will be widely diffused because nuclear energy will have found broader application for peaceful uses than it has now. Governments will still be governments. They will still seek to gain as much and lose as little as possible in their dealings with each other, even if they bargain in non-zero-sum fashion. Men will still be men. They will make love as well as war, each in its proper time and place and sometimes even simultaneously. These conditions, in turn, imply an evolving global and regional interdependence along some dimensions, but less interdependence along others—notably the military— at least as far as the nuclear powers are concerned. The multipolar international system of the present will slowly yield to a multibloc system.

Therefore, we confine our discussion to the marshaling of *nonmilitary* methods of limiting recourse to violence—of flattering, cajoling, blackmailing, and bribing governments rather than seeking to coerce them. In so doing we will be exploiting the ragged pattern of interdependence and the evident mixture of governmental motives and expectations. We shall also limit any dependence on the will of nuclear powers to use coercive methods, partly because of my innate doubts about the credibility of that will and partly simply because I prefer noncoercive means on moral grounds. Moreover, only multilateral means are discussed. Obviously, it ought to be possible for the United States, the Soviet Union, and other strong powers, unilaterally or in concert, to deter the use of violence by smaller powers. Deterrence could be achieved by the threat or the act of military intervention, by the refusal to furnish arms aid, or by cutting off such aid when it is already under way (as in the India-Pakistan war of 1965). It could also be achieved by curtailing or stopping nonmilitary aid and by manipulating commercial relations through comprehensive or selective embargoes and boycotts. However, such techniques have shown themselves to be quite ineffective *unless* the measures are respected by all major and middle-sized powers. To be sure, if the Soviet Union and the United States could act in concert vis-à-vis the Middle East, they could deter recourse to violence; but such concerts have been too intermittent and too shallow to have had a profound effect on the area. Hence, partly on the basis of such experience and partly because of my moral preference, the stress will be put on *multilateral* noncoercive means of deterring violence.

Who, then, is to be rewarded or reinforced? We cannot expect to reward countries already too wealthy or too powerful to be tempted by monetary means. Japan, West Germany, Italy, and Sweden have already passed the bounds of the blandishments we have in mind. The countries which can be expected to be influenced by these techniques must be sufficiently poor and weak as to be unable to budget for research and development purposes funds adequate to give them a small nuclear force. While India is a doubtful candidate here, the great bulk of the Third World countries would qualify. In short, we must assume, in order to make our projection in the least worthwhile, that the nuclear powers will wish to live up to the Non-Proliferation Treaty and, furthermore, will themselves refrain from causing major perturbations in the international system. The scheme examined here, then, will be confined to limiting the recourse to violence in relations among smaller and weaker states.

What are these countries to be rewarded for? Three types of activities or choices come to mind. They imply quite different modes of conduct and cannot be "scaled" in a linear fashion. One major type of activity is recourse to conventional military forces in the attainment of some governmental objective, whether through interstate operations or in support of an insurgent movement. Quite a different activity is suggested by the nuclear Non-Proliferation Treaty. Nonnuclear parties pledge not to manufacture nuclear weapons or to solicit aid for doing so. Hence we might be willing to reward states for observing the obligation they have assumed under NPT. However, treaties and men being what they are, we cannot take such a resolve for granted. Hence a third type of violence to be deterred through rewards or reinforcements is nonrecourse to nuclear weapons after NPT has been abrogated. It is entirely conceivable that a given reward might be effective in reinforcing a desire to observe NPT obligations but ineffective in deterring recourse to conventional forces in a border clash or military aid to ideologically kindred insurgents. Hence it is important to set out the hazards against which weaker nations may need to be protected before discussing the insurance of protection that might be available.

## II. MULTILATERAL PUNISHMENT, REWARD, AND REINFORCEMENT

### Punishment

To punish, in this context, means to withdraw or to withhold, without using military means, something strongly desired by the weaker or poorer countries. Many potential examples come to mind. A decision to suspend the operations of a development-aid consortium or to withdraw the benefits that come from membership in the International Bank or the International Monetary Fund is a form of economic punishment. Suspension of voting rights in international bodies is symbolically punitive, even if the real effect is not important. To refuse to make UN peacekeeping machinery available—that is, to permit the military adversary to achieve a crushing victory without UN intercession (as the UN might have permitted Israel to do in 1956 and 1967)—is a potential punishment of some moment. None of these modes of punishment has ever been used explicitly and overtly for one of the purposes listed above. Hence, once we contrast them with methods which have been used ineffectually, their possible importance in the future is to be borne in mind. In fact, the IBRD and IMF have come under increasing pressure for so far refusing to participate in any multilateral economic sanctions contemplated or recommended by the political organs of the UN.

International organizations have attempted to use noncoercive punitive measures on a number of occasions—never successfully unless the deprivation was, in effect, imposed by a hegemonial member state on which the victim was heavily dependent (as in the case of OAS sanctions against the Dominican Republic in 1960–1961). Economic punishment ordered by the UN against Rhodesia has had no serious effect. Similar measures recommended against Portugal and South Africa have not been consistently implemented by the membership. A novel punitive technique has been developed in the UN's struggle with Portugal and South Africa: giving technical assistance to insurgent groups after such a group has been recognized by the UN as the legitimate carrier of the demand for self-determination. No discernible effectiveness results from this practice.

Our analysis is focused on the future. Therefore we cannot confine our survey of methods of punishment to what is possible today. The further development of technology suggests several possible ways of increasing the leverage that can be exercised by multilateral agencies, particularly since the execution and implementation of such steps need not depend on the good will of the member states (as is the case now). It may be possible to develop a centralized monitoring or command-and-control system for equipment financed and operated under the auspices of UN economic and financial agencies. The sluice-gates on internationally financed dams may be subject to control from Geneva, oil rigs might be deployed on the deep ocean bottom from New York, weather satellites from Australia. UNIDO may one day get into the business of financing the construction of automated factories; the controls, however, might be kept in Vienna. All I mean to suggest here is that the evolution of technology may make greater noncoercive but punitive capacities available to international agencies in the same way that it has already increased the nonlethal resources of national authorities.

## Reward

To reward means to offer something which is desired by the recipient in exchange for conduct desired by the donor. In international politics, the distinction between "rewards" and "bribes" is somewhat elusive, unless the measures in question are executed under the auspices of an accepted body of law. Nonmilitary rewards are, of course, used routinely in the context of unilateral and bilateral foreign-aid policy. Their avoidance is the major claim to fame of the "nonpolitical" and "stringless" economic and technical aid dispensed by international agencies. Hence, it would require a major reorientation of attitudes to multilateralize foreign aid for purposes of rewarding desired military behavior.

Insofar as such a reward system involves the use of techniques now generally practiced, little need be said. Standard techniques of lending and granting development funds and of providing technical services for development could be made contingent on, for instance, the potential recipient's observation of the provisions of NPT. The political costs of doing so have been spelled out by the staff of the World Bank. Certainly, a major attitudinal breakthrough would be required before the major donors would consent to "politicize" the multilateral component of their aid package. But the time may come when such a step will appear more attractive than it does at the moment, particularly after the cohesion of present military blocs declines further, and after the world divides into more and more restless regional groupings which, through policies of skillful nonalignment, are able to put new kinds of pressures on the wealthy and strong. Politicized multilateral aid may become attractive then as a means of counteracting such pressures.

However, it is more interesting to speculate about some novel techniques of rewarding desired conduct. The inspiration for these speculations comes from the complex planning now going into the Second Development Decade. If we assume a certain minimal commitment to ever-increasing global activity designed to engage in a redistribution of economic capacity which would favor the underdeveloped nations—as we must—it follows that the capacity of international institutions for influencing recipient nations will also grow, even though these nations will increasingly share power in the making of redistributive decisions. We must rely on this commitment and the institutional involvements that will result from it for the efficacy of the rewards which follow.

United Nations institutions could guarantee specific nations a fixed growth rate for a certain period, say, a decade. The guarantee would be made meaningful by contributions pledged to the national-development plan in the form of appropriate aid consortia, loans, grants, and trade agreements (such as special preferences). The package would specify that the recipient will refrain from violating NPT and will otherwise abide by the rules of nonviolent international conduct except in self-defense. Conduct inconsistent with the pledges would result in an automatic interruption of the flow of economic benefits. The efficacy of such an approach would naturally depend on how seriously the developing nation took its own growth targets, though the international package would be likely to enhance the symbolic importance of the magic number.

More imaginative approaches to the issue of compensatory financing also come to mind. The wealthy could, in effect, insure the developing nations against certain kinds of hazards with the help of variously structured compensatory financing mechanisms. Among these hazards are contingencies which preoccupy planners in developing nations very much indeed, such as crop failures, the "brain drain," excessive population growth, and the progressive deterioration of the terms of trade, particularly because of the rapid development of synthetic substitutes for agricultural exports. The hazards themselves probably cannot be regulated or controlled through international action, at least not in the foreseeable future. But insurance against them is conceivable. The return for the reward, of course, would be military conduct consonant with the principles discussed.

There is still another way of rewarding the late developing nations. Such nations are increasingly worried about a lack of balance between rates and kinds of social development on the one hand and economic development on the other. All desire more science, more technology, and more education; all are worried about too much urbanization, too much social mobilization, and too many educated unemployables. Nobody seems to know how to draw the proper balance; therefore, parallel but uncoordinated development policies are pursued in the economic and the social domains. International agencies might work out appropriate formulas for determining the balance, as UNESCO has begun to do in the field of science policy and education. The formulas, in turn, are likely to be highly salient to the developing nations, since future social peace could depend on their success. Again, the multilateral aid package can be geared to the implementation of a given formula that a recipient government, once committed, can hardly afford to abandon without serious risk. The *quid pro quo* here is identical with that in the system proposed above.

### Reinforcements

Reinforcements[1] are incentives adopted by those with the proper resources to support behavior already in progress or already latent in the intentions of the recipient. Thus they neither punish nor reward in precisely the sense adopted above. The reinforcements of particular interest to us are methods of "social instrumentation" (Schwitzgebel's term) made possible by technology. They are social controls considered benign by those

[1]The idea of "reinforcement" here used is an adaptation of the concept developed by Robert Schwitzgebel. See his "Can We Automate the Good Society?" *Interplay* (February 1970), pp. 28, 34–37.

whose conduct is to be controlled. Schwitzgebel gives several examples. Clocks are a reinforcement for those who wish to be punctual but know themselves incapable of always living up to the wish. Daylight saving time makes it easier for people to be active after dinner though, presumably, they wished to be in their gardens anyway. Cash registers and credit cards are nonpunishing and nonrewarding incentives for honesty on the part of sales personnel. Social instrumentation of this kind can sometimes take the place of unpopular legislation. Since gun control is not popular in the United States, substituting tranquilizer guns for hunting rifles would be a form of reinforcement. Alternatively, once electronic monitoring of the use of hand guns becomes feasible, such monitoring may also be a form of reinforcement which could take the place of outright legislation against the sale of firearms. Proponents of such measures expect to be able to control social deviance without having to come to grips with their sources.

Some of the devices we discussed as rewards, such as growth targets, could, therefore, be considered as reinforcements as well. A more sweeping approach to peace and nonviolence has been proposed by several sources, including Schwitzgebel: that is, the United Nations Good Behavior Index. The suggestion is based on the assumption that one basic objective of all governments is to enjoy a good international image, to be respected as generous, peaceful, and law-abiding. Therefore, it should be possible to design forms of reinforcement for supporting the attainment of this objective. Such reinforcements would be aimed particularly at groups within nations most crucial in decision making and most subject to the desire to possess a good image. The Good Behavior Index would be based on the purposes spelled out in the UN Charter and in major UN documents; it would be a set of scales against which the actual conduct of governments could be measured, presumably by a respected private body such as the Nobel Prize committees. One such scale could then deal with the type of behavior of concern to us.

Self-administered and self-inspected arms-control agreements approximate the scenario suggested by the gun-legislation example; but implementation of NPT is dependent on international inspection, which is considered punishing by several governments. It follows, therefore, that to the extent that the enforcement of the treaty can be based entirely on automated devices and centralized monitoring linked to a public-performance index, reinforcement for compliance with NPT could be facilitated. Obviously we are far from that point at present. Hence it is impossible for us to rely solely on reinforcements, without rewards, if we wish to find noncoercive multilateral means for controlling international violence. Our subsequent discussion will consider both techniques jointly.

### The Limiting Condition: Interpenetration of Policy Domains

We are discussing the use of economic, social, and technological incentives for deterring governments from using their military capability. We cannot hope to take seriously any linking of rewards and reinforcements for such a purpose unless we insist on one fundamental condition: Governments must consciously tie their calculations of advantage, their informal cost-benefit analyses, to a holistic view of foreign policy under which the benefits of a military step would be considered along with the costs incurred in other foreign-policy domains. These costs, in turn, would make themselves felt primarily in fields of activity normally considered as domestic policy, such as economic development, education, and urban growth. A few examples will show that this condition is a very difficult assumption to meet.

Such a holistic view of national foreign policy would actually prevail if Egypt and Jordan were deterred from attacking Israel by being rewarded by the construction of the Aswan Dam and the Jordan River Valley project, respectively, and reinforced by the steadily improving international image they would probably enjoy as a result. But why could not Egypt and Jordan talk as if they were most anxious for the economic benefits implied and *also* plan war against Israel? Why must the military domain be linked with the economic and social? History shows that it was not, even though the economic development of both countries was demonstrably slowed down as a result of war and preparation for war.

In another example, a holistic view would prevail if the Indus Waters Project were considered by India and Pakistan as an activity preferable to fighting about Kashmir or the Rann of Kutch. If this attitude prevailed, an intensified economic interdependence, financed by the World Bank, would deter recourse to violence. Again, history showed clearly that Pakistan and India wanted both the benefits of the Indus Waters Project *and* war. Moreover, they got both. In a similar vein, we shall argue later that a combination of rewards and reinforcements clustering around the joint development of the Mekong River may deter recourse to further violence in Indochina. But such an argument rests on first overcoming the limiting condition of insufficient interdependence between policy domains.

Under what conditions can we then expect such interdependence to be recognized? Whenever countries are both poor and committed to dramatic means of overcoming poverty, military spending must be considered as closely linked to economic nonspending. Whenever countries profess strong nationalist objectives but know themselves incapable of marshaling the forces for realizing them, a similar calculus should prevail. Whenever countries are already deeply penetrated by international institutions and programs (such as the Congo was in 1961), it would seem that the necessary interdependence prevails. In the longer run—that is, after a certain degree of wealth, contentment, and security has been achieved—one would expect a poor nation to be increasingly reluctant to sacrifice these programs and institutions to military operations which would reduce levels of satisfaction. Moreover, once a certain enmeshment in international trade and communications has been achieved, it becomes painful for the recipient to break the strands, thus confirming interdependence. The relationship of Ireland, Norway, and Denmark to Britain illustrates such purely economic interdependence. If the occasion ever arose, one would expect Britain to be able to deter these nations by noncoercive means.

In short, our problem is insoluble unless we assume that the major domain of government policy in each country is not seen by decision makers as autonomous and separable from that of others. We assume that the domains are recognized as interdependent, or will be so recognized as soon as the first costs of not operating according to this assumption become apparent. An examination of some situations instructive for our purposes will show the weakness of the assumption. Weakness, however, does not mean that the limiting condition can never be met, though it does mean that our expectations should be modest.

## POLICY DOMAINS AND INTERNATIONAL REWARDS: LESSONS OF THE PAST

These situations to be considered here involve the alleged power acquired by international organizations by virtue of their ability to provide funds to needy governments. The IMF and the IBRD are the major actors; others are the central banks of the Group of Ten as institutionalized by the Bank for International Settlements, and international aid-consortia organized by the IBRD. These institutions are able to punish: they can withhold or withdraw funds when the debtor government fails to conform to specified rules of behavior. The rules of conduct applied, however, have thus far had nothing to do with recourse to violence; they have been confined to fiscal and monetary policy. If the power to punish has been ineffective in enforcing such rules, how much less effective is it likely to be when the objective is explicitly political and military? International agencies also have the power to reward: to make new credit available in recognition of faithful adherence to past obligations. The facts show that new credits are made available also in the absence of such faithful conduct. The combination of rewards and reinforcements, however, remains to be tested. Perhaps the regime for authorizing the issuing of Special Drawing Rights (SDRs) by the IMF represents such an instance, assuming that the representatives of the major governments take seriously the restrictions written into the potential access of debtors to SDRs.

The instances described here of the nonuse of the power to punish and reward are taken from the work of Susan Strange.[2] Britain received multilateral central-bank assistance four times between 1964 and 1968. "There
has been little of that correlation between performance and reward, or between failure and punishment, such as might have been expected if the su-
pervision had been really strict."[3] Beginning in 1965, India was under considerable pressure by its international aid consortium and the IBRD to
devalue the rupee and be friendly to foreign investors. Moreover, the
United States sought to suspend economic aid to India in order to stop the
war with Pakistan in that year. By 1967, however, India (even though the
rupee was devalued) managed to extract new international credits. International agencies wanted "at all cost to avoid the open and defiant declaration by the debtor of default on past loans. Thus while they have exerted
some influence on the debtor's financial policies, they have also helped to
wring concessions from the creditors."[4] The IMF's experience with Egypt
suggests the same lesson. That country defaulted on debt repayment in
1966, after several years of bitter recriminations between major donors
and the Nasser regime. The outbreak of war with Israel in 1967 was used
by the IMF as an excuse for Egypt's default and actually served as a preliminary step for the eventual rescheduling of new credits and debts! Miss
Strange's conclusion, after her examination of these and other recent instances of this kind, can hardly be stated better:

Indeed, the axiom of many business tycoons that you only achieve a secure success
when you have borrowed so much that the bank cannot afford to see you go
broke seems to apply almost equally to international relations—except that the
bankers are less able to stop you going broke if you insist on doing so.[5]

One might add only that the debtor's stranglehold on the international
community actually gets stronger when he insists on using violence against
his neighbors because he can then extract a reward for *misbehavior* by
claiming that peace cannot be restored unless the economy also improves.

In short, economic development and debt servicing have been autonomous policy domains; international agencies have not successfully meshed
them with political and military objectives. And when they have been
meshed by the unfolding of actual events, the military delicts have been
successfully used by the debtors to increase economic rewards rather than
strengthen the international agencies' ability to restrain military initiatives.

[2]Susan Strange, "The Meaning of Multilateral Surveillance," in Robert W. Cox (ed.), *International Organisation: World Politics* (London: Macmillan, 1969). See also Richard N.
Gardner, "The Politics of Liquidity," in the same volume.
    [3]Strange, p. 233.
    [4]Strange, p. 236.
    [5]Strange, p. 239.

One of the most dramatic instances of the failure of multilateral rewards to divert or delay the acquisition of new military capability is the case of Atoms for Peace. When, in 1953, the United States first proposed an international research-and-aid program designed to upgrade the ability of developing countries to utilize atomic energy for peaceful industrial purposes, it had several objectives in mind: (1) to demonstrate that the horrible aspect of nuclear knowledge was only one of several, and that such knowledge could be put to constructive uses; (2) to make a contribution to the international redistribution of knowledge and wealth; (3) to create the beginnings of an international machinery for inspecting the use made of fissile materials, and thus gradually approach an acceptance of the principle of inspection for arms-control purposes; (4) to prevent and delay nuclear proliferation by facilitating access to *peaceful* nuclear knowledge and equipment while barring use of that access for military purposes. In short, new and arcane knowledge and equipment were offered gratis as a reward for not putting the material to military uses. As we now know, the plan simply did not work because there is no meaningful distinction between knowledge useful for peaceful purposes and that useful for military ones. Many countries, but especially India, in taking advantage of the program eventually administered by the IAEA, *did* enhance their potential nuclear military capacity very appreciably. In other words, the program accelerated nuclear proliferation despite the intentions of its founders to avoid that very contingency.

These instances all dealt with relations between the wealthy and strong (and international agencies controlled by them) on the one hand, and the poor and weak on the other. Is the situation any different if we examine relations between strong and weak nations in settings in which both are reasonably wealthy? This perspective leads to an examination of systemic interdependence and the meshing of policy domains among the member nations of OECD. True, we have already excluded Japan, Germany, and Sweden from our list of nations possibly to be deterred from recourse to violence by noncoercive rewards and reinforcements. Nevertheless, their intimate involvement, through the European Common Market, EFTA, and the Group of Ten with the smaller nations of the "club of the rich" and with the United States commands a second look. There has been no recourse to violence in relations among these nations since 1945, and there is no suggestion that such a recourse is in anyone's mind now. Hence, an opportunity for exploiting domain interdependence is removed. As far as its relations with Soviet-bloc countries and China are concerned, the United States has actually used economic rewards to *increase* conventional military preparations in some cases. In others, notably the case of Japan and in the famous chicken war with the EEC, the United States has applied economic punishment while simultaneously extending military rewards through NATO and bilateral aid. In short, the history of the economic-military-policy complex among the OECD countries shows no trend toward an interdependence of policy domains as far as conventional military preparations against communist nations are concerned. Mutual deterrence is an irrelevant consideration because of the nature of ties in the area.

This is not necessarily the case with respect to NPT and its future. The United States, Britain, and France may possibly continue to provide military rewards to restrain a violation of NPT by Germany, Italy, Japan, and Sweden. But it is difficult to see how economic rewards and reinforcements could be used in view of several features of the economic relations and institutions among OECD countries which argue against an increasing interdependence of policy domains, despite the very high level of transactions among these nations. I am thinking of the weakened economic position of the United States vis-à-vis the others, and the growth of multinational corporations, Eurodollars and Eurobonds, and various institutionalized means of resolving international commercial conflicts, thus removing such conflicts from the bargaining arena and making them immune to punishments and rewards.

The United States is less and less able to punish and reward its closest allies, even assuming that she wishes to do so. Bearing down on Japan too hard over cottons might trigger a stronger neutralist-pacifist reaction in Japan, a desire *not* to rearm and oppose China. But if we use economic rewards (that is, admit competing Japanese goods without discrimination) to induce Japan to rearm along conventional lines while observing NPT, what assurances do we have that Japan will not accept the reward but go nuclear anyway? As far as international agencies, go, of course, Japan is in a better position to extend certain kinds of rewards than is the United States. And so, too, is Europe. American access to SDRs depends on the concurring vote of the EEC countries. American agricultural exports depend on the EEC's Common Agricultural Policy. American corporations depend on the continuation of a permissive investment climate in Europe. Who is able to reward or punish whom? There is nothing in this picture of admitted interdependence which might enable us to say that violations of NPT by European countries are subject to American manipulations based on economic policy. The limits on such European desires are to be found in the attitudes and ambivalent objectives of European elites, not in an American capacity to reward and reinforce outside the military domain.

The trend is toward increasing the autonomy of economic and commercial domains. The growing market for Eurodollars and Eurobonds escapes American and European regulative ability; it is independent of other economic and monetary forces, let alone military or political ones. The large multinational corporation, overwhelmingly American, is not an instrument of American foreign policy. It is an autonomous force which cannot be easily linked to a reward-and-reinforcement structure worked out by governments, unless the governments choose to reward the corporations. But even if such companies are embroiled in disputes with the host government, more and more devices are available for conflict resolution outside the political arena. We mention only a few. International credit insurance is likely to reduce acrimony over expropriation and nationalization as well as other forms of default. New conciliation and arbitration techniques are being developed and practiced in international trade, pioneered in some cases by the International Chamber of Commerce. Finally, there is the Convention on the Settlement of International Investment disputes, which is also likely to depoliticize much that now engenders controversy. The more autonomous the processes of conflict resolution, the more autonomous the policy domain is likely to be; hence, there will be fewer opportunities for exploiting interdependencies.

This line of reasoning suggests another possible lesson of the past. During the early and middle 1960s American officials (and their Soviet opposite numbers), as well as such groups as the Pugwash Conferences, made much of the possibility of taming the nuclear arms race by means of institutionalized international cooperation in science and technology. The argument seemed to suggest that successful international cooperation in such fields as weather control, the ocean bottom, application of science to economic development, space exploration, and world-population problems would create the trust and expertise necessary for eventually tackling the arms race. Coincidentally, such measures would also wean the poorer and weaker countries away from a preoccupation with nuclear weapons and therefore create the psychological substructure for a successful NPT system.

Several multilateral developments in fact took place in response to this line of reasoning: The inspection powers of the International Atomic Energy Agency were sharply increased; the institutional infrastructure for a World Weather Watch was set up under the auspices of the World Meteorological Organization; negotiations for a UN agency with powers over the seabed and the ocean bottom advanced steadily; many international agencies, but notably UNESCO, actively entered the field of diffusing technological knowledge and gearing it to economic development; WHO took a leading role in an international population-control policy. In short, the initial Soviet-American consensus on this nexus of issues resulted in the growth of international institutions and programs capable of rewarding and reinforcing national conduct which could wean weaker countries away from any fascination with nuclear weapons.

It is impossible to say whether such a weaning process has in fact been triggered. Successful scientific and technological cooperation has probably contributed to improving certain dimensions of Soviet-American relations by eliminating some sources of tension. But that is not our concern. Why should not India, Egypt, Israel, South Africa, or Brazil gladly avail themselves of the advantages of scientific cooperation and *still* ponder the wisdom of not observing NPT? Why link policy domains when one has much to gain by not doing so?

It appears that the past has few lessons which could encourage us in thinking along the lines of using economic and social rewards for military-political abstinence. If our line of analysis seems plausible, we must conclude that rewards work only if the interpenetration and interdependence of policy domains is actually perceived by important elites as being greater than autonomy. Moreover, such interdependence must be actively valued as being more important than the autonomy which might be within the grasp of some countries in terms of availability of resources. Two instances come to mind, though they are both partly speculative.

Within the network of expectations of future benefits and the recognition of past benefits which we call the European Common Market, there probably exists an appreciation on the part of important elites that interdependence is *and* should be greater than national autonomy in most policy domains. The post-Gaullist history of the EEC shows many examples of this appreciation, particularly since policy domains dealing with money, taxes, and research are increasingly linked with trade and commercial policy. There is even more talk than before about their inherent links with defense and foreign policy. What does this have to do with deterring recourse to violence or observing NPT? Let us assume that Germany and Italy, in the absence of a NATO or European defense posture considered adequate or credible, reluctantly consider opting for an independent nuclear deterrent. Let us note, first of all, that the pooled nuclear-research efforts have shown themselves more popular and more effective. How can Britain and France reward Germany and Italy for not infringing NPT? Not by economic means alone. Economic rewards (that is, not having to spend more for nuclear weapons at the expense of economic welfare) would have to be linked with a military umbrella of some kind, either unilateral or collective. The cost of building and maintaining such a deterrent force (that is, a merged Force de Frappe and Bomber Command) would be shared, thus reducing the cost which Germany and Italy would otherwise have had to bear alone had each decided to go nuclear. Other rewards for abstinence are readily suggested by interdependence in the fields of agriculture and industrial competition. Germany's share of the Common Agricultural Policy costs could be reduced; Italy's desire to invest in French industry might be accommodated, and production shares parceled out. The point to be kept in mind, however, is the impossibility of relying on economic rewards alone. The genuine military concerns of Italy and Germany would have to be met by *reinforcing* their reluctance to go nuclear; and this can be done only through military means. Unless we assume that such a reluctance exists, we could never hope to be successful.

India offers another speculative example. The major powers and the UN agencies were temporarily successful in 1965 in linking economic punishment with diplomacy in bringing the war with Pakistan to an end. The success was temporary because the punishment was soon lifted and more aid was offered than ever before, though hostilities did cease. Suppose we assume a scale of preference among Indian leaders which clearly makes them put economic development ahead of settling the Kashmir issue on their terms. This preference could be reinforced by external measures, such as guaranteeing the territorial status quo. It could be reinforced also by offering a nuclear umbrella designed to protect India against China, thus limiting the temptation to infringe NPT, although it is more than doubtful that this would restrain India from using nuclear weapons once NPT had been infringed. Finally, it would be easy to draw on the possible economic rewards discussed above in order to pay India for putting economic development ahead of settling accounts with Pakistan or spending heavily to buy security against China. And, even if such a scale of preference does not exist now, it is at least possible that it could be induced by offering appropriate rewards. Again, however, economic rewards *alone* are unlikely to suffice unless military reinforcements are also furnished, even if we grant that for Indian leaders an appreciation of interdependence among policy domains outweighs a drive for autonomy.

All we can say at this stage is that the success of our strategy depends crucially on cases such as these. And we must also say that in the present international system the essential condition in which interdependence outweighs the autonomy of policy domains does not exist.

## INTERDEPENDENT POLICY DOMAINS AND THE FUTURE

It is my contention that certain essential features of the international system in which we now live, and from which the lessons just analyzed have been taken, are undergoing a series of major changes that will result in a new system, labeled "multibloc." The current system is still multipolar because the United States and the Soviet Union continue to serve as leaders of nuclear alliances, but China has emerged as the leader of a putative bloc. And while the nonaligned nations lack a clear bloc leader (in fact, they deny being a bloc), Tito, Haile Selassie, Indira Gandhi, Kenneth Kaunda, and Julius Nyerere have sought to "speak for" the nonbloc. Perhaps Salvador Allende will join them, or General Velasco. In any event, the grouping has often acted as a bloc, and has thus made it inaccurate and misleading to speak of bipolarity except in terms of a nuclear second-strike capability. Moreover, the various kinds of capabilities—military, ideological-propagandistic, and economic—are distributed in a heterosymmetrical fashion among groups and alliances. Certain kinds of capabilities are concentrated in one group, other kinds in others; there is unlikely to be a pleasantly proportional, equal, or symmetrical distribution. I expect that in a multibloc system there will be an even less patterned distribution of capability than in the multipolar system, thus suggesting that we call it "asymmetrical." I offer an abbreviated scenario of this system:[6]

1. There will be neither world government nor a world empire. The superpowers will not be sufficiently in accord to rule the world by condominium. The small powers will not be sufficiently in accord to dominate the superpowers, even though they will be more energetic and stronger than in the current system. Supranational government (in the United Nations or elsewhere) will be no stronger in the realm of peacekeeping than it is now.

2. The character of national polities will have changed. Eastern European communist nations will still be authoritarian, but less totalitarian and will come to exhibit more and more of the life styles and attitudes of the "postindustrial" society. Indochina will be a united communist state, allied with neither Moscow nor Peking. Other Southeast Asian countries will continue to be authoritarian, while India will become more so. The countries of the West will be less cohesive internally, and therefore less willing to take energetic international action as the characteristics associated with high consumption and even higher self-indulgence become more marked.[7] Latin America will be divided between communist-ruled totalitarian polities and more or less democratic ones, professing an energetic development doctrine. In Africa, the bulk of the nations will alternate between mild authoritarian and rigid totalitarian forms of government. Japan, remaining democratic, will rediscover nationalism and a na-

---

[6]The passages which follow are taken from my *Tangle of Hopes: American Commitments and World Order* (Englewood Cliffs: Prentice-Hall, 1969), pp. 226–230. The system here described in the form of a scenario is very similar to two systems described by Morton Kaplan, labeled "unstable bloc" and "development world," respectively. See his "Constitutional Structures and Processes in the International Arena," in Richard A. Falk and Cyril E. Black (eds.), *The Future of the International Legal Order*, Vol. I (Princeton: Princeton University Press, 1969), pp. 173–78.

[7]I accept most of the implications of the scenario of the postindustrial society developed by H. Kahn and A. J. Wiener. See *The Year 2000* (New York: Macmillan, 1967), chapter 4.

tional mission as she becomes the fourth most powerful nation. China will show less and less evidence of any "permanent revolution," and become a more efficient and rapidly developing bureaucratic totalitarian entity.

3. The present blocs and regional organizations are more or less congruent with regard to military, ideological, and economic objectives; for example, the OAU represents all three (at a very general level of consensus) for Africa, the EEC for the continental European countries, COMECON and the Warsaw Pact for Eastern Europe. NATO and OECD also represent congruent policy domains for most members (excepting the European neutrals and Portugal). This is unlikely to be true in the next system. Regional organizations (and voting blocs in the UN) will proliferate along autonomous policy lines as economic development and world planning become recognized as independently necessary and desirable international activities. Hence we will see more common markets and free trade areas, *not* cleanly overlapping with military alliances. We will also see more military alliances and understandings, including collective and UN-guaranteed neutralization agreements. But these will not be led by the superpowers in all instances; nor will they neatly group whole continents. Several alliances may oppose each other in Africa and Latin America, divided by central ideological issues or purely local ones. Intervention will be frequent. NATO will have decayed. The various common markets of the developing nations will be loosely allied in UN organs for economic purposes only.

4. Nations will continue to use familiar means for attaining their objectives. But technology will give us more sophisticated devices than we now have for warfare, riot control, mind manipulation, technical assistance for economic development, mass education, and propaganda. Whether these technical developments imply a qualitative change in the nature of the system may well be doubted if we assume roughly equal access by all nations and blocs to the artifacts and techniques involved. The developing world will demand more aid of all kinds and more access to the markets of the developed. The industrial world will furnish more and more aid, but will also insist on spelling out conditions and limits. These transactions will go forward through bilateral as well as multilateral channels. While the West and the Soviet bloc will tone down their respective propaganda campaigns, no such restraint will be observed between the West and the Third World and among the various blocs of developing nations. The entire range of social- and human-rights policies will be infected with the concerns and charges elaborated in these propaganda campaigns. Argument will continue over the conditions governing private foreign investment. More acrimony will be heard over the most "egalitarian redistributive" way of applying new knowledge to economic and social development; solutions may well

confirm a decentralized and asymmetrical pattern of accommodation, eliminating both superpowers as the sole font of action and ultimate authority. And, it almost goes without saying, the agitation for the complete elimination of all kinds of colonial rule will continue, as will sporadic welfare designed to hasten the process or defend against it.

Will these objectives, alignment patterns, and methods imply more enmeshment—or less—in multilateral processes? Economic development, decolonization, world trade, the status of human rights, and the diffusion of scientific and technological knowledge will almost certainly involve continuous international negotiation, even culminating in confrontation—whether verbal or financial. The nature of the evolving human environment leaves little room to expect anything less. The exception to this projection is the preservation of peace itself: The different characters of the blocs and the asymmetric confrontation pattern between demands and means suggests that the bargaining pattern between demands and means suggests that the bargaining pattern between collective-security and decolonization or economic-development objectives is a thing of the past. For UN peacekeeping to work, we must have independent commitments of member nations, who accept it as good and desirable, not expediential, or dependent on payoffs in other issue areas. Such commitments are unlikely to exist in the multibloc system.

And this unlikelihood has immediate implications for the tasks the UN will be expected to carry out. The members will insist on using the organization for the completion of decolonization, for energetic industrialization policies, for social modernization, for the regulation of world trade and, finance, and even for propaganda broadsides in the field of human rights. The UN will almost certainly be used increasingly for social and economic planning and for the diffusion—controlled or not—of new knowledge. The point is, however, that each of these activities will be legitimate in its *own* right, with positive expectations attaching to *each* and little dependence on other issues or tasks. Therefore, the preservation of peace and the facilitation of peaceful change among the nations, *unless it too becomes an autonomous and legitimate task*, will not become legitimate by association with nonmilitary activities. There is nothing in the nature of a multibloc asymmetric system that gives us the right to expect such a development. As the tasks of the UN become autonomous, they also become self-encapsulating and self-sufficient, preventing the more precariously established tasks to profit from the success of the autonomous ones.

The implications of this projection now remain to be worked out. We wish to ascertain how likely it will be that noncoercive punishments, rewards, reinforcements, and rewards combined with reinforcements can be used multilaterally to deter recourse to force in international relations, and to enforce observance of the nonproliferation treaty, or nonuse of nuclear weapons in the event of infringements of the treaty. For this purpose we present the simple matrix in Table 1. But we must bear in mind that the capability for nuclear proliferation, technologically speaking, is assumed to be high. Moreover, we assume in this long-range scenario that policy domains are more autonomous, the world more fragmented into blocs, calculations of elites more instrumental and task-oriented, and that the willingness of the most powerful nations to intervene globally is sharply reduced. The willingness to intervene militarily on the part of the smaller nations, on the other hand, is proportionately less restrained.

Once NPT has in fact been infringed, our noncoercive multilateral techniques are less likely to deter the use of nuclear weapons in a world system more decentralized and asymmetric in terms of capabilities than that of the present. That does not mean that *coercive* techniques might not effectively deter a nuclear Japan, India, or Germany. It is quite possible, even likely, that new nuclear powers will respond to the logic of the balance of terror exactly as the superpowers have. It is all the more possible if the superpowers devise credible assurances of nuclear umbrellas for nations faithful to NPT (as they have not so far). This line of thought, however, takes us beyond the task we have set ourselves in this essay.

Nations will have few incentives in a future world system to heed multilateral blandishments to refrain from using conventional military coercion. Our projection of policy domains and interdependencies leads us to conclude that there will be less bargaining among and between domains and policy-specific preferences; it also leads us to conclude that the bloc structure of the system will make bargaining *across* domains more difficult than it now is. That being so, a regime would have to be passionately devoted to peace and nonviolence in order to be responsive to any of the four multilateral techniques of encouraging it. It is conceivable that a few small countries, probably not in the Third World, will be very responsive to the combination of rewards and reinforcements. But this possibility hardly entitles us to be encouraged about a general trend, particularly if no countervailing coercive techniques under multilateral auspices can be expected to flourish.

These conclusions leave us with the alternative of using noncoercive techniques with respect to shoring up observation of NPT. And here the picture looks somewhat brighter. Rewards alone cannot be expected to work. Punishment can be expected to work only when the likelihood of a nation's seeking a nuclear force is not very great to start with. Reinforcement alone may be effective with respect to a very special kind of nation, a kind that

TABLE 1. OBJECTIVES OF MULTILATERAL ACTION.

| | To Deter Use of Force | To Observe NPT | To Deter Use of Nuclear Weapons |
|---|---|---|---|
| Punish | *Under exceptional circumstances.* When elites entertain very strongly held welfare development aims which they are unwilling to sacrifice for territorial or prestige objectives. | *In some cases.* Poorest countries can be kept by economic punishment from investing research-and-development resources; more developed countries can get minimal resources without permanently sacrificing development through suffering delays. | *No.* Temptation for use strong in a sharp military crisis when survival is at stake; but punishment cannot respond to the long-range welfare aims associated with responsiveness to noncoercive sanctions. |
| Reward | *No.* Acceptance of the reward will enable the recipient all the more effectively to resort to force at a later point. | *No.* Acceptance of the reward will enable the recipient all the more effectively to violate NPT at a later point. | *No.* Same reasons as above. |
| Reinforce | *No.* Reinforcements, such as a high UN rating on love of peace, would have to be valued very highly indeed! | *Possibly.* When Elites entertain quasi-pacifist views and value ideational support from the UN, as perhaps in Sweden. | *No.* Same reasons as above. |
| Reward and Reinforce | *Under exceptional circumstances.* Countries valuing a high rating and anxious to minimize welfare losses might be expected to be willing to forego military/prestige gains. Denmark, Norway, Costa Rica, Zambia? | *Possibly.* If tied to neutralization and guaranteed rates of progress in a setting of elite commitment to national development undisturbed by international pressures. | *No.* Same reasons as above. |

is not likely to dominate international politics if our cynical view of men and their governments is well founded. But the combination of rewards and reinforcements is promising if it is handled by an imaginative international secretariat with a certain amount of independent resources at its disposal. And we must remember that the very concept of reinforcement assumes the prevalence of attitudes of restraint among ruling elites. One can imagine this combination of circumstances operating in the following settings.

Assume the continuation of a territorial stalemate in the Middle East for another five or six years plus an increasing weariness over unsettled conditions among the Israelis. Assume further that the pressure for domestic reform and higher standards of living in the Arab countries augments and challenges the values of the increasingly radical leadership in these countries, even to the extent that policies of external militancy can no longer be considered functional equivalents for domestic economic development. Under such conditions, the combination of economic rewards and ideological reinforcement might be used effectively to cool down the military situation and encourage Egypt and Israel to abide by NPT.

Or assume that Brazil's military dictatorship develops a taste for nuclear weapons thinking to use them to blackmail Peru, Bolivia, and Venezuela, who permit radical insurgents to use their territories. In addition, Brazilians may wish to have these weapons to give them a taste of *grandeur* of their own, finally demonstrating to them that they are approaching the great destiny which has been held out to them since independence. A combination of rewards (a development program underwritten by international agencies on a sliding scale—the better the performance the greater the external support) and status reinforcements could be devised. It is true that Brazil might then use conventional forces to deal with her neighbors, but the nuclear-development threat would still have been averted.

Another potential setting for the combination of rewards and reinforcements is Southeast Asia. In the following section I present a scenario of possible action, designed to end the war and stabilize the area, which covers both the deterrence of conventional force and the implementation of NPT. Moreover, unlike the reasoning above, it addresses an immediate situation in the present international system.

### THE MEKONG RIVER AS A SOURCE OF REWARD AND REINFORCEMENT

Again we must start with a number of assumptions which might not stand the test of actual behavior: A general conference on Indochina will be held which the Saigon and Cambodian regimes are compelled to attend.

The United States is determined to disengage by the fall of 1972. While publicly the United States continues to take the stance of wishing to assure the territorial integrity of South Vietnam and Cambodia, the tacit expectation is otherwise. American leaders are assumed to be willing to permit a coalition government to take over in Saigon, knowing that the coalition will give way to a communist regime within a year or two. The same is true in Cambodia. In Laos the status quo is ritually legitimated once more, with the tacit expectation that communist victories in Cambodia will soon result in a victory of the Pathet Lao. In short, it is tacitly expected that within a few years of the American withdrawal Indochina will be re-united under communist auspices. As a result of this expectation, American policy will be designed primarily to prevent the following developments: (1) Indochina must not fall under Chinese influence; (2) Thailand, Burma, Malaysia, and Indonesia must not be subjected to invasions and insurgent movements; (3) Indochina must not go nuclear. Hence the purpose of the general conference is to make possible the gradual and relatively peaceful communization of Indochina by ending the war, installing coalition governments, and neutralizing the whole area militarily. Naturally, we assume that Hanoi would withdraw its forces with alacrity if presented with this opportunity, thus enabling the United States to claim that the achievement of neutralization and coalition governments represent an American victory.

Neutralization is crucial in our scenario. Without effective neutralization the United States has no incentive to reward Hanoi and Sihanouk. Without neutralization the other Southeast Asian nations would probably oppose a general conference aimed at making life easier for Hanoi and Washington. Without neutralization the danger of Chinese domination would be overwhelming. But why would neutralization be attractive to Hanoi? It would probably not be, and that is why we need a reward and reinforcement mechanism.

Put differently, we must contrive a number of rewards which would persuade the leaders in Hanoi to accept a neutralized Indochina, and we must also reinforce their desire to bring about the rapid modernization of Indochina. We can link rewards and reinforcements with appropriate policies of guaranteed economic development under multilateral auspices, even under multilateral control. On the other hand, and in a different sense, we must also reward and reinforce the United States. The reward would not be aid furnished by the United Nations or the Asian Development Bank. The primary rewards for the United States would be guarantees against increasing Chinese influence in Indochina and the endangering of Thailand. The reinforcement, moreover, would be the fact that American contributions to the economic modernization of Indochina would be only a fraction of the expense of the war. While neutralization would neither reward nor reinforce the Soviet Union, it would presumably be acceptable as long as Moscow had no great interest in the area. China can be expected to oppose the arrangement; implementation would therefore have to occur over Chinese opposition. If China threatened military intervention, the economic reward structure here outlined would have to be initiated after an American military demonstration against China.

Neutralization would take the form of an agreement between the three Indochina regimes (now coalitions) not to seek military aid from or ally with any third country, and to ratify NPT. A second agreement would be concluded by the three Indochinese governments on the one hand and the remaining Southeast Asian governments on the other, reaffirming the Five Principles of Coexistence and abjuring intervention in each other's affairs, including support to insurgents. A third agreement would provide the teeth of the matter; The UN Security Council would adopt a resolution creating a permanent conciliation commission which would investigate (at the initiative of the Secretary-General) any alleged infraction of the two agreements; if the commission found the infraction to have taken place, and one of the Indochinese regimes (or the final communist regime) was to blame, the flow of rewards previously authorized would be cut back or stopped without requiring debate or vote by the Security Council. A fourth and final agreement would bind the United States and the Soviet Union to come to the assistance of the Indochinese states (or their successor) if threatened by any other state in the region, whether the threat were nuclear or conventional.

The centerpiece in this projected reward-and-reinforcement structure for the communists in Indochina is the Mekong River project, already under construction for almost a decade. It is a remarkable fact that civil war in Laos, Thailand, Cambodia, and South Vietnam—the four riparians—has not so far seriously interfered with the construction of dams, reservoirs, power plants, or survey work. When completed, the project will be the largest international comprehensive river development scheme ever attempted, combining irrigation, flood control, the generation of power, agricultural expansion, and navigational improvements.[8] If properly exploited and geared to the over-all growth plans of the four countries, it could become the single most important pole of development, feeding the expanding population as well as providing the source for expanding exports. Presumably, inheriting intact a partly completed system of dams, power plants, and training centers would be a considerable prize for Hanoi once communist responsibility extends beyond fighting a war and comes to include

[8]On the scheme, see W. R. Derrick Sewell and Gilbert F. White, "The Lower Mekong," *International Conciliation*, No. 558 (May 1966); and C. Hart Schaaf and Russell H. Fifield, *The Lower Mekong* (Princeton, N.J.: Van Nostrand, 1963).

the administration and systematic development of South Vietnam and Cambodia.

I propose that the Mekong River project—already financed almost exclusively as a result of UNDP projects, World Bank loans, Asian Development Bank support, and bilateral contributions coordinated by a consortium of donors—be made the key to enforcing the neutralization agreements. As long as the agreements were faithfully implemented, the UN system would commit itself to contributing annually to a program calculated to achieve a given growth rate. It would also commit itself to compensatory financing in the event of balance-of-payments difficulties, deterioration of the terms of trade, or damage due to typhoons or other catastrophes. A bonus in benefits could be devised for overfulfillment of growth targets, as well as for every year during which no complaints of treaty violations were received. Violations of the agreements would be met with an automatic reduction of benefits. We would seek, therefore, to bribe the communist leadership into devoting itself to the peaceful modernization of Indochina, a goal to which the leadership is already clearly committed in any case.

Whether any part of this plan can actually be implemented is far from clear. But unless we use some imagination in projecting the possibilities of conflict management, we are compelled to rely exclusively on coercive techniques to inhibit nuclear proliferation—techniques which are even less likely than the suggested plan to be used in practice. Should we therefore simply shrug our resigned shoulders and accept the inevitability of proliferation? It is not yet that late. But, as our extended and hopeful Southeast Asian scheme shows, not even the successful combination of noncoercive rewards and reinforcements can take the place of military guarantees. At best, it can complement them and make the acceptance of them less bitter.

CHAPTER 11

Richard Rosecrance

# *Reward, Punishment, and the Future*

## SUMMARY

This book has reviewed the probable impact of future technology and weapons upon international stability. It has also focused upon means for regulating the system, now and in the future. Many propositions have been offered by the separate contributors. Some are agreed and some are in dispute. Perhaps the proposition which would command most general assent is this: The impact of the spread of nuclear weapons upon the central system (or supergame) is likely to be destabilizing.

Donald Brennan believes that the spread of weapons and technology will make possible a catalytic attack in which an anonymous third power strives to simulate an attack by one of the two major powers on the other. Such a contingency is the more likely if the two superpowers are engaged in a crisis or confrontation. Because of the danger of third-party attacks, Brennan believes that ballistic-missile defense would be a worthwhile investment.

Malcolm Hoag deplores the impact that the spread may have on superpower capabilities. After an attack by a smaller nuclear state, either the United States or the Soviet Union might not have enough residual capacity to deter the other. Thus the development of Chinese, and later perhaps Japanese, forces may threaten the stability of the central game.

Morton Kaplan contends that a "rational" unit-veto system would not witness more recourse in the future to weapons of mass destruction, but speculates that the attainment of power by "romantic" nationalist leaders in the less developed countries may make the rational model inapplicable.

George Quester believes that a system of twenty nuclear powers would be stable internationally if the only putative aggressors were individual nation-states. If one state attacked another, sideline powers might rob the victor of his inheritance. Various unorthodox means of retaliation are conceivable in which even a small nuclear power might eventually wreak ven-

175

geance upon an attacker. If multilateral aggression, or nuclear "ganging up," occurs, however, retaliation would be much more difficult. Aggressive alliances could make the system much more unstable.

Kenneth Boulding contends that all powers will be reduced to a status of conditional viability once nuclear weapons are generally possessed, and that arms races will be much less likely to reach points of stability or equilibrium.

John Harsanyi notes that the differential capacities which would exist in the central or supergame as new nuclear powers were added would foster instability and perhaps lead to preemptive attacks. Alliances might mitigate this danger if they were defensive, or not too unequal in size.

Reinhard Selten and Reinhard Tietz argue that differential strength is likely to produce instability. The Selten-Tietz model, however, assumes that all powers having one bomb can retaliate. These authors would therefore not predict instabilities where all powers had at least one bomb.

While most of our theorists reason that the supergame will be less stable as nuclear weapons spread, there is divergence over the impact of the spread of weapons upon the entire system (supergame and subgame). Harsanyi and Selten and Tietz develop models in which instability increases with the increase in the differential in strength. Whatever may be the differential among nuclear powers, the difference between nuclear and nonnuclear powers is greater. Thus the spread of nuclear weapons is seen as fundamentally equalizing in the overall game. Relationships of 1-0 are transformed into 1-1 relationships. A central disagreement thus emerges among our contributors. Harsanyi and Selten and Tietz might argue that the number of conventional wars and conflicts in which major powers are embroiled against nonnuclear states (for example, Vietnam, Eastern Europe, the Sino-Indian border) would be prevented by the spread of weapons to nonnuclear powers. Other theorists would undoubtedly contend that the absence of nuclear capability in the past has not fostered conflict with those powers which possess weapons. Many neutralist countries without weapons are not the object of attack by nuclear powers. Some theorists would be likely to assert that as long as these powers remain nonnuclear, they have the protection and indulgence of the entire system. Once they acquire bombs, however, they will be expected to stand on their own. In addition, under certain contingencies the greatest nuclear powers might even have to contemplate an attack from a new nuclear state. Thus the Indian, Japanese, or Western European force would have to be taken into account in the counterforce and retaliatory calculations of the United States, the Soviet Union, and China. Under these circumstances, a new nuclear power could actually lose security by developing weapons.

There appears, in consequence, to be a difference between those theorists who look at the over-all game of international politics and those who assert that there are two specific games (the supergame and the subgame). The latter argue that subgame powers generally do not have to fear attack from powers in the supergame. Thus subgame powers do not have to develop nuclear capabilities to deter or prevent attack. They could rely on *de facto* nuclear guarantees or great-power abstention. Even if great powers were occasionally involved in conventional military operations against smaller nonnuclear states, they would not use their nuclear capabilities. If the smaller states went nuclear, however, conventional conflicts might be likely to escalate. Thus, the nonnuclear states should stay their hand.

The former argue that the over-all game is primary even though certain instabilities might be introduced at the supergame level if additional countries acquire nuclear weapons. From the standpoint of subgame states, nuclear weapons might be desirable. Subgame nations might not be able to count on good will, or upon the avoidance of great-power intervention in the subgame. The great powers have in fact intervened militarily in various nonnuclear areas of the globe. If the subgame states acquire nuclear weapons, they could deter great-power intervention, conventional or nuclear. Thus the acquisition of nuclear weapons could stabilize the over-all game even though it would make for greater inequalities among nuclear states.

It is, of course, possible that both groups of theorists are right in their separate propositions. The supergame theorists regard central nuclear stability as of overriding importance. They are willing to tolerate a certain amount of instability between great and small powers. They would not like to see weapons spread. The over-all-game theorists see the differences between super- and subgames as primary, and place most stress upon remedying inequalities at this level. Thus it might simultaneously be true that as new nuclear powers are added (1) the supergame becomes less stable and (2) the over-all game (between super- and subpowers) becomes more stable.

There is a third realm for investigation—that is, between the subgame powers themselves. The acquisition of weapons would surely destabilize subgame relationships insofar as nuclear weapons had not yet penetrated to these areas. The spread of weapons would merely further inequalities of strength. Thus, three propositions might be entertained simultaneously:

(1) The supergame becomes less stable with the spread of weapons.

(2) The subgame becomes less stable with the spread of weapons.

But (3) the over-all game (between super- and subpowers) becomes more stable with the spread of weapons.

## THE N-POWER GAME

Having speculated about different levels of games in international politics, let us return to the supergame, to the game of the major powers, since this game, after all, has the greatest consequence for the future of mankind. The results of military conflict at the supergame level could be decisive for the rest of the world. Any increased probability of conflict at this level creates a very negative expectation in decision-theory terms. In terms of the calculus-of-probability ($x$) results, the supergame is actually more important than the over-all game. Since the results of subgame-versus-supergame conflicts are not all that disastrous and have been entirely in the conventional or guerilla-warfare field, a diminished probability of such conflict does not reduce negative expectations as much as an increased probability of conflict at the supergame level increases them. Thus:

$$\Delta P_{sc} \times R_{sc} < \Delta P_{oc} \times R_{oc}$$

(where $P_{sc}$ is probability of supergame conflict, $R_{sc}$ is results of supergame conflict, $P_{oc}$ is the probability of over-all conflict, and $R_{oc}$ is results of over-all conflict.) Thus even if the change in $P_{sc}$ ($\Delta P_{sc}$) is no larger than the change in $P_{oc}$ ($\Delta P_{oc}$), the system is still worse off if nuclear weapons spread.[1]

We have seen that in the supergame (involving powers with nuclear weapons) stability is likely to decrease with the spread of weapons. *Inter alia*, this is because the spread of weapons will add differential capabilities to the supergame. The greater the inequality in supergame capabilities, the greater the instability. While this result will hold for the entire supergame, it may not apply to restricted parts of it. Suppose a world with five equal nuclear powers. Among these powers, equal capabilities would deter an attack launched by a single state. Alliances among groups of powers, however, could change this situation.

Assume a Harsanyi $c$ ratio of 3; that is, three powers attacking together can eliminate the nuclear force of one defending state. Under these circumstances any alliance of two states would be purely defensive. Such an alliance could be used to prevent three other powers from ganging up on one, but it could not be used for offensive or aggressive purposes. An alliance of four powers, on the other hand, could only be aggressive. Since superiorities of $4:1$ would not be needed for defense and retaliation, any four-power coalition would exist for the purpose of knocking out the remaining state. An alliance of five powers would confer general peace, and would be tantamount to universal arms control at the strategic level.

If the critical ratio $c$ were 2, the situation would be ambiguous. An alli-

---

[1]The change in $P_{sc}$ will be an increase. The change in $P_{oc}$ will be a decrease.

ance of two powers might be formed to attack one of the remaining states, or it might be designed to prevent two other powers from attacking one of two remaining states. Under these conditions the normal alliance configuration would be $2:2:1$. This situation would permit either of the two alliance pairs to attack the remaining single power. If one of the alliance combinations desired to help protect the remaining power, they might include it in the alliance, giving rise to a $3:2$ combination. Aggression would then be impossible. Alliances of four or five powers would not occur unless world arms control or disarmament were sought. If the $c$ ratio were 4, any alliance of four would clearly be aggressive, and any alliance of two or three purely defensive. If the $c$ ratio were 1, an alliance of two powers could be either defensive or aggressive. An alliance of two could protect against an attack by one power, but could not deter attacks by two or three powers. Under such conditions defense equals aggression. Any power which is sure it cannot be attacked must be in an alliance which is capable of knocking out other states. No alliance combinations can stabilize such a system. If $c$ were 5, on the other hand, stability would exist for all states without recourse to alliance. In the examples above, $c$ ratios of 2 and 1 generate conditions in which alliances can be either aggressive or defensive. Uncertainty and tension would be very high in such systems.

The situation worsens if five lesser and unequal states are added to the system of five equal great powers. $C$ ratios and alliance systems which would be stabilizing among the big five would be destabilizing with respect to the five lesser nuclear states. Alliances among the lesser states might be stabilizing, but any alliance blocs among the five larger powers would be likely to undercut the deterrent viability of some of the lesser five.

States which are sure they cannot meet rational deterrent-retaliatory criteria might seek to preempt the initiative of possible enemies by striking first. Unorthodox means of attack might be used, such as clandestine introduction of bombs into the cities of a major opponent power. If a state sought to "punish" or to wreak vengeance upon an enemy, it might engage in anonymous or catalytic attacks, posing the problem, Retaliation against whom? As a general rule it would appear that the more states fail to get over the orthodox deterrent threshold, the more likely they will be to resort to unorthodox means of nuclear delivery and retaliation. This likelihood in turn would greatly contribute to the tension, uncertainty, and insecurity of the nuclear supergame. The only way in which stability might be maintained in such circumstances would be for some of the big five powers to ally with some of the little five, forging perhaps two or three giant blocs. This is by no means a likely or probable outcome, however, since the big five powers would be seeking alliances among themselves to guard their own security. Some of these alliances or blocs among the big five would be likely to be capable of major and successful attacks upon one or more members of the little five.

## EQUILIBRATING THE SYSTEM:
## PUNISHMENT AND REWARD

In the light of future strategic uncertainty and insecurity, means other than manipulation of the punishment structure of world politics must be found to produce stability. Some such means were investigated or commented upon by contributors to this volume. Richard Gardner contends that economic rewards may influence purely economic strategies of game players. The economic techniques of international organizations however are much less likely to affect the political policies of nation-states, a conclusion in which Ernst Haas heartily concurs. Most difficult of all is the manipulation of political reward to influence political policies. The international system does not have powerful instruments at its command in the political arena. It cannot redistribute political payoffs for member states. In addition, Haas raises the valid point that states may decide to capture both the economic benefits offered by international organizations and the rewards to be had from separate national action against the international framework. The less developed countries are not likely to be dissuaded from a nuclear course by economic blandishments offered by the International Bank or the United Nations Special Fund. More important still, as Susan Strange has pointed out, international debtors have great leverage on multilateral financial institutions. Debt rescheduling and further extensions of credit may follow disruptive actions on the world stage by debtor nations. In the 1930s, the indebtedness of Hitler's Germany to Western countries and to Eastern Europe did not restrain Germany's international policies; it may rather have reduced international influence in coping with German expansion. Haas, in particular, makes the point that in many international situations there is no "interpenetration of policy domains" in national decision making. If political-military and economic policy domains are separate, then a state will not hesitate out of fear of losing an economic benefit to engage in disruptive actions in the political-military sphere. Since the political-military arena is primary and economic welfare secondary, the first will not be sacrificed to the second. States which might appear to be most amenable to international financial restrictions often are not. A state with a great deficiency in foreign exchange will not usually alter its political policies to gain access to hard currencies. Such a state is likely to have already become used to living on the margin of subsistence. It has less to lose than a more developed nation, and thus may be more impervious to manipulation of the international reward structure. Highly developed states also may not be subject to the reward and reinforcement operations of multilateral agencies. They have less need for economic and financial support.

These considerations do *not* lead to the inexorable conclusion that reward and reinforcement structures are not useful supplements to punishment strategies as a means of equilibrating the international system. One of the typical deterrent paradigms stresses that stability depends upon the margins between three variables: value of peace, value of first strike, and value of second strike.[3] Under normal circumstances, $V_p$ (value of peace) $> V_{fs}$ value of first strike) $> V_{ss}$ (value of second strike). The value of peace or the *status quo* is usually preferable to initiating war, particularly nuclear war. On the other hand, if war is likely, it is better to strike first than to be struck (and therefore only strike second). For deterrent purposes one wants to have the greatest possible margin between $V_p$ and $V_{fs}$. One also wants to have the greatest equality possible between $V_{fs}$ and $V_{ss}$. With a large difference between $V_p$ and $V_{fs}$, one would not be tempted to initiate war. If there is an approximation to equality between $V_{fs}$ and $V_{ss}$, on the other hand, one would still not strike first; one could afford to wait and to strike second. Both relationships would prevent initiation of aggressive military action in world politics.

The Soviet Union and the United States have only partially manipulated this paradigm. Typically, the United States Department of Defense has concentrated upon maintaining a high $V_{ss}$ for the United States and a low $V_{fs}$ for the Soviet Union. The Russians have concentrated upon reducing the American $V_{fs}$ outcome and in raising the Soviet $V_{ss}$ utility. Very occasionally, former U.S. Secretary of Defense McNamara talked of increasing the Soviet $V_{ss}$ position, and certainly in his later years in the Department of Defense he was prepared to concede the Russians a full second-strike capability and to refuse to take American steps to reduce the Soviet second-strike payoff. But defense planners in Moscow or Washington did nothing to take into account or to manipulate the respective $V_p$'s. Yet, if the Soviet Union and the United States are to be deterred over the long term from striking one another, and if other nuclear powers are to refrain as well, it will be partly because the status-quo situations which powers enjoy do not tempt them to aggression. This calculus is peculiarly important when one considers that the Japanese decision to strike Pearl Harbor was not the result of sanguine anticipation of $V_{fs}$, but rather of very pessimistic assessments of the Japanese $V_p$. In the long run the Japanese believed that the entire Co-Prosperity Sphere would be undermined and that the position in China would collapse if they did not attack the United States.

[3] See Daniel Ellsberg, *The Crude Analysis of Strategic Choices* (The RAND Corporation, P-2183, 1960).

Similar, though not identical, expectations were held by the Austrians on the eve of World War I. Austrian Minister for Foreign Affairs Berchtold seems to have been convinced that the Austrian Empire could not co-exist with a highly nationalistic Slavic state on its southern frontiers. Thus, Serbia had to be punished or humiliated at all costs. Neither the Austrians nor the Germans seem to have held high hopes for the utility they would derive from a $V_{fs}$ alternative. What seems to have been decisive, at least in Austrian calculations, were the long-term risks of not striking Serbia and the gradual erosion of Austrian power and political cohesion. Both wars, in short, were partly due to calculations of a drastic future decline in the $V_p$ utilities of the major protagonists. It is possible that, if they had not fore-seen such catastrophic decreases in their positions, they would not have struck and thereby precipitated world war.

Even Hitler's Germany was greatly influenced by what Hitler and his cohorts considered to be an unsatisfactory German position in Europe and the world. In the German case, however, it would have been impossible to remedy German dissatisfactions without encroaching on the liberties of other European states. On the other hand, if the Weimar German regime had been placated at the international level, the impetus to Nazism in for-eign policy would have been removed. A general rule seems to be that values of peace should not be allowed to deteriorate too markedly. If they do, new regimes bent on radical adventurism or aggression may come to power. As an international policy, appeasement would have succeeded admirably in 1921 or even 1929. But it could not work in 1936.

Thus the question is not whether marginal increments in reward or rein-forcement affect marginal changes in pacific or cooperative behavior. In many circumstances, as Haas correctly points out, a nation will seek and obtain rewards, but still proceed with sectarian or uncooperative behavior. But one should not expect "conditioned reflex" reactions in international relations. The cooperative behavior will not be proportionate to and follow immediately after international reward. In some cases, one should expect marginal behavior to be considerably more antisocial than absolute or total behavior. Nations do not like to be grateful. They do not like to have their policy affected by outside forces and institutions. When it appears that others are using blandishments to influence immediate actions, the nation in question may delight in frustrating their desires. Further, rewards have difficulty governing behavior which is antisocial but not really destructive. The spread of nuclear weapons, as we have seen, is probably destabilizing in the supergame, but it is not the same as the initiation of war. On the other hand, the launching of aggressive war hazards much more than marginal rewards. It places the entire value of the *status quo*, the value of peace, in jeopardy. If the value of peace is high, aggressive war will be less tempting;

if it is low, it will be more tempting. Nations that have little to lose are often willing to risk all they have.

The central problem of the future system of multipolarity is likely to be that the waging of aggressive war under certain circumstances will not result in losing all the values of peace. Because of problems of deterrent credibility, the danger of anonymous attack, and the sheer inadequacy of retaliatory capabilities, *some* nations under some circumstances may be able to attack others, even with nuclear weapons, and get away with it. Thus, in terms of our deterrent paradigm, a nation may not lose all $V_p$ while gaining in $V_{fs}$. Under these circumstances, of course, heightening $V_p$ through reward and reinforcement strategies would not rule out aggressive choices or war.

This condition does not mean that reward is irrelevant; nor does it prove that aggression will be a chronic feature of the future multipolar environment. In the previous bipolar system, deterrent credibility was presumably provided by the *certainty* of punishment if certain aggressive or provocative military actions were taken. If the United States were attacked, if Europe were invaded, an aggressor could presumably count on receiving retaliation. This degree of certainty not only helped to affix penalties on aggression; it also clarified those actions which a state could engage in *without* suffering retaliatory punishment. The maxim appeared to be, "Do $X$ and you will certainly be hit; do not do $X$ and you will certainly not be hit." In the future, as we have seen, the credibility of deterrent punishment—that is, the certainty of retaliatory punishment—will be lower than it has been in the past. But the system of multipolarity will itself be *uncertain*. Once military action is taken, given the existence of five powers and ten possible relationships, an aggressor just cannot know what will happen. His opponent may not retaliate upon him, but someone else might. His nuclear attack upon one power may lead to a series of nuclear attacks by other powers; the position he will finally derive in economic, military, and status terms will be unclear, even opaque. He cannot foresee the consequences of his own action. Therefore he cannot know in advance that his value of peace will remain unchanged, even though it is possible that it will stay the same. Too many other actors exist to deprive him of the favorable payoffs he seeks. The system may be not unlike that of diplomacy in 1876–1878, when the Russians thought simply in terms of humiliating and defeating Turkey. Owing to the intervention of other great powers, however, their gains were pared down at the conference table. After the Congress of Berlin in 1878 the Russians had gained little, and they had expended large reserves of blood and treasure. Nor would the multipolar situation of the future be like that of the 1930s. From Hitler's point of view, the key to the polity of the thirties was *certainty*. He believed he could predict exactly the way Britain and France would respond to his ventures and threats. He was emboldened to press further precisely because he thought that his enemies would not fight. His own certainty (which turned out to be fallacious) made him believe that he could preserve the values of peace while gaining those of military threat and attack. Until 1939, it appeared as if he had calculated correctly.

The multipolar situation of 1980–1990 will be much more uncertain, in this sense, than was the system of the 1930s. There will be a greater number of participant major powers; their capabilities will be far greater. If their weapons are used against an aggressor, his disutilities will be catastrophic. At minimum, aggressors will not be able to calculate that gains can be surely or certainly procured. This does not mean that recourse to the *fait accompli* will not be more characteristic than it has been in recent years. It does not mean that there may not be aggressors which attack and largely gain their objectives. But the *uncertainty* of the future system must give an aggressor pause. He must be willing to calculate that he might lose his status quo values in an attempt to gain first-strike values. Given this possibility the use of reward to build values of peace among multipolar powers will be a significant inhibitory factor in preventing wholesale aggression. Reward and reinforcement may not be significant in a short-run instrumental (*quid pro quo*) sense, but they may be very important as a means of raising the value of the *status quo*. The more one has invested in a particular international system, and the greater the status one enjoys, the less willing one should be to change that status through the use of large-scale violence. It is in this way that reward and reinforcement may become a crucial means of equilibrating the international system and an essential supplement to the role of punishment in world politics.

Reinhard Selten and Reinhard Tietz

# *A Formal Theory of Security Equilibria*

## 1. IRREVERSIBLE GAMES

An *irreversible game*, $G = (X,A,u)$, is defined as follows: (I) The *state set* $X$ is a finite set; the elements $x$ of $X$ are called *states*. (II) The *attainability function* $A$ assigns a subset $A(C,x)$ of $X$ to every pair $(C,x)$ containing a coalition $C$ and a state $x$. (A coalition $C$ is a subset of the set $N$ of the integers $1,\ldots,n$.) The set $A(C,x)$ is called the *attainability set* of $C$ and $x$. The attainability function satisfies the following conditions: (1) $x \notin A(C,x)$ for every pair $(C,x)$. (2) There is one and only one state $o$ which is in no attainability set $A(C,x)$; this state $o$ is called the *initial state*. (3) There is no chain of $m$ pairs $(C^1,x^1),\ldots,(C^m,x^m)$ such that $x^{k+1} \in A(C^k,x^k)$ for $k = 1,\ldots,m - 1$ and $x_1 \in A(C^m,x^m)$; this is true for $m = 2, 3, \ldots$

(III) The *utility vector function* $u$ assigns to every state $x \in X$ a utility vector $u(x) = [u_1(x),\ldots,u_n(x)]$; the utilities $u_i(x)$ are real numbers; the function $u_i$ is called the *utility function of player i*.

It can be seen easily that the models described in Section 2 of Chapter 7 are covered by this definition. In the following we shall use several obvious generalizations of the definitions given in Section 2. Thus, for example, we shall say that $y$ is attainable from $x$ for $C$ if $y$ is in $A(C,x)$. A state $z$ is called a *technical end state* if no $x \in X$ is attainable from $z$. Because of condition (3) for the attainability function $A$—this condition may be called the acyclicity of $A$—there must be always at least one technical end state. If this would not be true, we would be able to construct an infinite series of states $x_1,x_2,\ldots$, such that $x_{k+1}$ is attainable from $x_k$ for $k = 1,2,\ldots$; because of (3) this series cannot contain the same state more than once, which is impossible because $X$ is finite.

The acyclicity of $A$ is very important for our definition of an irreversible game. It is crucial for the development of our theory. In the models of Section 2 of Chapter 7, this acyclicity is caused by the irreversibility of the use of atomic weapons.

The intuitive interpretation of an irreversible game is essentially the same as that of the models of Section 2. At any state $x$, a coalition $C$ may be formed in order to achieve a transition from $x$ to a state $y$ in $A(C,x)$, but agreements which transcend the limited goals of such coalitions are excluded. It is important that the players may always choose to do nothing and that therefore a play might be "absorbed" by a state $x$, which is not a technical end state. The utility functions $u_i$ express the preferences which the players would have for the states $x$ in $X$ if all these states would be equally likely to remain stable once they have been attained.

## 2. DESIRABLE PROPERTIES OF EQUILIBRIUM SECURITY LEVELS

In this section we shall introduce our new solution concept which is based on the concept of "equilibrium security levels."

The term "security level" is sometimes used for certain maximum pay-offs; the value of a coalition in the characteristic function computed according to the method of von Neumann and Morgenstern is a security level of this kind.[1] We shall use the term security level in a somewhat different sense. Our security levels are supposed to have certain equilibrium properties, which justify the term "equilibrium security levels." In the following discussion we shall often drop the word "equilibrium" and simply speak of security levels in situations where we mean equilibrium security levels.

In an irreversible game the players know that eventually a state $z$ must be reached, which will remain unchanged. A play, which begins at the initial state $o$, may pass a number of states $o, x^1, \ldots, x^m$; this sequence of states must stop somewhere, because of the acyclicity of $A$ and the finiteness of $X$. If the sequence does not stop before, it cannot go further than to a technical end state. Let us call the state $x^m$ where the play stops in the sense that it remains unchanged, the *end state* of the play. Of course, the end state of a play need not necessarily be a technical end state.

If player $i$ wants to evaluate his situation at a state $x$, he must look at the end states which eventually might be reached from $x$. If he is interested in a conservative estimate of his chances at $x$ he can try to compute a "security level" $v_i(x)$, which is the minimum utility he can guarantee for himself at the end state of the play if the other players do not act in a way which can be exluded by theoretical considerations. This definition is only an informal one; it has no precise meaning as long as we do not specify which theoretical considerations can be used in order to exclude

[1] John von Neumann, and Oskar Morgenstern, *Theory of Games and Economic Behavior*. 3rd ed. (Princeton, N.J.: Princeton University Press, 1953).

actions that are possible according to the rules of the game. In this respect we are willing to make a strong assumption, which we shall call the "principle of security-level maintenance." In order to apply this principle one has to know the security levels $v_i(x)$. Therefore, the task of computing security levels involves a certain circularity; one has to determine security levels, $v_i(x), \ldots, v_n(x)$ for all states $x \in X$ which are in equilibrium relative to each other. This is the reason for the name "equilibrium security levels."

The principle of security-level maintenance assumes that a player does not want to do anything that would lower his security level. We do not assume that the behavior of the players is a function of the security levels alone, but we do assume that the security levels limit the behavior of the players. This means that the security level has the character of an aspiration level which will not be allowed to decrease if it can be avoided.

Especially if we think of an application to the models of Section 2 of Chapter 7, our assumption about the behavioral consequences of the security level is not unreasonable. If utility differences are a matter of life and death, it seems to be advisable to form a conservative estimate of the situation and to limit the range of possible decisions by this estimate.

It is important to keep in mind that we do not assume a principle of maximization of security levels. In our theory the players do not know exactly what determines the behavior of the other players; they know that nobody would do anything that would lower his security level, but every decision which does not violate this principle must be expected as possible.

We now shall give a formal definition of the principle of security level maintenance:

*Principle of Security-Level Maintenance:* A transition from a state $x = (x_1, \ldots, x_n)$ to a state $y = (y_1, \ldots, y_n)$ is possible if and only if there is a coalition $C$ with $y \in A(C, x)$ and

$$v_i(y) \geq v_i(x)$$

for all $i \in C$.

If a transition from $x$ to $y$ is possible according to the principle of security-level maintenance, we call $x$ *labile* against $y$ and $C$. The state $x$ is called *labile* if according to the principle of security-level maintenance at least one transition from $x$ to a state $y$ is possible. In this connection we use the word "labile" instead of "unstable" because we do not want to imply that a labile state cannot be the end state of a play. If a state is labile, transitions to other states are possible but they do not have to occur.

For an outside observer, all transitions from a state $x$ to a state $y$ against which $x$ is labile must be expected as possible, but player $i$ does not have to consider the same set of possibilities because he can prevent those transitions for which his cooperation is needed. On the other hand, player $i$ cannot assume that he will be able to achieve transitions for which he needs the cooperation of other players. If we want to determine the security levels $v_i(x)$ at a state $x$, we have to take into account these features of the situation.

Let $L_i(x)$ be the set of all states $y$, such that there is a coalition $C$ with $i \notin C$ for which $x$ is labile against $y$ and $C$. We call $L_i(x)$ the *lability set* of player $i$ at $x$. Clearly player $i$ cannot prevent an end state from being reached where he gets the minimum of the $v_i(y)$ for all $y \in L_i(x)$. But if the other players decide not to form a coalition with $i \notin C$, he may not even be able to get this minimum. In this case the minimum utility he can enforce may be determined as follows: Let $A_i(x)$ be the set of all states $y$ with $y \in A((i), x)$ and $v_i(y) \geq u_i(x)$. [Here $(i)$ is the coalition formed by player $i$ alone.] We call $A_i(x)$ the *action set* of player $i$ at $x$.

Define

$$m_i(x) = \begin{cases} u_i(x) & \text{for } A_i(x) = \phi. \\ \max_{y \in A_i(x)} v_i(y) & \text{for } A_i(x) \neq \phi. \end{cases} \qquad (1)$$

Clearly, $m_i(x)$ is the amount which player $i$ can enforce if the other players decide not to form any coalition. Define

$$1_i(x) = \begin{cases} m_i(x) & \text{for } L_i(x) = \phi \\ \min_{y \in L_i(x)} v_i(y) & \text{for } L_i(x) \neq \phi \end{cases} \qquad (2)$$

It is a consequence of our intuitive explanation of the equilibrium-security-level concept and the principle of security-level maintenance that the security levels must have the following equilibrium property:

*Equilibrium property:* For all states $x \in X$ we have

$$v_i(x) = \min [m_i(x), 1_i(x)] \qquad (3)$$

for $i = 1, \ldots, n$.

Player $i$ cannot prevent a transition from $x$ to a state $y \in L_i(x)$. Therefore $v_i(x)$ is not greater than $1_i(x)$. If $m_i(x)$ is smaller than $1_i(x)$, player $i$ can always enforce $m_i(x)$, if the other players do not do him the favor of going to a state $y \in L_i(x)$. He may either stay at $x$ and get $u_i(x)$, or go to a state in $A_i(x)$ and secure the maximum of the $v_i(y)$ over all $y \in A_i(x)$.

A state $x$ for which there is no state $y$ against which $x$ is labile is called stable. Such states are also called *security equilibria*. If a state $x$ is stable, the sets $A_i(x)$ must be empty [$x$ is labile against any $y \in A_i(x)$], and the sets $L_i(x)$ must be empty too. Therefore, for stable states we have $m_i(x) = u_i(x)$ and $v_i(x) = m_i(x)$ because of (1) and (2). Consequently, it follows from the equilibrium property that

$$v_i(x) = u_i(x) \qquad \text{for } i = 1, \dots, n \tag{4}$$

is true for every stable state $x$.

As we shall see, it is always possible to compute a *system of security-level functions*, $v = (v_1, \dots, v_n)$, satisfying our equilibrium property. The security-level functions may not always be uniquely determined by the equilibrium property, but we shall achieve uniqueness by an additional plausible assumption.

### 3. THE COMPUTATIONAL DEFINITION OF EQUILIBRIUM SECURITY LEVELS

Our method for computing equilibrium security levels is more than a computational device. From an intuitive point of view, it is the only sensible method to compute equilibrium security levels; therefore it may be regarded as the definition of the concept of equilibrium security levels.

It is necessary to precede the description of our algorithm with some additional definitions about irreversible games. A *complete* set of states is a subset $Y$ of $X$ with the following property: from a state $y \in Y$ no state $z$ is attainable which is not also in $Y$. A state $x$ is called a *predecessor* of a complete set $Y$ if $x$ is not in $Y$ and if $Y$ contains all states $z$ which are attainable from $x$.[2] Obviously we get a complete set if we add a predecessor of $Y$ to a complete set $Y$.

It can be seen easily that every complete set $Y$ which is not equal to the set $X$ of all states has at least one predecessor. If such a set $Y$ had no predecessor, we could construct a sequence of states $x^1$, $x^2, \dots$ with $x^k \in X - Y$ such that $x^{(k+1)}$ is attainable from $x^k$ for $k = 1, 2, \dots$. But because of the acyclicity of $A$ and the finiteness of $X$ this is not possible.

Our method for computing equilibrium security levels is described by the flowchart in Figure 1. The computation begins at rectangle 1, where an arbitrary technical end state $y$ is selected, and $Y$ is determined as the set which contains $y$ as its only element. Every technical end state is stable because no state is attainable from a technical end state. Therefore, according to the equilibrium property (3), the security levels of $y$ are $v_i(y) = u_i(y)$. In rectangle 2 these values are given to the security levels of $y$.

In hexagon 3 the question is asked whether $Y$ is equal to the state set $X$. If the answer is "no," an arbitrary predecessor $x$ of $Y$ is selected in

---

[2] Note that a technical end state is a predecessor of *any* complete set not containing that technical end state.

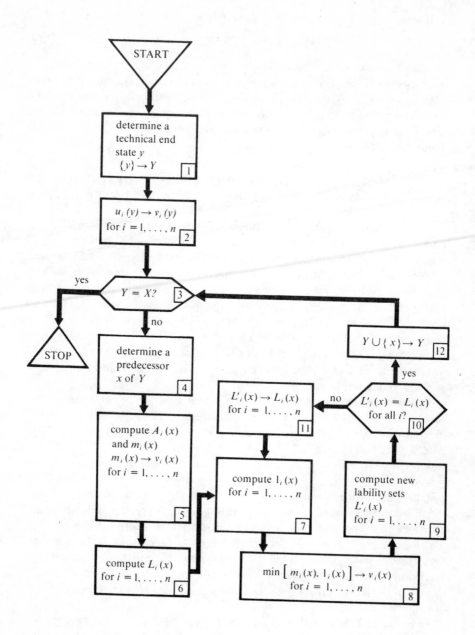

rectangle 4. In the course of the computation, $Y$ will always be a complete set (this is trivial in the beginning). A predecessor can always be found as long as we do not have $Y = X$.

In rectangle 5 an iterative subprocess begins which determines the security levels of $x$. This is done in a way which secures that the equilibrium property (3) is satisfied. The formulas (1), (2), (3) can be regarded as simultaneous equations for the $v_1(x), \ldots, v_n(x)$. All states $y$ which are attainable from $x$ must be in $Y$ because of the completeness of $Y$. In the course of the computation, $Y$ is always the set of those states whose equilibrium security levels have already been computed. (As soon as the equilibrium security levels have been determined for a state $x$, this state is added to $Y$ in rectangle 12.) Therefore, with the exception of $v_1(x), \ldots,$ $v_n(x)$, all security levels which occur in formulas (1), (2), and (3) are known when the computation of the $v_1(x), \ldots, v_n(x)$ begins. But the right side of (2) nevertheless depends on the unknown variables $v_1(x), \ldots, v_n(x)$, because the security levels of $x$ occur in the definition of the sets $L_i(x)$.

The simultaneous equations (1), (2) and (3) are solved by an iterative method. In order to compute the $A_i(x)$ and the $m_i(x)$ we do not have to know the $v_i(x)$, but in order to compute the $L_i(x)$ and the $l_i(x)$ directly we would have to know the $v_i(x)$. Our iterative method begins in rectangle 5 where the $A_i(x)$ and the $m_i(x)$ are computed and the initial values $m_i(x)$ are given to the $v_i(x)$. Then in rectangle 6 preliminary lability sets $L_i(x)$ are determined on the basis of the assumption $v_i(x) = m_i(x)$. In rectangle 7 the preliminary sets $L_i(x)$ are used for the computation of preliminary $l_i(x)$ and in rectangle 8 new preliminary security levels $v_i(x)$ are determined.

The new $v_i(x)$ are the basis of the computation of new preliminary lability sets $L_i'(x)$ in rectangle 9. The new $v_i(x)$ are not greater than the initial values $m_i(x)$. Therefore it follows from the definition of the lability sets that we must have $L_i'(x) \supseteq L_i(x)$ for $i = 1, \ldots, n$. In hexagon 10 the question is asked: Do we have $L_i'(x) = L_i(x)$ for $i = 1, \ldots, n$? If we do, the values for the $v_i(x)$, computed in rectangle 8, satisfy the equilibrium property (3), and the computation of equilibrium security levels for $x$ is finished. If at least one of the $L_i'(x)$ contains more states than the corresponding $L_i(x)$, a new cycle of the iterative process begins in rectangle 11, where the $L_i(x)$ are redefined; the new $L_i(x)$ are the old $L_i'(x)$. In rectangle 7 new $l_i(x)$ are computed from the new $L_i(x)$. The cycle is repeated until we have $L_i'(x) = L_i(x)$ for $i = 1, \ldots, n$. Then a new set $Y$ is formed in rectangle 12 by adding $x$ to the old set $Y$. As $x$ is a predecessor of the old $Y$, the new set $Y$ is a complete set too.

It can be shown easily that the iterative process for the computation of the $v_i(x)$ must stop after a finite number of cycles. As we have seen, we have $L_i'(x) \supseteq L_i(x)$ for the $L_i'(x)$ computed in the first cycle. The same must be true for all other cycles too, because $l_i(x)$ and $v_i(x)$ cannot become greater if $L_i(x)$ has been enlarged by the preceding cycle, and the $L_i(x)$ cannot lose states if some or all of the $v_i(x)$ have become smaller. As long as the iteration does not stop, at least one of the $L_i(x)$ must grow with every new cycle. As there are only a finite number of states, the iteration must stop after a finite number of cycles.

The whole computational process stops when we have $Y = X$, which means that the $v_i(x)$ have been computed for all $x \in X$.

It can be shown that the result of the computation does not depend on the selection of the initial technical end state $y$ and on the sequence in which predecessors are added to $Y$. In order to see this, we assume that $v = (v_1, \ldots, v_n)$ and $v' = (v_1', \ldots, v_n')$ are two different systems of equilibrium security level functions which are both computed by the method described by the flow chart in Figure 1. Let $x^1$ be a point with $v'(x^1) \neq v(x^1)$. The complete sets to which $x^1$ is added after the computation of $v(x^1)$ and $v'(x^1)$ may be different from each other, but both of them must contain all those states which are attainable from $x^1$. Obviously, among these states there must be at least one state $x^2$, for which we have $v(x^2) \neq v'(x^2)$, because otherwise we could not compute different security-level vectors $v(x^1)$ and $v'(x^1)$ by our method. In the same way it follows that from $x^2$ a state $x^3$ with $v(x^3) \neq v'(x^3)$ must be attainable; we could construct an infinite sequence $x^1, x^2, x^3, \ldots$ with $v(x^k) \neq v'(x^k)$ for $k = 1, 2, 3, \ldots$, such that $x^{k+1}$ is attainable from $x^k$. But because of the acyclicity of $A$ and the finiteness of $X$, this is not possible. Therefore by our method only one system $v = (v_1, \ldots, v_n)$ of equilibrium-security-level functions can be computed. Of course, this does not exclude the possibility that other such systems which also satisfy the equilibrium property (3) can be computed by other methods.

## 4. A MAXIMUM PROPERTY

It can be shown by a simple example, that the system of security-level functions computed by the method in the preceding section is not always the only one satisfying the equilibrium property (3). Our example is an extremely simple case of the models in Section 2, Chapter 7. There are only 2 countries—country 1 and country 2. Each of both countries has 1 bomb $(b_1 = b_2 = 1)$. Both countries are assumed to have the indifference utility function (see Section 1, above).

Table 1 contains the four states of this model together with the utility vectors $u(x) = [u_1(x), u_2(x)]$ and the security levels computed by the method in the preceding section. An additional column contains "alternative security levels," which also satisfy the equilibrium property (3).

TABLE 1. A SIMPLE EXAMPLE FOR ALTERNATIVE SECURITY
LEVELS LACKING THE MAXIMUM PROPERTY

| States | Utility Vectors | Security Levels | Alternative Security Levels |
|--------|-----------------|-----------------|-----------------------------|
| (0,0) | (3,3) | (3,3) | (2,2) |
| (0,1) | (3,1) | (2,2) | (2,2) |
| (2,0) | (1,3) | (2,2) | (2,2) |
| (2,1) | (2,2) | (2,2) | (2,2) |

In Table 1, the state (2,1) is a technical end state; for this state, the security levels must be equal to the utilities. The state (2,1) is in the action sets $A_1((2,0))$ and $A_2((0,1))$. Therefore, the states (2,0) and (0,1) are labile against (2,1). According to the formulas (1), (2), and (3), the security-level vector for the states (2,0) and (0,1) must be (2,2). But for the state (0,0) these formulas do not determine unique security levels. If security levels are computed by the method described in the preceding section, we get (3,3) for the state (0,0); but the vector (2,2) would also satisfy the equilibrium property.

If both players have the security level 3 for the initial state (0,0), then (0,0) is stable. If the security levels for (0,0) are (2,2), then (0,0) is labile against the states (0,1) and (2,0). It seems to be intuitively clear that it is more adequate to regard (0,0) as stable. Our example describes a very simple deterrence situation. If deterrence is believed to work anywhere, it should work here. The security-level vector (2,2) for (0,0) would correspond to a situation in which each country expects that the other country will not be deterred, and that therefore nothing is to be lost by attacking first. But if each of both countries expects the principle of deterrence to work, it will indeed work and the adequate security level for (0,0) will be 3 for both players.

The two countries of our example must coordinate their expectations. The situation is similar to that of a noncooperative game with several equilibrium points. If among several equilibrium points there is exactly one which is "dominant," in the sense that for all players the pay-off at this equilibrium point is not smaller than the pay-off at each of the other equilibrium points, the vector of all players' expectations at this dominant equilibrium point is the obvious rational solution.[3] A similar principle may also be applied to our example where (3,3) is better for both players than (2,2).

[3]This is true if the game is in normal form. For games in extensive form we must distinguish between "perfect" and "nonperfect" equilibrium points; a perfect equilibrium point is an equilibrium point which induces equilibrium points on every subgame. Only perfect equilibrium points can be regarded as strictly noncooperative solutions for extensive games. See Reinhard Selten, "Spieltheoretische Behandlung eines Oligopolmodells mit Nachfrageträgheit—Teil I" *Zeitschrift für die gesamte Staatswissenschaft*, 121 (1965), pp. 301–324.

It is not always possible to find a dominant equilibrium point in a non-cooperative game with several equilibrium points. Fortunately, the situation is more favorable in the case of equilibrium security levels. We can prove the following theorem:

*Theorem:* Let $G = (X,A,u)$ be an irreversible game and let $v = (v_1, \ldots, v_n)$ be the system of security-level functions computed for this game by the method in Section 3. For any other system of security-level functions $v' = (v'_1, \ldots, v'_n)$ for $G$, which also satisfies the equilibrium property (3), the following is true: If $Y$ is a complete set of states for $G$, such that $v(y) = v'(y)$ for every $y \in Y$, and if $x$ is a predecessor of $Y$, then we have

$$v_i(x) \geq v'_i(x) \qquad \text{for } i = 1, \ldots, n. \tag{5}$$

*Proof:* Let $L_i^{(1)}(x)$ be player $i$'s preliminary lability sets computed on the basis of the assumption $v_i(x) = m_i(x)$ in rectangle 6 of the flow chart in Figure 1. Let $L_i^v(x)$ be player $i$'s lability set relative to the system $v' = (v'_1, \ldots, v'_n)$. All states $y$ which are attainable from $x$ are elements of $Y$; for these states we have $v(y) = v'(y)$. Because of (3) the inequality $v'_i(x) \leq m_i(x)$ holds for $i = 1, \ldots, n$. Consequently each of the $L_i^{(1)}(x)$ must be a subset of the corresponding $L_i^v(x)$. This follows from the definition of the lability sets.

The $l_i^{(1)}(x)$ computed from the $L_i^{(1)}(x)$ in rectangle 7 cannot be smaller than the $l_i^v(x)$ which result from the application of the definition of $l_i(x)$ to the $L_i^v(x)$. From the $l_i^{(1)}(x)$ and the $m_i(x)$ "first-cycle approximations" $v_i^{(1)}(x)$ to the $v_i(x)$ are computed in rectangle 8. Because of $l_i^{(1)}(x) \geq l_i^v(x)$ we must have $v_i^{(1)}(x) \geq v'_i(x)$.

Consider a case where the computation of $v(x)$ does not stop before it reaches the $k$th cycle. For such cases let $v_i^{(k)}(x)$ be the approximation to $v_i(x)$ computed in the $k$th cycle. In order to prove the theorem it is sufficient to show that $v_i^{(k)}(x) \geq v'_i(x)$ is always true. We know that this inequality holds for $k = 1$. If the inequality is true for $k$, and if the iteration does not stop before the $(k + 1)$th cycle, the inequality is true also with $k + 1$ instead of $k$. This can be shown as follows: From the $v_i^{(k)}(x)$ new preliminary lability sets are computed in rectangle 9; let us call these sets $L_i^{(k+1)}(x)$. From the $L_i^{(k+1)}(x)$ new approximations to the $l_i(x)$ are computed in rectangle 7; let us call these approximations $l_i^{(k+1)}(x)$. Because of $v_i^{(k)}(x) \geq v'_i(x)$, the $L_i^{(k+1)}$ must be subsets of the corresponding $L_i^v(x)$. Therefore we must have $l_i^{(k+1)}(x) \geq l_i^v(x)$, which implies $v_i^{(k+1)}(x) \geq v'_i(x)$. This completes the proof.

The theorem which has just been proved justifies our point of view—that equilibrium security levels should be computed according to the method of Section 3. Therefore we shall use the name "equilibrium security levels" only for the security levels defined in this way.

The property of the equilibrium security levels which is expressed by the theorem will be called the *maximum property*. We think that the maximum property is a desirable property. If for a state $x$ there are several security-level vectors satisfying the equilibrium property relative to given security-level vectors for the states attainable from $x$, the players must coordinate their expectations at one of these vectors. Because of the theorem, among these vectors they will always find one which for all of them contains security levels at least as high as each of the other vectors. This vector seems to be the natural focus point for the coordination of the players' expectations because they are interested in high security levels. They do not necessarily want to maximize their security levels, but they will try to maintain a security level once it has been reached. In this sense, their behavior is oriented towards higher security levels.

The equilibrium property and the maximum property taken together uniquely determine the equilibrium security levels. This is an immediate consequence of the theorem.

## 5. SOME ADDITIONAL ASPECTS OF THE THEORY

Let $G = (X, A, u)$ be an irreversible game. After the equilibrium-security-level vectors $v(x) = [v_1(x), \ldots, v_n(x)]$ have been computed for all states $x \in X$, it is easy to determine which states are stable and which states are labile against other states. As we have already seen, there must always be at least one stable state, because every technical end state is stable.

If we look at the example of Table 1, we see that the stable state $(2, 1)$ will never be reached from the initial state $(0, 0)$ because $(0, 0)$ itself is stable. This shows that not all stable states are equally important. Therefore we have to introduce some further definitions in order to complete our theory.

Let $x^1, \ldots, x^k$ be a sequence of states, such that $x^j$ is labile against $x^{j+1}$ for $j = 1, \ldots, k - 1$. We shall call such a sequence a *lability chain* from $x^1$ to $x^k$. A state $x$ which is not the initial state $o$ is called *rationally expectable* if there is at least one lability chain from $o$ to $x$. The initial state $o$ is also called *rationally expectable*.

The rationally expectable states are those which can be reached without violation of the principle of security-level maintenance. If the initial state $o$ is stable, then $o$ is the only rationally expectable state. We call an irreversible game $G = (X, A, u)$ *stable* if the initial state of $G$ is stable. If $G$ is not stable, $G$ is called *labile*.

Let $R$ be the set of all rationally expectable states for an irreversible game $G$. If $G = (X, A, u)$ is labile, it still makes a difference whether $R$ is a relatively small or a relatively large subset of $X$. The number of states in $R$ divided by the number of states in $X$ might be regarded as a measure of the degree of lability.

For the models of Section 2 in Chapter 7 we can define a more interesting measure of the degree of lability. This measure is the average number of destroyed countries at rationally expectable stable states.

Stable states which are not rationally expectable may still be of some interest. If there is some small probability that one player or a group of players will act irrationally in the sense of a deviation from the principle of security-level maintenance, then it is important to know which stable states may be rationally reached after an irrational action. The possibility of irrational actions has often been used as an argument against the proliferation of atomic weapons. Therefore it is important that the consequences of irrational actions can be investigated within the framework of our theory.

We call a sequence of states $x^1, \ldots, x^k$ an *attainability chain* from $x^1$ to $x^k$, if $x^{j+1}$ is attainable from $x^j$ for $j = 1, \ldots, k - 1$. Let $w$ be a state in state set $X$ of $G = (X, A, u)$ and let $Y$ be the set which has $w$ and all those states $y$ as elements for which an attainability chain from $w$ to $y$ exists. If we restrict the regions on which the functions $A$ and $u$ are defined to the states in $Y$, we get the *restricted attainability function* $A'$ and the *restricted utility-vector function* $u'$. The set $Y$ and the functions $A'$ and $u'$ are the constituents of the *subgame* $G_w = (Y, A', u')$ of $G$ at the state $w$.

This definition of a subgame is analogous to the definition of subgames of games in extensive form. Extensive forms may have vertices at which there is no subgame, but there is a subgame at every state of an irreversible game. In this respect irreversible games are similar to extensive forms with perfect information.

Our original explanation of the concept of equilibrium security levels (given at the beginning of Section 2) may be reformulated as follows: *The equilibrium security level* $v_i(x)$ *is the highest minimum utility which player* i *can guarantee for himself at the end state of a play in the subgame at* x, *if the other players do not violate the principle of security-level maintenance.* We shall show that this proposition is correct.

As we have said in section 2, the fact that a state $x$ is labile does not mean that this state $x$ cannot be an end state of a play. Every rationally expectable state may be the end state of a play which does not violate the principle of security-level maintenance. This is important for the interpretation of the above proposition.

In order to give the proposition a more precise meaning we must introduce some further definitions. Let us first define a function $p_i$ which assigns to every state $x$ a state $y = p_i(x)$; for $m_i(x) = u_i(x)$ the state $p_i(x)$ is the state $x$ itself; for $m_i(x) > u_i(x)$ let $p_i(x)$ be an arbitrary fixed state $y \in A_i(x)$ with $v_i(y) = m_i(x)$. We call $p_i$ the *maximizing strategy* for player $i$. The intuitive idea behind this definition is the following: $p_i$ describes a strategy for player $i$ which tells him what he will do at a state $x$ if the other players do not achieve a transition to another state before he has a chance to act. If $x = p_i(x)$, he will do nothing; if $p_i(x)$ is different from $x$, he will go to $y = p_i(x)$.

Similarly, we define a function $q_i$, which we call a *minimizing strategy* of the other players. $q_i$ assigns $x = q_i(x)$ to $x$ for $L_i(x) = \emptyset$ or $m_i(x) < l_i(x)$. For $L_i(x) \neq \emptyset$ and $l_i(x) \leq m_i(x)$, the function $q_i$ assigns a state $y = q_i(x)$ with $y \in L_i(x)$ and $v_i(y) = l_i(x)$ to $x$. This may be interpreted as a strategy which tells the other players what they will do if they can act before player $i$ has a chance to do something.

We shall say that a state $x$ is *i-maxlabile* against a state $y$ if $y \in L_i(x)$ or $y = p_i(x)$ with $y \neq x$ is true. A state is called *i-minlabile* against a state $y$ if either (a) or (b) is true: (a) $y \neq x$ and $y = q_i(x)$. (b) $x = q_i(x)$ and $y$ is a state which is attainable from $x$ for player $i$ alone. A sequence $x^1, \ldots, x^k$ is an *i-maxlability chain*, if $x^j$ is *i*-maxlabile against $x^{j+1}$ for $j = 1, \ldots, k - 1$. Similarly an *i-minlability chain* is a sequence $x^1, \ldots, x^k$ where $x^j$ is *i*-minlabile against $x^{j+1}$ for $j = 1, \ldots, k - 1$.

Let $R_i(x)$ be the set of all states $y$ with the following two properties: (1) $y = x$, or an *i*-maxlability chain from $x$ to $y$ exists. (2) $y = p_i(y)$. Intuitively, the set $R_i(x)$ is the set of all possible end states for plays which have reached $x$ if player $i$ uses the maximizing strategy and the other players follow the principle of security-level maintenance.

Let $S_i(x)$ be the set of all states $y$ with the following two properties: (1) $y = x$, or an *i*-minlability chain from $x$ to $y$ exists. (2) $y = q_i(y)$. Intuitively, $S_i(x)$ is the set of all possible end states for a play which has reached $x$ if the minimizing strategy is used against player $i$; here it is not assumed that player $i$ follows the principle of security-level maintenance, but the minimizing strategy remains within the limits drawn by this principle.

It can be shown that the following two inequalities are satisfied:

$$v_i(x) \leq \min_{y \in R_i(x)} u_i(y); \tag{6}$$

$$v_i(x) \geq \max_{y \in S_i(x)} u_i(y). \tag{7}$$

This means that player $i$ can at $x$ guarantee at least $v_i(x)$ by using the maximizing strategy; but because of (7) he cannot guarantee more since he cannot prevent the use of the minimizing strategy by the other players. With (6) and (7) we now have a more precise formulation of the proposition stated above.

Let us first prove (6). Clearly, we have $v_i(y) > v_i(x)$ if $x$ is $i$-maxlabile against $y$, because for $y \in L_i(x)$ the inequality $v_i(y) \geq l_i(x)$ holds, and for $y = p_i(x)$ we have $v_i(y) = m_i(y) \geq v_i(x)$. It follows from the property (1) of the states in $R_i(x)$ that $v_i(y) \geq v_i(x)$ is true for every $y \in R_i(x)$. Because of property (2) we have $u_i(y) = m_i(y) \geq v_i(y)$ and therefore $u_i(y) \geq v_i(x)$ for every $y \in R_i(x)$. This yields (6).

Inequality (7) can be proved in a similar way. If $x$ is $i$-minlabile against $y$, then we have $v_i(y) \leq v_i(x)$, because $v_i(y)$ is equal to $l_i(y)$ for $L_i(x) \neq \emptyset$ and $l_i(x) \leq m_i(x)$ and because $v_i(y)$ cannot be greater than $m_i(x)$ for $x = q_i(x)$. Therefore we have $v_i(y) \leq v_i(x)$ for every state $y \in S_i(x)$. Because of property (2) of the states in $S_i(x)$, the security level $v_i(y)$ of a state $y \in S_i(x)$ must be equal to $m_i(y)$, which means that $v_i(y) \geq u_i(y)$ is true. Consequently we have $u_i(x) \leq v_i(x)$ for every $y \in S_i(x)$. This yields (7).

In the next section we shall use the inequalities (6) and (7), in order to prove some interesting results about the deterrence models discussed in Section 2 of Chapter 7.

Another aspect of our theory which we would like to make clear concerns the interpretation of the utility functions. Consider a very simple case of the model in Chapter 7, Section 2, where there are only 2 countries, named 1 and 2, which both have the indifference utility function. Country 1 has one bomb ($b_1 = 1$) and Country 2 has no bomb ($b_2 = 0$). There are only two states, the initial state $(0, 0)$ and a technical end state $(0, 1)$. Country 1 is indifferent between the states $(0, 0)$ and $(0, 1)$, but nevertheless $(0, 0)$ is labile against $(0, 1)$. The objection might be raised that $(0, 0)$ should be regarded as stable because Country 1 has no reason to use its bomb. Our answer to this objection is the following: Country 1 has no reason to use its bomb, but this does not mean that it has a reason not to use its bomb. Country 1 is indifferent between the states $(0, 0)$ and $(0, 1)$. It is inherent in the concept of indifference that a subject who is indifferent between two alternatives might choose one or the other. If Country 1 is really indifferent between the states $(0, 0)$ and $(0, 1)$ it cannot be predicted whether or not it will use its bomb.

## 6. A THEOREM ON THE DETERRENCE MODELS PRESENTED IN CHAPTER 7, SECTION 2

It is not always necessary to compute the equilibrium security levels of all states in order to decide whether a deterrence model is stable or not.

Many cases can be easily solved with the help of a theorem which we shall prove in this section.

Consider an irreversible game $G = (X, A, u)$ which is derived from a model in the class of models described in Chapter 7, Section 2. In the following we shall use the short name *deterrence games* for such games. Let $b_i(x)$ be the number of bombs which are still in the possession of player $i$ at state $x$. [Formally $b_i(x)$ is $b_i$ minus the number of components in $x$ which are equal to $i$.] Let $X'$ be the set of all states $x \in X$ with the property that for $i = 1, \ldots, n$ country $i$'s component $x_i$ satisfies $x_i = 0$ if $b_i(x) > 0$. The countries which have bombs are undestroyed at every state $x \in X'$. We call $X'$ the *reduced state set*. If we restrict the regions on which the functions $A$ and $u$ are defined to the states in $X'$, we get the attainability function $A'$ and the utility function $u'$ for the reduced set. We call $G' = (X', A', u')$ the *reduced game* of $G$. The reduced game generally has a smaller number of states than the original one but the attainability relations and the utilities for the states $x \in X'$ are the same in both games.

The reduced game may not always be an irreversible game in the sense of the definition in Section 1 of this appendix, because it may contain more than one "initial state" which is not attainable from any other state. In this case $G'$ is decomposible into several irreversible games.

The following theorem makes it possible to solve the reduced games instead of the original games; this is a considerable computational advantage.

*Theorem:* Let $G = (X, A, u)$ be a deterrence game where the utility functions $u_1, \ldots, u_n$ of all players satisfy the conditions (a) and (b) of Appendix Section 2 (motive of self-preservation and motive of retaliation). Let $G' = (X', A', u')$ be the reduced game of $G$. Then the following is true: (1) A state $x$ is rationally expectable in $G$ if and only if it is rationally expectable in $G'$. (2) The equilibrium security levels for the states in $X'$ are the same in $G'$ and $G$.

*Proof:* Let $x$ be a state in $X'$ and let $y$ be a state in $X - X'$. Assume that $y$ is attainable from $x$ for a coalition $C$. Let $T$ be the set of all players $i$ with $b_i(x) > 0$. The coalition $C$ must contain players who are in $T$, because otherwise no state would be attainable for $C$. The action of $C$ which achieves $y$ must involve the use of bombs by members of $C$, which are in $T$ against countries in $T$ which are not in $C$. This follows from the definition of $X'$. Therefore $T$ contains at least one pair of two players $j$ and $k$ with $j \in C$, $k \in N - C$ and $y_k = j$. Because of $j \in C$ we have $y_j = 0$; members of the same coalition do not destroy each other.

Let $\bar{u}_i$ be the maximum utility which country $i$ can have for a state $w = (w_1, \ldots, w_n)$ with $w_i \neq 0$. We shall prove that $v_j(y) \leq \bar{u}_j$ is true for the player $j$ whose existence was demonstrated above.

At the state $y$ country $k$ can use its bomb in order to destroy country $j$. If this is done a new state $z$ is reached which differs from $y$ only in the $j$th component which is $z_j = k$. For all states $w$ in $S_k(z)$ [for definition of $R_i(x)$ and $S_i(x)$ see Section 5 above] we must have $u_k(w) > u_k(y)$ because of the motive of retaliation. It follows from inequality (7) that $v_k(z) > u_k(y)$. Therefore $z$ is in $A_k(y)$. Let $z'$ be a state in $A_k(y)$ with $m_k(y) = v_k(z')$. Obviously we must have $z'_j = k$ for the $j$th component of $z'$ because of the motive of retaliation. $z'$ is in $L_j(y)$ and therefore $y$ is $j$-maxlabile against $z'$. It follows from inequality (6) that $v_j(y) \leqq u_j(z')$. $z'_j = k$ has the consequence $u_j(z') \leqq \bar{u}_j$. Therefore we have $v_j(y) \leqq \bar{u}_j$.

Let us now look at the iterative determination of $v(x)$. The computation of preliminary lability sets in rectangle 6 of Figure 1 above is based on the assumption of $v_i(x) = m_i(x)$. It follows from $x \in X'$ and from assumption (a) of Appendix Section 1 that we have $u_i(x) > \bar{u}_i$ for all $i \in T$. If a state $y$ is attainable from $x$ for a coalition $C$, then, as we have seen, $C$ contains a player $j \in T$ with $v_j(y) \leqq \bar{u}_j$. For this player $j$, $v_j(y) < u_i(x)$ and therefore $v_j(y) < m_j(x)$ is true. It follows that neither the action sets $A_i(x)$, nor the preliminary lability sets computed in rectangle 6, contain any states which are in $X - X'$.

If $x$ is a technical end state in $G' = (X', A', u')$, this means that $v(x) = u(x)$, and thus that $x$ is stable because only states in $X - X'$ are attainable from $x$. We shall use this fact in order to prove that $v_i(x) > \bar{u}_i$ for all $i \in T$ is true for every $x \in X'$. Let $x^1, x^2, \ldots x^r$ be the states in $X'$ and assume that they are numbered in such a way that $x^1, \ldots, x^k$ is a complete set in $G'$. It is always possible to number the states in $X'$ this way; one has to begin with a technical end state $x^1$ and give the number $k$ to a predecessor of the set containing the states $x^1, \ldots, x^{k-1}$. As we have seen, $v_i(x^1) = u(x^1)$ is true because $x^1$ is a technical end state in $G'$. For $x \in X'$ we always have $u_i(x) > \bar{u}_i$ for $i \in T$; this follows from $x_i = 0$ and assumption (a) of Appendix Section 1. Therefore $v_i(x^1) > \bar{u}_i$ for all $i \in T$.

Assume that $v_i(x^s)$ for all $i \in T$ and for $s = 1, \ldots, k - 1$. Consider the iterative determination of $v(x^s)$. The action sets and the preliminary lability sets computed in rectangle 6 do not contain states in $X - X'$. Therefore, every state $w$ in these sets satisfies $v_i(w) > \bar{u}_i$ for all $i \in T$. Consequently the first-cycle approximations for $v_i(x^s)$ computed in rectangle 8 are greater than $\bar{u}_i$ for $i \in T$. The preliminary lability sets computed on the basis of these approximations also cannot contain states from $X - X'$. Therefore, if second-cycle approximations are determined for $v_i(x^s)$, they will also be greater than $\bar{u}_i$ for $i \in T$. The same arguments apply to the third-cycle approximations, and so on. Hence we have $v_i(x^s) > \bar{u}_i$ for all $i \in T$. Consequently $v_i(x) > \bar{u}_i$ for all $i \in T$, and for all $x \in X'$.

From $v_i(x) > \bar{u}_i$ for $i \in T$ and $x \in X'$ it follows that a state $x \in X'$ cannot be labile against a state $y \in X - X'$. A coalition $C$ for which $y$ is attainable from $x$ must have a member $j$ with $v_j(y) < \bar{u}_j$. Therefore the lability sets and the action sets for a state $x \in X'$ are the same in $G$ and $G'$. In both games the equilibrium security levels can be computed in the same way, beginning with a technical end state and augmenting each new complete set in $G'$ by a predecessor. It follows that statement (2) of the theorem is true. Statement (1) is also true, because a lability chain beginning at $o$ must obviously remain in $X'$. This completes the proof.

The theorem has an obvious intuitive interpretation: The possession of at least one bomb protects against attacks. A country does not have to have more than one bomb in order to deter all potential attackers.

The theorem has an interesting consequence. If $G = (X, A, u)$ is a deterrence game satisfying the conditions of the theorem, then the following corollary is true:

*Corollary:* If $b_i > 0$ for $i = 1, \ldots n$, then the game is stable.

In the case of the corollary no state in $X'$ is attainable from $o$. This means that $o$ must be stable.

## 7. ADDITIONAL REMARKS ON THE DETERRENCE MODELS PRESENTED IN CHAPTER 7, SECTION 2

The corollary of the last section was important for the discussion of the sources of stability in Section 5 of Chapter 7. The following remark concerns another result mentioned there.

*Remark* (stability by good will): A deterrence game is stable if every country has the good-will utility function. This can be proved as follows: If every country has the good-will utility function, then $u_i(o) > u_i(x)$ for all $x \neq o$ and for $i = 1, \ldots, n$. Therefore it follows from inequality (6) that $v_i(x)$ is smaller than $u_i(o)$ for all $x \neq o$. Consequently $o$ is stable.

Generally it is easy to give intuitive explanations for our results once they have been computed, but without computation or proof one can never know whether an intuitive argument is correct. In order to illustrate this, we may look at some examples. In these examples we shall always assume that all players have the indifference utility function; therefore we can simply speak of the game $b = (b_1, \ldots, b_n)$ if $b_i$ is the initial stockpile of player $i$.

As we have seen in Chapter 7 Section 4, the game $(0, 1, 1)$ is stable because of the scarcity of bombs. Now let us look at the game $(0, 1, 1, 1)$. Surprisingly, this game is labile. One of players 2, 3, and 4 can attack player 1, whereby a stable state is reached; those two players who still have bombs deter each other. Now consider the game $(0, 0, 1, 1)$. This game is labile, because players 3 and 4 can form a coalition in order to destroy countries 1 and 2, whereby a technical end state is reached. The game $(0, 0, 1, 1, 1)$ is stable. If a coalition formed in order to attack one or two of the countries which do not have bombs, the attacker or attackers would become defenseless against a possible attack by a player who still has a bomb. (Five-country examples can still be computed within a reasonable time, if the total number of bombs is low.) The game $(0, 1, 1, 1, 1)$ is also stable because of similar reasons, but the game $(0, 0, 0, 1, 1)$ is labile.

# *Additional Readings*

Aron, Raymond. *Peace and War*. Garden City, N.Y.: Doubleday, 1966. The author presents an exceedingly rich and varied examination of the principles and methods of peace, including the role of polarity, militarism, ideology, population, and economic development. Fundamentally, he concludes that only the maintenance of the deterrent balance and a resolute willingness to keep abreast of the enemy in every sphere of operations can assure peace.

Adelson, Alan M. "Please Don't Steal the Atomic Bomb." *Esquire*, Vol. 71, (May, 1969), pp. 130–133, 144. A quite pessimistic account of the difficulties in keeping control over fissionable materials within states, as criminal or secessionist elements try to acquire atomic bombs for their own purposes.

Bader, William B. *The United States and the Spread of Nuclear Weapons*. New York: Pegasus, 1968. A basic account of American reasoning on the proliferation problem and the pros and cons of a Non-Proliferation Treaty (NPT) with special reference to specific "*n*th" countries.

Baldwin, Hanson W. "If Sixteen Countries Had the Bomb." *The New York Times Magazine*, February 12, 1961, p. 74. After reviewing the psychological, political, and military effects of nuclear dispersion, the author concludes that the danger of catalytic war has been exaggerated, though the possibilities of accident or escalation are increased.

Barnaby, C. F., ed. Preventing the Spread of Nuclear Weapons. London: Souvenir Press, 1969. A collection of articles prepared for a Pugwash panel on the prospects for the NPT, as well as on the difficulties inherent in controlling or living with proliferation whether or not the treaty is accepted.

Beaton, Leonard. *Must the Bomb Spread?* Hammondsworth, England: Penguin, 1966. A full account of the technological and political prospects for the spread of fissionable materials and the bombs into which they can be assembled.

Boulding, K. E. *Conflict and Defense*. New York: Harper, 1962. An essay on the theory of viability of states, given different geographic and military-technological conditions. Fundamentally it hypothesizes that strength varies inversely with distance and concludes that the three determinants of viability are: (1) home-base strength, (2) distance between national competitors, and (3) the rate of decline of strength with distance. He considers that modern weapons, given low rates of decline, make the problem of unconditional viability much more difficult.

Bozeman, Adda B. *The Future of Law in a Multicultural World*. Princeton, N.J.:

Princeton University Press, 1971. The author concludes that personal and familial orientations in the less developed countries will continue to prevent common agreement upon international legal standards and their application. Communist states, whose approach to law is on class bases, cannot accept legal restraints. In the West, respect for law within society is declining. For all these reasons legal approaches to international order are likely to be less successful in the future.

Brennan, Donald G. "The Risks of Spreading Weapons: A Historical Case." *Arms Control and Disarmament*, Vol. 1 (1968), pp. 59–60. An account of historical examples where the existence of nuclear weapons in a national arsenal was exploited in a "civil war" situation.

Brody, Richard A. "Some Systemic Effects of the Spread of Nuclear Weapons Technology: A Study through Simulation of a Multi-Nuclear Future." *The Journal of Conflict Resolution*, Vol. 7 (1963), pp. 663–753. This is the first work to utilize recent internation simulation techniques to study the possible effects of nuclear diffusion. This study used 357 Chicago high-school students, who simulated national decision makers. Beginning with a postulated two nuclear powers in a tight bipolar system, the study concludes that the diffusion of nuclear weapons has the effect of fragmenting this bipolarity and reducing the cohesion of each bloc. In addition, each bloc feels external threat reduced, international threat increased.

Burns, Arthur Lee. "From Balance to Deterrence: A Theoretical Analysis." *World Politics*, Vol. 9 (July 1957), pp. 494–529. A world comprised of many globally deterrent powers (that is, wide proliferation of sophisticated nuclear forces will not be unstable, as long as sudden technological innovations are precluded). It is assumed that the presently deterrent powers realize the futility of global war and act accordingly (that is, the "balance of terror" effectively precludes major war), and that future deterrent powers will find themselves in the same situation.

Cockcroft, Sir John D. "The Perils of Nuclear Proliferation." In Nigel Calder, ed., *Unless Peace Comes: A Scientific Forecast of New Weapons*. New York: Viking Press, 1968, pp. 30–42. An increase in the number of countries possessing nuclear arsenals is dangerous for it would substantially enlarge the risk of global nuclear war. Smaller countries armed with nuclear weapons might not develop the sophisticated command-and-control systems needed to minimize the danger of accidental war and might be tempted to use them irresponsibly.

Coffey, Joseph I., "Threat, Reassurance, and Nuclear Proliferation." In Bennett Boskey and Mason Willrich, eds., *Nuclear Proliferation: Prospects for Control*. New York: Dunellen, 1970, pp. 119–132. Acceptance of the NPT or other barriers to nuclear proliferation will depend importantly on the political threats various nations face, and the forms of alternative reassurance they receive. If such assurance can be arranged, nuclear weapons options may not be exercised.

Conrad, Thomas M. "Do-It-Yourself A-Bombs." *Commonweal*, Vol. 90 (July 25, 1969), pp. 455–457. There are many autonomous organizations like the Mafia that could afford the price and become potential nuclear powers. The introduction on the market of relatively cheap and quick nuclear bombs would enable these organizations to blackmail whole cities with the threat of nuclear destruction.

Haas, E. B. *Tangle of Hopes*. Englewood Cliffs, N.J.: Prentice-Hall, 1969. The author considers the "enmeshment" of the United States in the tangled web of international organizations. In part, this "enmeshment" has disciplined, limited and altered U.S. policy. In part, it has caused the U.S. to become involved in international conflicts and issues that lie well beyond the contours of its immediate interests. The author discerns no trend toward either a "constitutionalization" of U.S. policy or toward that of the international environment as a whole.

Halperin, Morton H. *China and Nuclear Proliferation*. Chicago: University of Chicago Center for Policy Study, 1966. A discussion of Chinese statements and attitudes on further proliferation of nuclear weapons, suggesting that Peking may see some benefits in such further weapons spread, given its goals in world politics.

Harrison, Stanley L. "The Elusive Goal of Non-Proliferation." In United States Naval Institute, Annapolis *Proceedings*, Vol. 95 (April 1969) pp. 26–37. The proliferation of nuclear weapons is inevitable for both political and technical reasons, and the nonproliferation treaty (NPT) only confounds the problem by refusing to acknowledge this. The longstanding American policy of opposing proliferation should be abandoned in favor of a more realistic effort to "channel and control the inevitable."

Hoag, M. W. "On Stability in Deterrent Races," *World Politics*, Vol. 13 (July 1961), pp. 505–527. The author illustrates different weapons-technological scenarios and shows how deterrence and defense have become dissociated. He also exposes the vulnerability of certain forms of offensive weapons systems.

Hoffmann, Stanley, "Nuclear Proliferation and World Politics." In Alastair Buchan ed. *A World of Nuclear Powers?* Englewood Cliffs, N.J.: Prentice-Hall, 1966, pp. 89–121. A comprehensive and abstract discussion of changes to be anticipated in the international system if additional countries are allowed to acquire atomic and hydrogen bombs after China and France.

Iklé, Fred Charles. "*N*th Countries and Disarmament." *Bulletin of the Atomic Scientists*, Vol. 16 (December 1960), pp. 391–394. Without minimizing the dangers inherent in the proliferation of nuclear weapons, the author argues that such proliferation does not end chances for peace and arms control.

Kaplan, M. A. *System and Process in International Politics*. New York: Wiley, 1957. The author offers six analytical models of the international system, two of which have had historic counterparts. His "unit veto" system in which the means of mass destruction are possessed by every member is seen to be tension-ridden and ultimately catastrophically unstable.

Kaplan, Morton A. "Weaknesses of the Nonproliferation Treaty." *Orbis*, Vol. 12 (Winter 1969), pp. 1042–1057. Several factors are necessary for the success of the nuclear nonproliferation treaty: a universal nuclear test ban, a super-power condominium, and a U.S. and/or Soviet guarantee to defend the victims of aggression. These requirements cannot be satisfied. The belief that a a Soviet-American condominium could last for 25 years disregards "the complexities, ambiguities, absurdities and novelties that help to make up the historical process."

Knorr, K. and Verba, S. *The International System*. Princeton, N.J.: Princeton University Press, 1961. This series of essays is both methodological and substantive. Methodologically, the contributors consider whether a general theory of international relations is possible and of what it would consist. Game theoretical models are stressed as an illuminating technique. Substantively, the authors consider various types of international systems: historical, industrial-agricultural, and transitional.

Maddox, John. "The Nuclear Club." *Listener*, Vol. 81 (June 5, 1969), pp. 773–775. The forces that determine the extent of nuclear proliferation are not so much technical as political and military. A nation acquires nuclear weapons not merely because it has the technical means to do so but because it believes that nuclear weapons will be useful in a given international environment.

National Planning Association. *1970 Without Arms Control*. Planning Pamphlet No. 104. Washington, D.C., 1958. One of the original pessimistic predictions on the spread of nuclear weapons. While some "arms control" has occurred to keep the nuclear club in 1970 still limited to five members, the potential members are very much the ones listed in this report.

Osgood, R. E. and Tucker, R. W. *Force, Order and Justice*. Baltimore: Johns Hopkins Press, 1967. The authors conclude that there are not special moral or legal limitations on the use of force except those that derive from the situational context. They find bipolarity a stable international pattern and are not convinced that nuclear multipolarity would be more stable.

Quester, George H. "Is the Non-Proliferation Treaty Enough?" *Bulletin of the Atomic Scientists*, Vol. 23 (November 1967), pp. 35–37. The Non-Proliferation Treaty may depend overly much on the common-sense assumption that civilian and military nuclear activities are easily distinguished. If this is not true, the treaty may not be effective.

Riker, W. *The Theory of Political Coalitions*. New Haven: Yale University Press, 1962. The author asserts a theory of "minimum winning coalitions" among players of zero-sum games where side-payments are permitted. Applied to international relations this theory would predict small, but winning coalitions, and an attempt to reduce the size of large winning coalitions.

Rosecrance, R. N. *Action and Reaction in World Politics*. Boston: Little, Brown, 1963. The author surveys nine systems of international relations which have existed since 1740. Basically, he concludes that the immediate post-war tripolar system has broken down and that there are now fewer controls on U.S. and Soviet policy than previously existed. The spread of nuclear weapons to smaller states is seen as a reversal of previous precedents in which the instruments of great destructiveness were possessed only by major powers who had a stake in the maintenance of the international system.

————, ed. *The Dispersion of Nuclear Weapons*. New York: Columbia University Press, 1964. This collection of essays on the probabilities and effects of the spread of nuclear weapons basically concludes (1) that incentives to proliferation are likely to be high and that a variety of other nations will acquire nuclear weapons capabilities; and (2) that the consequences of that spread upon the central balance is likely to be less destabilizing than had previously been supposed.

Singer, Max. "A Non-Utopian, Non-Nuclear Future World." *Arms Control and Disarmament*, Vol. 1 (1968), pp. 79–97. A nonnuclear world—a world with only a few nuclear powers and no tendency toward the general spread of nuclear arms—requires both global recognition that such proliferation "would be bad for the world" and "a general desire to make world politics proceed much as they would if nuclear weapons had never been invented." A presump-

tion herein is that these weapons be maintained solely to prevent or counter
the use of others of their kind and that no other political or military benefits—
namely, no "positive benefits"—be drawn from them.

United Nations, Department of Political and Security Council Affairs. *Effects of
the Possible Use of Nuclear Weapons and the Security and Economic Implications for States of the Acquisition and Further Development of These
Weapons.* New York, 1968. A definitive collection of cost estimates on national nuclear weapons programs, unfortunately, perhaps, showing that the
marginal costs of plutonium warheads per se are not very high, although delivery systems may be more expensive.

United Nations Association of the United States of America. *Stopping the Spread
of Nuclear Weapons.* New York, 1967. A thoughtful statement of the need
for action in preventing further spread of nuclear weapons, arguing that the
Nuclear Non-Proliferation Treaty is a very good way to do this.

Wohlstetter, Albert, "Nuclear Sharing: NATO and the $N + 1$ Country," *Foreign
Affairs*, Vol. 39 (April 1961), pp. 355–387. A persuasive presentation of
American arguments against national nuclear forces for individual members
of NATO, citing the costs and difficulties of going from simple bombs to an
effective military force.

# Index

*(continued)*